Goochem in Mokum
Wisdom in Amsterdam

Oudtestamentische Studiën

OLD TESTAMENT STUDIES PUBLISHED ON BEHALF OF THE SOCIETIES
FOR OLD TESTAMENT STUDIES IN THE NETHERLANDS AND
BELGIUM, SOUTH AFRICA, THE UNITED KINGDOM AND IRELAND

Editor

B. Becking (*Utrecht*)

Editorial Board

P. Van Hecke (*Leuven*)
H.F. Van Rooy (*Potchefstroom*)
H.G.M. Williamson (*Oxford*)

VOLUME 68

The titles published in this series are listed at *brill.com/ots*

Goochem in Mokum
Wisdom in Amsterdam

Papers on Biblical and Related Wisdom Read at the Fifteenth Joint Meeting of the Society for Old Testament Study and the Oudtestamentisch Werkgezelschap, Amsterdam, July 2012

Edited by

George J. Brooke and Pierre Van Hecke

with the assistance of

Bob Becking and Eibert Tigchelaar

BRILL

LEIDEN | BOSTON

Library of Congress Cataloging-in-Publication Data

Names: Joint Meeting of the Society for Old Testament Study and the
 Oudtestamentisch Werkgezelschap in Nederland en België (15th : 2012 :
 Amsterdam, Netherlands) | Brooke, George J., editor. | Hecke, P. van
 (Pierre), editor.
Title: Goochem in mokum, wisdom in Amsterdam : papers on biblical and related
 wisdom read at the fifteenth joint meeting of the Society of Old Testament
 study and the Oudtestamentisch Werkgezelschap, Amsterdam, July 2012 /
 edited by George J. Brooke and Pierre van Hecke ; with the assistance of
 Bob Becking and Eibert Tigchelaar.
Description: Leiden ; Boston : Brill, [2016] | Series: Oudtestamentische
 studiën = Old Testament studies, ISSN 0169-7226 ; v. 68 | Includes
 bibliographical references and index.
Identifiers: LCCN 2016001752 (print) | LCCN 2016013891 (ebook) | ISBN
 9789004314764 (hardback : alk. paper) | ISBN 9789004314771 (E-book)
Subjects: LCSH: Wisdom—Biblical teaching—Congresses. | Bible. Old
 Testament—Criticism, interpretation, etc.—Congresses.
Classification: LCC BS1199.W57 J65 2016 (print) | LCC BS1199.W57 (ebook) |
 DDC 223/.06–dc23
LC record available at http://lccn.loc.gov/2016001752

Want or need Open Access? Brill Open offers you the choice to make your research freely accessible online in exchange for a publication charge. Review your various options on brill.com/brill-open.

Typeface for the Latin, Greek, and Cyrillic scripts: "Brill". See and download: brill.com/brill-typeface.

ISSN 0169-7226
ISBN 978-90-04-31476-4 (hardback)
ISBN 978-90-04-31477-1 (e-book)

Copyright 2016 by Koninklijke Brill NV, Leiden, The Netherlands.
Koninklijke Brill NV incorporates the imprints Brill, Brill Hes & De Graaf, Brill Nijhoff, Brill Rodopi and Hotei Publishing.
All rights reserved. No part of this publication may be reproduced, translated, stored in a retrieval system, or transmitted in any form or by any means, electronic, mechanical, photocopying, recording or otherwise, without prior written permission from the publisher.
Authorization to photocopy items for internal or personal use is granted by Koninklijke Brill NV provided that the appropriate fees are paid directly to The Copyright Clearance Center, 222 Rosewood Drive, Suite 910, Danvers, MA 01923, USA. Fees are subject to change.

This book is printed on acid-free paper and produced in a sustainable manner.

Contents

Introduction VII
  Bob Becking

The Book of Ben Sira: Some New Perspectives at the Dawn of the 21st Century 1
  Pancratius C. Beentjes

The Place of Wisdom in the Formation of the Movement behind the Dead Sea Scrolls 20
  George J. Brooke

The Wisdom of Job's Conclusion (Job 42:1–6) 34
  David J.A. Clines

Ecclesiastes as Mainstream Wisdom (Without Job) 43
  Katharine J. Dell

Unity, Date, Authorship and the 'Wisdom' of the Song of Songs 53
  J. Cheryl Exum

The Substance of Job: Beginnings and Endings 69
  Jan Fokkelman

An Awfully Beastly Business: Some Thoughts on *behēmāh* in Jonah and Qoheleth 82
  Alastair G. Hunter

Ecclesiastes Among the Tragedians 95
  John Jarick

The Disturbing Experience of Eliphaz in Job 4: Divine or Demonic Manifestation? 108
  Mart-Jan Paul

Acquiring Wisdom: A Semantic Analysis of Its Metaphorical Conceptualisations 121
  Pierre Van Hecke

Aristobulus and the Universal Sabbath 138
   J. Cornelis de Vos

Divine Judgment and Reward in Ecclesiastes 155
   Stuart Weeks

Index of Authors 167
Index of Textual References 170

Introduction

Bob Becking

The fifteenth joint meeting of the Society for Old Testament Study and the Oudtestamentisch Werkgezelschap took place in the city of Amsterdam as a satellite programme to the International Meeting of the Society of Biblical Literature. After the meeting, it was agreed upon that the proceedings would be published, as usual, in the series Oudtestamentische Studiën/Old Testament Studies. The chairmen of both societies, George Brooke and Pierre Van Hecke, accepted the responsibility to act as editors of the volume. Due to unforeseen circumstances at the personal level, both editors could not find time enough for the editorial duty they received. The editorial board of the series Oudtestamentische Studiën/Old Testament Studies was pleased by the offer of Eibert Tigchelaar to edit the manuscripts. Some of them were already sent in soon after the meeting and others only after the sixteenth joint meeting took place. We would like to thank Eibert for his generous and unselfish contribution.

In Bargoens, the cant spoken in Amsterdam in Jewish circles and beyond, the city of Amsterdam is called Mokum. The word is derived from Hebrew *māqôm*. For many Jews Amsterdam was 'the place'. Other Dutch cities were also named Mokum: Delft was known as *mokum dollet*. Amsterdam, however, is the only city still nicknamed Mokum. The same slang has given the Dutch language the untranslatable word 'goochem'. The noun has its roots in Yiddish and is eventually derived from Hebrew *ḥokmāh*, 'wisdom', and *ḥākam*, 'wise'. In Dutch the word has a positive as well as a negative connotation and refers to everything between 'wise', 'smart', and 'canny'.

In choosing 'Goochem in Mokum' as title of this volume the city of Amsterdam and its long Jewish tradition is honoured. It goes without saying, that the authors of this volume have taken 'goochem' in its positive sense.

The Book of Ben Sira: Some New Perspectives at the Dawn of the 21st Century

Pancratius C. Beentjes

1   Introduction

The past decades have seen an immense progress in the study of the book of Ben Sira, which has been amply documented in an avalanche of overviews, dictionaries, congress volumes, *Festschriften*, and doctoral theses, as listed in the appendix to this article. It is impossible, therefore, even to try to present here an overall view of all those recent publications and their specific topics.

Just one general remark, however, is in order here. The discovery of fragments of a Hebrew Ben Sira scroll at Masada in 1964 by Yigael Yadin,[1] the publication of these fragments,[2] as well as the publication of the great Psalms Scroll from Qumran Cave 11, containing parts of the Hebrew text of Sir. 51:13–30, were crucial landmarks in the study of the book of Ben Sira.[3]

The Ben Sira texts from Masada and Qumran provide conclusive evidence that the Hebrew text of the mediaeval Ben Sira manuscripts, which had been discovered in the Cairo Genizah in 1896 and later on in a number of libraries, reflects to a high degree Second Temple forms of the text. As a result, it was no longer necessary to spend nearly all research time to defend the reliability of the Hebrew Ben Sira manuscripts.

As a result, from the mid-sixties of the twentieth century onwards, a major shift in the study of the book of Ben Sira took place. Text critical problems no longer monopolized the conversation; scholarly research shifted towards theological and literary topics. The first substantial fruits of this 'theological turnover' were Josef Haspecker's dissertation and Johann Marböck's Habilitationsschrift.[4] Since then, a continuous current of literary, historical, theological, and sociological studies were brought to the fore.

---

1 Sir. 39:27–32; 40:10–19; 40:26–44:15.17.
2 Y. Yadin, *The Ben Sira Scroll from Masada with Introduction, Emendations and Commentary*, Jerusalem 1965 [= *Masada VI*, Jerusalem 1999, 151–225].
3 J.A. Sanders, *The Psalms Scroll of Qumran Cave 11 (11QPsª)* (DJD, 4), Oxford 1965, 79–85.
4 J. Haspecker, *Gottesfurcht bei Jesus Sirach: Ihre religiöse Struktur und ihre literarische und doktrinäre Bedeutung* (AnBib, 30), Rome 1967; J. Marböck, *Weisheit im Wandel: Untersuchungen zur Weisheitstheologie bei Ben Sira* (BBB, 37), Bonn 1971 [= BZAW, 272, Berlin 1999].

This paper will pay attention to a couple of notions that have a *theological* impact, have amply been discussed in the past and for some reason have recently been discussed anew. It concerns the topics of (1) Ben Sira and priesthood and (2) Ben Sira's correlation of Wisdom and Torah.

2   Ben Sira and Priesthood

Without a shadow of doubt, even a cursory reading of the book of Ben Sira brings to light 'the author's outspoken enthusiasm regarding the Jerusalem priesthood and the Temple cult'.[5] In particular, passages such as Sir. 7:29–31 ('Fear God, revere his priests'), Sir. 34:21–35:12 (the offering of sacrifices), Sir. 45:6–25 (Aaron and Phinehas), and Sir. 50:1–24 (Simon, the High Priest) are solid evidence to substantiate this view.[6] 'It is obvious that Ben Sira held the priesthood and the cult in very high esteem. In the hymn of the fathers a disproportionate amount of space is devoted to the priesthood in the person of Aaron and Phinehas and ... the tribute to Simon is perhaps the most glowing piece of all'.[7]

The question of why Ben Sira was focused in such a way on priesthood and cult has triggered a vivid debate that has already been going on for a long time. It is all about the issue of whether Ben Sira was a priest himself or not. As a matter of fact, an early hint is already found in the colophon of the Greek translation of the book of Ben Sira. Whereas the majority of manuscripts in Sir. 50:27 have the rendering 'Jesus, son of Sirach Eleazar, the one from Jerusalem' (ὁ Ἱεροσολυμίτης), in Codex Sinaiticus (prima manus) we find ἱερεύς ὁ σολυμειτης.[8]

Among the advocates that Ben Sira was a priest are, for instance, Gerhard Maier, John Sawyer, Burton Mack, Helge Stadelmann, and Saul Olyan.[9] Other

---

[5] B.G. Wright, '"Fear the Lord and Honor the Priest": Ben Sira as Defender of the Jerusalem Priesthood', in: P.C. Beentjes (ed.), *The Book of Ben Sira in Modern Research: Proceedings of the First International Ben Sira Conference Soesterberg, Netherlands* (BZAW, 255), Berlin 1997, 189–222 (192).

[6] D. Skelton, 'Ben Sira's Imaginative Theodicy: Reflections on the Aaronide Priesthood under Gentile Rule', *Restoration Quarterly* 51 (2009), 1–12.

[7] J. Priest, 'Ben Sira 45:25 in the Light of the Qumran Literature', *RevQ* 5 (1964–1965), 111–18 (117).

[8] For the rather complicated and divergent versions of this colophon, see F.V. Reiterer et al., *Bibliographie zu Ben Sira* (BZAW, 266), Berlin 1998, 1–10.

[9] G. Maier, *Mensch und freier Wille nach den jüdischen Religionsparteien zwischen Ben Sira und Paulus* (WUNT, 12), Tübingen 1971, 34 ('Infolgedessen nehmen wir an, daß Ben Sira Priester gewesen sein muß'); J.F.A. Sawyer, 'Was Jeshua Ben Sira a Priest?' in: *Proceedings of the Eighth*

scholars, such as Rudolf Smend, Theophil Middendorp, and Patrick Skehan are a little bit cautious, but in fact they are of the same opinion.[10]

An argument that is often put forward in favour of Ben Sira being a priest is that out of all biblical ideologies of priesthood the Jerusalem sage stands closest to the thought of P.[11] This view, however, is not as sound as it looks. First, unlike P, Ben Sira does not deal with the Levites at all.[12] The one and only time the name of Levi is mentioned in the book of Ben Sira is found in Sir. 45:6b where Aaron is introduced: 'Aaron from the tribe of Levi'.

In my view, both the fact that Ben Sira's vocabulary is close to the thought of P and that he quite emphatically lays stress upon priesthood, High Priesthood, and cult do not necessarily mean that he himself must have been a priest. Indeed, recently a circumstantial analysis by F.V. Reiterer has adduced conclusive evidence which makes it difficult to believe Ben Sira was a priest himself. Reiterer carefully studies the passage on Aaron in Sir. 45:6–22, specifically the *vocabulary* of this extensive pericope, which produces quite spectacular

---

World Congress of Jewish Studies, Division A: The Period of the Bible, Jerusalem 1982, 65–71, at 66 ('The simplest explanation would be that this wisdom teacher was also a member of the priestly aristocracy'); ibid., 67 ('One further piece of evidence for the priestly pedigree of Ben Sira is his name. All four names recorded in the various manuscripts appear to be typically Zadokite'). B.L. Mack, *Wisdom and the Hebrew Epic: Ben Sira's Hymn in Praise of the Fathers*, Chicago 1985, 1 ('written by a Jewish priest in Jerusalem'). H. Stadelmann, *Ben Sira als Schriftgelehrter* (WUNT, 2.6), Tübingen 1980, 12 ('scheint es uns...in ihm einen priestlichen Schriftgelehrten und Weisen zu sehen'); ibid., 14 ('Denk man sich Ben Sira entsprechend als Priester...'); ibid., 14 ('Ein weiterer Umstand, der es nahelegt, die standesmäßige Herkunft Ben Siras im Priestertum zu suchen...'); ibid., 25 (' dann legt sich...nahe, in Sirach selbst einen Sōfēr zu sehen, der...von Hause aus Priester war'); ibid., 174 ('Es handelt sich hier gewissermaßen um das Mahnwort eines Priesters (Ben Siras) an seine priesterlichen Kollegen'). S.M. Olyan, 'Ben Sira's Relationship to the Priesthood', *HTR* 80 (1987), 261–86, at 263 ('his place in the priesthood of his days...').

10 R. Smend, *Die Weisheit des Jesus Sirach...erklärt*, Berlin 1906, xiv ('vermutlich priestlicher...Herkunft'); T. Middendorp, *Die Stellung Jesu Ben Sira zwischen Judentum und Hellenismus*, Leiden 1973, 60 ('so darf mit Fug eine persönliche Beziehung zum Priesterstande angenommen werden...'); ibid., 61 ('Vermutlich war der Schulbetrieb Ben Siras eng verbunden mit der Priesterschaft'). P.W. Skehan, A.A. Di Lella, *The Wisdom of Ben Sira* (AB, 39), New York 1987, 518 ('Ben Sira, who is presumed to have been of a priestly family himself,...').

11 Olyan, 'Ben Sira's Relationship', 273, 275; H.-J. Fabry, 'Jesus Sirach und das Priestertum', in: I. Fischer, et al., *Auf den Spuren der schriftgelehrten Weisen. Fs J. Marböck* (BZAW, 331), Berlin 2003, 265–82, at 273 ('Dass er sprachlich ganz in der Nähe der Priesterschrift steht, ist schon mehrfach herausgestellt worden').

12 Fabry, 'Jesus Sirach', 273 ('Im Gegensatz zu P halt er jedoch von den Leviten nichts...').

results.[13] According to Reiterer, a 'detailed investigation shows that we have to pay attention to features that are at first glance unremarkable'.[14] Let us have a look at some examples.[15]

(1) Sir. 45:7a
The Holy One exalted Aaron from the tribe of Levi.
He set him as a perpetual ordinance,
He gave him authority, and He ministered to him in his glory. (45:6a–7c)

'Perpetual ordinance' is the rendering of the Hebrew collocation חק עולם, which in the Hebrew Bible is a fixed phrase that without exception refers either to ordinances that Aaron and his sons have to fulfill (Exod. 30:21; Lev. 6:15) or to those parts of offerings that Aaron and his sons will claim for ever (Exod. 29:28; Lev. 6:11; 7:34; 10:15; 24:19; Num. 18:8. 11. 19). 'It is therefore a fixed phrase with an established application'.[16]

In Sir. 45:7a, however, the collocation חק עולם has a bearing on Aaron who is installed by God as a 'perpetual ordinance'. Commentators have noticed this remarkable characterization.[17] 'Ben Sira is not interested in the priesthood or the offerings, but in the figure and the role of Aaron!'.[18]

(2) Sir. 45:7d
ויאזרהו בתועפות ראם   He girded him with horns of a wild ox.

Two observations relating to Sir. 45:7d are in order here. First, in the Hebrew Bible the verb אזר ('to gird') nowhere occurs in a ritual context. The technical term for the priestly girding is חגר which, however, is nowhere to be found in the book of Ben Sira. The occurrence of the noun אזור ('girdle') in 45:10c shows that Ben Sira used the stem אזר on purpose.

---

13 F.V. Reiterer, 'Aaron's Polyvalent Role according to Ben Sira', in: J. Corley, H. van Grol (eds), *Rewriting Biblical History: Essays on Chronicles and Ben Sira in Honor of P.C. Beentjes* (DCLS, 7), Berlin 2011, 27–56.
14 Ibid., 34.
15 As a consequence, both the examples and the wording of the following paragraphs rely heavily on Reiterer's essay.
16 Ibid., 33.
17 I. Lévi, *L'Ecclésiastique ou la Sagesse de Jésus, fils de Sira* (BEHE.R, 10,1), Paris 1898, 96 ('Construction étrange'); N. Peters, *Das Buch Jesus Sirach oder Ecclesiasticus übersetzt und erklärt* (EHAT, 25), Münster 1913, 387 ('Hier ist der Ausdruck auf Aharon selbst übertragen...'; Smend, *Die Weisheit.. erklärt*, 428. 'Aaron ist selbst חק genannt...').
18 Reiterer, 'Aaron's Polyvalent Role', 33.

THE BOOK OF BEN SIRA

Second, the collocation 'horns of a wild ox', which is found in Num. 23:22 and 24:8 as a metaphor to describe God's royal power and invincibility, has been used in Sir. 45:7d to present Aaron. In the Hebrew Bible the wild ox is never mentioned in cultic contexts. Therefore, its metaphorical usage in Sir. 45:7d should not be understood as cultic either. Here, too, Ben Sira has created his own particular perspective.

(3) Sir. 45:7e–45:9a

וילבישהו פעמונים   He clothed him with bells. (Sir. 45:7e)
ויקיפהו פעמונים   He surrounded him with bells. (Sir. 45:9a)

Ben Sira seems to be fascinated by the bells which surrounded Aaron. Though the Hebrew Bible mentions 'golden bells' on the lower hem of the priestly robe (Exod. 28:33–34; 39:25), neither the collocation 'to be clothed with bells', nor the expression 'to surround someone with bells' are found in it. Therefore, Ben Sira's portrayal of Aaron is unique again.

(4) Sir. 45:8a–b

וילבישהו כליל תפארת   ויפארהו בכבוד ועוז

He clothed him with complete beauty / he adorned him with glory and strength.

It should come as no surprise that similar phrases relating to priestly or liturgical matters are nowhere to be found in the Hebrew Bible. Ben Sira's 'focus is on power and influence and not on the religious aspects of liturgy'.[19]

These four examples suffice to show that in his description of the priestly garments Ben Sira often deviates from the vocabulary and expressions of the Pentateuch. We fully agree with Reiterer who considers Ben Sira as someone who offers a description of the priest's garments from a distance and who neither had special knowledge of 'detailed questions covering religious ritual', nor employed 'any technical terms for the ritual, although we would expect them'.[20] It appears that Ben Sira did not have a good knowledge of priestly clothing. It is hard to believe, therefore, that he was a priest himself.

Since for Ben Sira the priest is not primarily a representative of the cult, a further explanation is required. During the last two decades, the discussion relating to the topic of priesthood in the book of Ben Sira has broadened.

---

19   Ibid., 39.
20   Ibid., 47.

Research into the meaning and background of such contemporary writings as *The Book of the Watchers* (1 Enoch 6–36), *The Astronomical Book* (1 Enoch 72–82), the *Testaments of the Twelve Patriarchs* and the *Aramaic Levi Document* has quite unmistakably brought to light that in Ben Sira's day there was heavy controversy over the legitimacy of the Jerusalem priesthood and cult.[21] 'In each case, the conclusions point to groups of priests and/or scribes, who are either supportive of or stood opposed to those priests who control the cult in Jerusalem'.[22]

A passage from the book of Ben Sira (45:25) supports the interpretation that Ben Sira portrayed Aaron and his descendants as *political* representatives rather than as representatives of the cult. This passage, however, is a famous *crux interpretum*. What strikes one most in Sir. 45:25 is that Ben Sira for the first time in the *Hymn to the Fathers* abandons the strictly chronological order which is so characteristic of this hymn. Subsequent to the passage on Phinehas (45:23–24), which has been composed with the help of a selection of cola from Num. 25:11–13, Sir. 45:25 all of a sudden introduces the theme of God's covenant with David.[23] This untimely mention of David—to whom in 47:1–11 a lengthy passage will be devoted—must therefore play a special role in the context of the Phinehas pericope. The Hebrew text of Sir. 45:25 (Ms. B.) runs as follows:

וגם בריתו עם דוד　　בן ישי למטה יהודה
נחלת אש לפני כבודו　　נחלת אהרן לכל זרעו

The third colon of this verse has substantial text critical problems. In my doctoral dissertation, I argued that this Hebrew text of 45:25c should be taken

---

21　See especially Olyan, 'Ben Sira's Relationship', 275–81; Wright, 'Fear the Lord'; B.G. Wright, 'Putting the Puzzle Together: Some Suggestions Concerning the Social Location of the Wisdom of Ben Sira', in: SBL *Seminar Papers 1996*, Atlanta 1996, 133–49 (142–46) (repr. in: B.G. Wright, L.M. Wills [eds], *Conflicted Boundaries in Wisdom and Apocalypticism* [SBLSS, 35], Atlanta 2005, 89–112); Fabry, 'Jesus Sirach und das Priestertum', 280–81.

22　Wright, 'Putting the Puzzle', 142; see also B.G. Wright, 'Ben Sira and *The Book of Watchers* on Legitimate Priesthood', in: J. Corley, V. Skemp (eds), *Intertextual Studies in Ben Sira and Tobit: Essays in Honor of A.A. Di Lella* (CBQMS, 38), Washington 2005, 241–54.

23　For the composition of Sir. 45:23–24 see P.C. Beentjes, 'Canon and Scripture in the Book of Ben Sira (Jesus Sirach / Ecclesiasticus)', in: M. Saebø (ed.), *Hebrew Bible / Old Testament. The History of Its Interpretation*, Vol. I/2: The Middle Ages, Göttingen 2000, 591–605 (601–2). See also K.E. Pomykala, 'The Covenant with Phinehas in Ben Sira (Sirach 45:23–26; 50:22–24), in: Pomykala (ed.), *Israel in the Wilderness: Interpretations of Biblical Narratives in Jewish and Christian Traditions* (TBN, 10), Leiden 2008, 17–36.

more seriously than had been done before.[24] Up to then, no single scholar or commentator had been able to propose a meaningful interpretation of this colon. Therefore, various textual emendations have been suggested to solve this problem.[25]

The opening cola (45:25ab) refer to David, and the last one (45:25d) is devoted to Aaron. The cola 45:25c and 45:25d have a parallel structure. Therefore, all commentators take for granted that 45:25c relates to David, and assume a comparison between the succession in the lineage of David (45:25c) and the one in the lineage of Aaron (45:25d). Indeed, both the Greek and the Syriac translation would seem to confirm that these cola present a comparison.

καὶ διαθήκη τῷ Δαυιδ	And a covenant with David,
υἱῷ Ιεσσαι ἐκ φυλῆς Ιουδα	son of Jesse from the tribe of Judah;
κληρονομία βασιλέως	an inheritance of a king
υἱοῦ ἐξ υἱοῦ μόνου·	is a son from a son only,
κληρονομία Ααρων	an inheritance of Aaron
καὶ τῷ σπέρματι αὐτοῦ.	is also to his seed.

ܘܐܦ ܕܘܝܕ ܒܪ ܐܝܫܝ	And also David, son of Jesse,
ܘܐܬܪܐ ܕܡܠܟܐ ܒܠܚܘܕܘܗܝ ܝܪܬ	the inheritance of kings he alone inherited;
ܘܐܬܪܐ ܕܐܗܪܘܢ	but the inheritance of Aaron
ܠܗ ܘܠܙܪܥܗ	is to him and his seed.

On the basis of these two versions, several proposals have been submitted to reconstruct the 'original' Hebrew text of 45:25c. Since both the Greek and the Syriac version have the notion 'alone', it has often been suggested to alter כבודו ('his glory') into לבדו ('alone'), and to substitute לבנו ('his son') for לפנו ('in his presence').[26] However, a more fundamental question has consistently been left

---

24 P.C. Beentjes, *Jesus Sirach en Tenach: Een onderzoek naar en een classificatie van parallellen, met bijzondere aandachtvoor hun functie in Sirach 45:6–26*, Nieuwegein 1981, 175–200.

25 An overview is offered by A. Caquot, 'Ben Sira et le Messianisme', *Sem* 16 (1966), 43–68, esp. 59–64; Priest, 'Ben Sira 45:25'.

26 See, e.g., K.E. Pomykala, *The Davidic Dynasty Tradition in Early Judaism: Its History and Significance for Messianism* (SBLEJL, 7), Atlanta 1995, 132–44; M. Pietsch, »*Dieser ist der Sproß Davids...*« *Studien zur Rezeptionsgeschichte der Nathanverheißung im alttestamentlichen, zwischentestamentlichen und neutestamentlichen Schrifttum* (WMANT, 100), Neukirchen 2003, 164–75.

unanswered, namely in what way could the 'original' Hebrew text of 45:25c have been corrupted to the extant text of Ms. B.

I therefore decided to investigate whether the discovered Hebrew text could have a meaningful sense *within the Phinehas passage*. This proves to be possible if one abandons the idea that 45:25a is the start of a new sentence. Instead, one may look upon 45:25a as the *immediate continuation* of 45:24cd. A translation of 45:24c–25b would then run as follows:

> So that he [Phinehas] and his descendants
> should possess the high priesthood forever,
> and even His covenant with David,
> the son of Jesse of the tribe of Judah.

This translation, which up to then had not been considered in scholarly discussion, would explain why the Hebrew of 45:25ab has no verb: these cola form a *subordinate clause* to 45:24c. The Greek text, too, appears to contain a similar lead. Nearly all Greek manuscripts have an accusative (διαθήκην), which all commentators immediately amended to a nominative.[27] The mere fact, however, that the vast majority of the Greek manuscripts in Sir. 45:25a render an accusative is significant and should be given due consideration. It could indicate that Ben Sira's grandson, as the translator of the Greek text, indeed understood διαθήκην as the object of a preceding verb, even though the Greek syntax of 45:24 does not allow for that kind of dependence.

If one relates God's covenant with David (45:25a) to the institution of the High Priesthood (namely, by transferring it to Phinehas), then the purport of 45:25c becomes perfectly clear, without the necessity of emendations of the Hebrew text. There is no longer any need to emend אש ('fire') into איש ('man'),[28] because the colon is not connected to David, but to Phinehas and his descendants, and can therefore be interpreted within the sphere of the high priestly institution, namely the cult:

> the inheritance of fire before his glory,
> the inheritance of Aaron for all his descendants.

---

27 See J. Ziegler, *Sapientia Iesu Filii Sirach* (Septuaginta Vetus Testamentum Graecum, 12,2), Göttingen 1965, 340.

28 Nowhere in the Hebrew manuscripts of Ben Sira is אש found as a defective reading for איש.

In that way, the mention of Aaron in the passage on Phinehas not only refers to the preceding lengthy pericope on Aaron (45:6–22), but also ties in with the notion of 'inheritance' that in 45:22 constitutes the culmination of the passage on Aaron.

The notion of 'fire' plays an important role in Num. 17:1–15, but Sir. 45:6–22 contains no reference at all to this biblical passage. In his portrayal of Aaron, Ben Sira may have deliberately omitted an allusion to that text, since he wanted to link the notion of 'fire' with the special theme he created for 45:25.

It appears that Ben Sira in 45:25 transfers God's covenant with David to the High Priesthood of Aaron, Phinehas and his descendants: 'that what was once promised to the Davidic dynasty has now been "inherited" by the Aaronite high-priesthood'.[29] Against this background, it becomes evident why Ben Sira in 45:12 portrays Aaron, the High Priest, with 'a diadem of precious gold' (עטרת פז), a collocation that is unique and is only found in Ps. 21:4, where it has a bearing on a *king*!

The same is true for Sir. 45:15, where the collocation 'as permanent as the heavens' (כימי שמים) is said of Aaron and his descendants. This, too, is a unique biblical wording, which is found in Ps. 89:30 with respect to *King David*.[30] Now one can understand why Ben Sira in his portrayal of David refers neither to Nathan nor to God's promise of a permanent Davidic dynasty. In Ben Sira's view, God's covenant with David has been *transferred* to the Aaronite dynasty.[31]

James Martin, the first scholar to agree with my interpretation of Sir. 45:25, has an interesting remark: '... corresponding to what we might call the "Davidising" of the Aaronite (high-)priesthood, there is in the David pericope what we might call the "Aaronising" of David, with ... an emphasis being laid on his role in the establishing of the cult'.[32]

Finally, Sir. 50:24 should be adduced as solid evidence that 'the office of king, secured by the Davidic covenant, is for Ben Sira now located in the office of high priest'.[33] It is not by chance, of course, that in 50:24d the collocation

---

29   J.D. Martin, 'Ben Sira's Hymn to the Fathers: A Messianic Perspective', in: A.S. van der Woude (ed.), *Crises and Perspectives* (OTS, 24), Leiden 1986, 107–23 (115).

30   An overview of David in the Psalter is offered by E. Ballhorn, 'Um deines Knechtes David willen (Ps 132,10): Die Gestalt Davids im Psalter', *BN* 76 (1995), 16–31.

31   It is no accident, of course, that exactly the same phrase—'as permanent as the heavens' (כימי שמים)—is used again in Sir. 50:24d, which is the concluding line of Ben Sira's praise of Simeon the High Priest.

32   Martin, 'Ben Sira's Hymn', 115.

33   Pomykala, *Davidic Dynasty*, 143.

כימי שמים ('as permanent as the heavens')[34] is used with respect to Phinehas, as in 45:15 it was with regard to Aaron.[35] Again, we find a clue that this collocation, which originally referred to the Davidic dynasty (Ps. 89:30), has been transferred to the high priestly dynasty.

Most probably, in Sir 45:25, Ben Sira upholds a tradition which is already documented in the third century BCE. In the so-called *Aramaic Levi Document*, the figure of Levi and the Levitical line have been given a particularly central status.[36] In ALD 11:6–7, Judah's royal blessing is transferred to Kohath, Levi's second son and the ancestor of the high priestly line, by means of a midrash on Gen. 49:10.[37]

Ben Sira, however, did not just adopt this tradition, he also made some adjustments; instead of Kohath, he favoured Aaron and Phinehas. In Sir. 50:24b, for instance, we come across the collocation ברית פינחס ('the covenant with Phinehas'), a combination that is unknown to the Hebrew Bible and is therefore to be considered a creation by Ben Sira himself. By means of this unique collocation, the author refers back to 45:24 in a twofold way. First, the name of Phinehas in 50:24 directly calls to mind the crucial passage on this High Priest in chapter 45. Second, Sir. 50:24 contains the only mention of ברית ('covenant') after its occurrence in Sir. 45:24–25.

Ben Sira might even have had political reasons for heaping praise on Phinehas. In Samaritan tradition Phinehas is held in high esteem.[38] It is possible that by laying stress on Phinehas and the covenant of high priesthood, Ben Sira steals a march on the Samaritans. The Jerusalem sage claims that in no

---

34 In their analysis of Sir. 45:15, a lot of commentators do not even mention that the collocation בימי שמים is also found in Sir. 50:24.

35 It is not impossible that the phrasing אשר לא יכרת לו ולזרעו (Sir. 50:24c) has been inspired by 1 Kgs 9:5b (לא יכרת לך איש מעל כסא ישראל). If so, this is one more 'royal text' that has been transformed into a 'high priestly' one!

36 I like to thank professor Michael Stone (Hebrew University, Jerusalem) for his reference to this document.

37 See J.C. Greenfield, M.E. Stone, E. Eshel, *The Aramaic Levi Document: Edition, Translation, Commentary* (SVTP, 19), Leiden 2004, 35, 94–95, 184–88; H. Drawnel, *An Aramaic Wisdom Text from Qumran: A New Interpretation of the Levi Document* (JSJSup, 86), Leiden 2004, 145–50, 307–9.

38 'Five inscriptions from the walls of the sacred precinct of the sanctuary on Mt. Gerizim mention priests: four of them concern the priest Pinḥas [nos. 24, 25, 384, 385], who was possibly the high priest'; J. Dušek, *Aramaic and Hebrew Inscriptions from Mt. Gerizim and Samaria between Antiochus II and Antiochus IV Epiphanes* (Culture and History of the Ancient Near East, 54), Leiden 2012, 83. I like to thank my colleague Prof. Bob Becking for his comment relating to this question.

way was it an exclusive northern tradition, but it belonged to the high priesthood of Jerusalem. He works this out in a twofold way. First, the ברית פינחס is mentioned in Sir. 50:24 as part of the conclusion of the Praise of Simon the High priest. Second, this collocation is immediately followed by the marked proverb relating to 'the foolish people that dwells in Shechem' (Sir. 50:26b). I therefore fully agree with M. Goff that 'Ben Sira's connection of Simon to Phinehas may be a polemical adaptation of Samaritan tradition, although this cannot be proven'.[39]

To conclude: the assertion that Ben Sira himself must have been a priest is not tenable. On the contrary, there is solid evidence that his presentation of Aaron and his descendant Phinehas were rather political, since in his day there were serious controversies over the High Priesthood. Ben Sira wanted to emphasize both the southern claim to and the royal status of the high priest.[40]

3   Ben Sira's Correlation of Wisdom and Torah

A second major theological topic in the book of Ben Sira is the correlation of Wisdom and Torah. Eckhard Schnabel's doctoral thesis, which no doubt is the most detailed investigation of the subject, claims that the vast majority of scholars recognise and acknowledge 'the complete identification of law and wisdom by Ben Sira'.[41] He adduces no less than seven passages being 'explicit evidence' for such a 'clear and direct identification of wisdom and law': Sir. 15:1; 17:11; 19:20; 21:11; 24:23; 34:8; 45:5c–d.[42] Moreover, '[t]welve passages presuppose, imply, or result in the identification of law and wisdom': Sir. 1:26; 2:15–16; 6:36; 15:15; 19:24; 24:22; 24:32–33; 33:2–3; 38:34–39:8; 44:4c; 51:15c–d; 51:30a–b.[43]

Until then many scholars were adherents of that point of view.[44] In the beginning of the nineties, however, there began a turning point. One of the first

---

39   M. Goff, '"The Foolish Nation That Dwells in Shechem": Ben Sira on Shechem and the Other Peoples in Palestine', in: D.C. Harlow et al., *The "Other" in Second Temple Judaism: Essays in Honor of John J. Collins*, Grand Rapids 2011, 173–88 (185).

40   See A. van der Kooij, 'The Greek Bible and Jewish Concepts of Royal Priesthood and Priestly Monarchy', in: T. Rajak et al., *Jewish Perspectives on Hellenistic Rulers* (HCS, 50), Berkeley 2007, 255–64.

41   E. Schnabel, *Law and Wisdom from Ben Sira to Paul* (WUNT, 2.16), Tübingen 1985, 89 n. 443.

42   Ibid., 69–73.

43   Ibid., 73–77.

44   To mention just a few advocates: O. Kaiser, 'Die Begründung der Sittlichkeit im Buche Jesus Sirach', *ZThK* 55 (1958), 51–63, at 56 ('Hier tritt die Identifikation der Weisheit mit dem mosaischen Gesetz deutlich zutage'); F. Christ, *Jesus Sophia: Die Sophia-Christologie*

scholars who offered a more thoughtful approach to this topic was Gabriele Boccaccini, who reached the conclusion that it 'is not an identification, but a complex play of balances within the synergetic prospect proposed to humankind as the road to salvation'.[45] Therefore, he preferred the term 'asymmetrical relationship'.[46] About a decade later, the debate intensified and a growing number of scholars dissociated themselves from the traditional point of view.[47]

bei den Synoptikern (ATANT, 57), Zürich 1970, 36 ('Die Weisheit ist identisch mit dem Gesetz, dem Buche des Bundes'); B.L. Mack, *Logos und Sophia: Untersuchungen zur Weisheitstheologie im hellenistischen Judentum* (SUNT, 10), Göttingen 1973, 23 ('Bekanntlich wird im Sirachbuch die Weisheit mit dem Gesetz identifiziert'); M. Hengel, *Judaism and Hellenism*, London 1974, 138–39; M. Küchler, *Frühjüdische Weisheitstraditionen: Zum Fortgang weisheitlichen Denkens im Bereich des frühjüdisches Jahweglaubens* (OBO, 26), Göttingen 1979, 31–45; J. Blenkinsopp, *Wisdom and Law in the Old Testament* (Oxford Bible Series), Oxford 1983 (1995), 166 ('The really novel element in Ben Sira's poem comes in the second part (vv. 23–34) in which he identifies this pre-existent Wisdom with Torah...'); Marböck, *Weisheit im Wandel*, 90; J. Marböck, 'Gesetz und Weisheit. Zum Verständnis des Gesetzes bei Jesus Ben Sira', *BZ* 20 (1976), 1–21 (8) [= Marböck, *Gottes Weisheit unter uns*, 52–72 (59)]; G.T. Sheppard, *Wisdom as a Hermeneutical Construct: A Study in the Sapientializing of the Old Testament* (BZAW, 151) Berlin 1980, 63 ('... full identification... between the book of the Torah and Wisdom'). G. Schimanowski, *Weisheit und Messias*, Tübingen 1985, 57 ('Die Identifikation von Weisheit und Tora kommt nicht überraschend'); J.R. Busto Saiz, 'Sabiduría y Torá en Jesús Ben Sira', *EstB* 52 (1994), 229–39 ('para Ben Sira, la sabiduría se identifique con la Torá', 235); Y.A.P. Goldman, 'Le texte massorétique de Qohélet, témoin d'un compromise théologique entre les "disciples des sages" (Qoh 7,23–24; 8:1; 7:19)', in: Goldman et al., *Sôfer Mahîr: Essays in Honour of Adrian Schenker* (VTS, 110), Leiden 2006, 69–93 (76); J.J. Collins, *Jewish Wisdom in the Hellenistic Age* (OTL), Louisville 1997, 49–61; L.G. Perdue, *Wisdom Literature: A Theological History*, Louisville 2007, 247 ('Sir. 24:23–29 identifies Wisdom with the Torah...'). Most recently, D. Penchansky, *Understanding Wisdom Literature: Conflict and Dissonance in the Hebrew Text*, Grand Rapids 2012, 6 ('... Ben Sira equates Woman Wisdom with Torah...').

45   G. Boccaccini, *Middle Judaism: Jewish Thought, 300 BCE to 200 CE*, Minneapolis 1991, 81–99.
46   Ibid., 88.
47   J. Rogers, '"It overflows like the Euphrates with understanding": Another Look at the Relationship between Law and Wisdom in Sirach', in: C.A. Evans (ed.), *Of Scribes and Sages: Early Jewish Interpretation and Transmission of Scripture* I (SSEJC, 9; LSTS, 50), London 2004, 114–21; Rogers, 'Wisdom in Sirach', *JNSL* 30 (2004), 61–79; F.V. Reiterer, 'Neue Akzente in der Gesetzvorstellung: תורת חיים bei Ben Sira', in: M. Witte (ed.), *Gott und Mensch im Dialog* II (BZAW, 345/2), Berlin 2004, 851–71; T. Veijola, 'Law and Wisdom: The Deuteronomistic Heritage in Ben Sira's Teaching of the Law', in: J. Neusner et al., *Ancient Israel, Judaism, and Christianity in Contemporary Perspective* (FS K.J. Illman), New York 2006, 429–48 [= T. Veijola, *Leben nach der Weisung: exegetisch-historische Studien zum*

Since scholars unanimously point to Sir. 24:23 as the most crucial passage on how law and wisdom are correlated, we have to take a quick look at this verse.

Ταῦτα πάντα βίβλος διαθήκης θεοῦ ὑψίστου,
νόμον ὃν ἐνετείλατο ἡμῖν Μωυσῆς
κληρονομίαν συναγωγαῖς Ιακωβ,

All this is the book of the covenant of God Most High,
the Law which Moses commanded us
as an inheritance for the communities of Jacob.

Quite a few scholars claim that (a substantial part of) this verse must be secondary. Their arguments, however, differ; to mention just a few of them: (1) The first line is a gloss;[48] (2) In the book of Ben Sira tristichoi cannot be genuine;[49] (3) Nowhere in the book of Ben Sira is διαθήκη used for the covenant with Israel or Moses;[50] (4) Sir. 24:23a is a later addition caused by Bar. 4:1.[51] No doubt the most interesting argument, however, is the contention that the pronoun ἡμῖν ('us') in Sir. 24:23b does not fit in the context, since Ben Sira uses that pronoun only in prayers.[52]

In my view, however, it is precisely the occurrence of 'us' in the Ben Sira text that should be considered an argument *in favour* of its originality, because

---

Alten Testament [W. Dietrich, M. Marttila, eds] (FRLANT, 224), Göttingen 2008, 144–64]; F.V. Reiterer, 'Das Verhältnis der חכמה zur תורה im Buch Ben Sira: Kriterien zur gegenseitigen Bestimmung', in: G.G. Xeravits, J. Zsengellér (eds), *Studies in the Book of Ben Sira: Papers of the Third International Conference on Deuterocanonical Books, Shime'on Centre, Pápa, Hungary, 18–20 May, 2006* (JSJSup, 127), Leiden 2008, 97–133; F.V. Reiterer, 'The Interpretation of the Wisdom Tradition of the Torah within Ben Sira', in: A. Passaro, G. Bellia (eds), *The Wisdom of Ben Sira: Studies on Tradition, Redaction, and Theology* (DCLS, 1), Berlin 2008, 209–31; Adams, *Wisdom in Transition*, 198–204; Schmidt Goering, *Wisdom's Root*.

48 J.K. Zenner, 'Zwei Weisheitslieder', ZKT 21 (1897), 551–58 (554).
49 Peters, *Das Buch Jesus Sirach*, 203 ('Nirgends ist aber in Ekkli sonst ein Tristichon als ursprünglich sicher überliefert'); Rickenbacher, *Weisheitsperikopen*, 127, 130–31.
50 Rickenbacher, *Weisheitsperikopen*, 166–67.
51 Peters, *Das Buch Jesus Sirach*, 203; Rickenbacher, *Weisheitsperikopen*, 127; M. Gilbert, 'L'éloge de La Sagesse (Siracide 24)', RTL 5 (1974), 326–48 (337).
52 Rickenbacher, *Weisheitsperikopen*, 127. In Deut. 33:4, Codex Vaticanus has the reading ὑμῖν, just as Codex Venetus and some minuscles in Sir. 24:23; Ziegler, *Sapientia Iesu Filii Sirach*, 240.

it creates a tension, which is caused by the insertion of the quotation from Deut. 33:4 (LXX).[53]

καὶ ἐδέξατο ἀπὸ τῶν λόγων αὐτοῦ
νόμον, ὃν ἐνετείλατο ἡμῖν Μωυσῆς,
κληρονομίαν συναγωγαῖς Ιακωβ.

and he received of his words
the law which Moses commanded us,
as an inheritance to the assemblies of Jacob.[54]

However, if one reads the previous verses (24:19–22) as an invitation by Lady Wisdom, a particular question comes to mind. For it is obvious that Lady Wisdom's invitation which ends in verse 22 is *incomplete*: 'He who obeys me will not be ashamed, and those who work with me will not sin'. There can be no doubt that the audience at this point expected to hear from Lady Wisdom herself how her invitation can be accepted and in what way it is to be substantiated.[55] The answer to this crucial question is unequivocal: 'the book of the covenant of the Most High / the law that Moses commanded us' (24:23).

That an identification of wisdom and Torah is impossible is established by the subsequent passage (Sir. 24:25–27). The subject of this passage is either βίβλος ('book') or νόμος ('law'), or both. It is the Torah that supplies wisdom, it

---

[53] In fact, this feature bears a close resemblance to Sir. 45:21a where suddenly the verb is in third person *plural*. The criteria Devorah Dimant has formulated are completely valid for Sir 24:23. The phrases from Deut. 33:4 are literally reproduced in Sir. 24:23, even with the remarkable 'us'; there is also explicit mention of the same agents (God, Moses) and addressees ('us', and the communities of Jacob). Both passages have a common literary feature; they are part of a poetic text; D. Dimant, 'Use and Interpretation of Mikra in the Apocrypha and Pseudepigrapha', in: M. Mulder, H. Sysling (eds), *Mikra. Text, Translation, Reading and Interpretation of the Hebrew Bible in Ancient Judaism and Early Christianity* (CRINT, 2,1), Assen 1988, 379–419.

[54] Sheppard, *Wisdom as a Hermeneutical Construct*, 63 ('Consequently, Dt. 33:4 has, by its placement in Sir. 24:23, been given a new redactional setting which successfully reveals the writer's own particular interpretation of it. For the writer, Dt. 33:4 is not only a statement about the Torah, but it is a commentary on the proximity of Wisdom in the history of Israel').

[55] See P.C. Beentjes, '"Come to me, you who desire me…": Lady Wisdom's Invitation in Ben Sira 24:19–22', in: R. Egger-Wenzel, K. Schöpflin, J.F. Diehl (eds), *Weisheit als Lebensgrundlage: Festschrift für F.V. Reiterer zum 65. Geburtstag* (DCLS, 15), Berlin 2013, 1–11.

is the source of wisdom, the source of understanding, and the source of education. And it is not by chance that this explanation is presented with the help of paradisiacal and primordial metaphors, since in a subtle way they harken back to what Lady Wisdom has said about her origin (24:9a).

In 2004 Jessie Rogers devoted two articles to the question of the relationship of Law and Wisdom. In my view his following descriptions are spot on:

> The close association between Law and Wisdom in Sirach is undisputed, but there is a growing realization that the relationship is more nuanced than the term 'identification' would imply. The question of how Wisdom relates to Law in Sirach is crucial for an understanding of the nature of Wisdom in this work. If the concepts were identified in the strict sense of the word, then Wisdom in Sirach would be completely nationalized and the sage would be a Scripture scholar.[56]
>
> The implication need not be that the *content* of Wisdom and Law are identified in a one-to-one correspondence (i.e. that the Law alone is the locus of Wisdom). In this regard it is significant that *fulfilling* the law and *keeping* the commandments are most often linked with *acquiring* wisdom.[57]
>
> The Law is an already-given gift, which everyone may obey, but Wisdom remains something to be sought after, but not granted to all by virtue of its autonomy with respect to the relationship between human beings and God.[58]
>
> For Ben Sira, who is steeped in the sapiential tradition, Wisdom remains the primary category, and provides the hermeneutical tool through which to read the sacred texts... Law in Sirach is one concrete expression of Wisdom which exists before and beyond it and which can never be fully exhausted by it.[59]

This line of thought is also upheld by Samuel Adams. He opposes the view of scholars like Schnabel and Hengel that universal wisdom came only to dwell in Israel and specifically on Zion in the temple. 'Such arguments,' he says, 'attach an ideology of "only-ness" to the book of Ben Sira' and such 'a rigid dichotomy between "profane wisdom" and Torah-centered "piety" also misses the mark'.[60]

---

56   Rogers, 'It overflows', 114.
57   Rogers, 'Wisdom', 74.
58   Ibid., 75.
59   Rogers, 'It overflows', 120.
60   Adams, *Wisdom in Transition*, 200.

Adams lays stress upon the fact that 'the Torah is encompassed by a more universal Wisdom in Ben Sira, and not vice versa'.[61]

A substantial and fresh approach to interpreting Ben Sira's correlation of Wisdom and Torah is offered by Greg Schmidt Goering. He argues that any simple identification of Wisdom and Torah in the book of Ben Sira is problematic, because Wisdom is characterized there as universally available to all human beings, whereas Torah, on the other hand, is characterized as the particular preserve of Israel. In order to avoid this collapse of one category into another, Schmidt Goering suggests that Ben Sira views Wisdom and Torah not as identical but rather as correlated or congruous. In order to emphasize this new approach, he offers an investigation into the concept of 'election' which enables a profitable discussion on the relationship of Wisdom and Torah in the book of Ben Sira.

Ben Sira distinguishes between human beings on the basis of two unequal allotments of divine wisdom. One involves a general outpouring of wisdom upon all creation, including all humanity (Sir. 1:9b–10a). The other consists of a special distribution of an extra measure of wisdom to a select group of humanity (Sir. 1:10b). While most scholars interpret this classification dualistically, Schmidt Goering argues that Ben Sira bases the distinction on an idea of election that has no implication of dualism. That is, Israel's election does not include a rejection of the non-elect. The notion that a doctrine of opposites lies at the heart of Ben Sira's view of the world is strongly rejected, even with respect to the famous passage in Sir. 33:7–15, which according to the author was his "aha!" moment for finding an interpretative key.[62]

Ben Sira regards both allotments of wisdom as forms of divine revelation. The outpouring of wisdom upon all creation constitutes a 'general wisdom' that is available to all humanity through the natural world. However, the lavish distribution of wisdom upon the elect constitutes a 'special wisdom' to which Israel alone is privy. This view complicates most scholars' facile description that Ben Sira characterizes wisdom as either universal or particular. The sage develops his understanding of the relationship between the elect and special wisdom through the metaphor of inheritance.[63]

Ben Sira's description of Israel's special wisdom as an inheritance suggests a portion to be preserved and transmitted within a lineage from generation to generation. Therefore, Schmidt Goering seeks to identify the mechanisms that

---

61   Ibid., 203.
62   Schmidt Goering, *Wisdom's Root*, ix.
63   נחלה is found in Sir. 8:10; 9:6; 42:3; 44:8, 11, 23; 45:20, 22(2x), 25(2x); 46:8, 9; κληρονομία is found in Sir. 9:6; 22:23; 23:12; 24:7, 12, 20, 23; 41:6; 42:3; 44:11, 23; 45:20, 22, 25(2x); 46:8, 9.

the sage envisioned as the proper means of safeguarding special wisdom and handing it on from generation to generation among the elect. In order to typify Ben Sira's view, it appears that the role of the king and, to a certain extent, the family in the book of Ben Sira is marginalized in favour of the scribes and the priests as preservers and transmitters of wisdom.

Ben Sira most often associates fear of YHWH with special wisdom. Since non-Jews are the recipients of general wisdom, the nations have the capacity to fear YHWH in the general sense of experiencing awe at creation and, as a result, recognizing his sovereignty as creator of the world. If, however, the awesomeness of creation does not move the Gentiles to fear YHWH, then God's miraculous rescue of his oppressed people becomes necessary (Sir. 35:22–36:22). In this way, the elect, as recipients of divine deliverance, play a passive role in bringing about the eschatological reality in which all nations recognize YHWH as sole deity.

Finally, the question under discussion has taken an important step forward on the *lexical level* by way of F. Reiterer, who in a detailed investigation studied all Ben Sira passages in which 'law' and 'wisdom' occur, both in Hebrew, Greek and Syriac. His conclusion is quite spectacular: 'Es gibt keine direkte Parallelsetzung von σοφία / חכמה und νόμος / תורה im Buch Ben Sira ... Für eine Identifikation von חכמה / σοφία und תורה / νόμος konnte kein Beleg gefunden werden'.[64]

4 Conclusion

No doubt Ben Sira research has entered into a new phase, since nowadays text critical studies are no longer the only avenue towards a better understanding of this wisdom document. As a result of archaeological discoveries of texts, substantial progress on historical, sociological and lexical grounds has been made. These results have also contributed to a better understanding and fine tuning of the theological message of the book of Ben Sira and, most recently, to the conclusion of the non-priestly decent of its author.

Appendix: Recent Literature on the Book of Ben Sira

Overviews: D.J. Harrington, 'Sirach Research since 1965: Progress and Questions', in: J. Kampen, J.C. Reeves (eds), *Pursuing the Text: Studies in Honor of Ben Zion Wacholder*

---

64   Reiterer, 'Das Verhältnis', 133.

(JSOTSup, 184), Sheffield 1994, 164–76; A.A. Di Lella, 'The Wisdom of Ben Sira: Resources and Recent Research', *Currents in Research: Biblical Studies* 4 (1996), 161–81; F.V. Reiterer, 'Review of Recent Research on the Book of Ben Sira (1980–1996)', in: P.C. Beentjes (ed.), *The Book of Ben Sira in Modern Research* (BZAW, 255), Berlin 1997, 23–60; P.C. Beentjes, 'Some Major Topics in Ben Sira Research', *Bijdragen* 66 (2005), 131–44 [= P. Beentjes, *"Happy the One who Meditates on Wisdom". Collected Essays on the Book of Ben Sira* (CBET, 43), Leuven 2006, 3–16]; N. Calduch-Benages, 'La situació actual dels estudis sobre el llibre del Siràcida (1996–2000)', *RCatT* 26 (2001), 391–98; M. Gilbert, 'Où en sont les études sur le Siracide?' *Bib* 92 (2011), 161–81.

Dictionaries: A.A. Di Lella, 'Wisdom of Ben Sira', *ABD* 6, New York 1992, 931–45; M. Gilbert, 'Jesus Sirach', *RAC* XVII, Stuttgart 1995, col. 878–906; M. Gilbert, 'Siracide', *DBSup* XII/71, Paris 1996, col. 1390–1437; J. Marböck, 'Sirach/Sirachbuch', *TRE* XXXI/1–2, Berlin 2000, 307–17; F.V. Reiterer, 'Jesus Sirach / Jesus Sirachbuch / Ben Sira / Ecclesiasticus', *WILAT*, Stuttgart 2007.

Congress volumes: F.V. Reiterer (ed.), *Freundschaft bei Ben Sira: Beiträge des Symposions zu Ben Sira Salzburg 1995* (BZAW, 244), Berlin 1996; P.C. Beentjes (ed.), *The Book of Ben Sira in Modern Research: Proceedings of the First International Ben Sira Conference Soesterberg, Netherlands* (BZAW, 255), Berlin 1997; R. Egger-Wenzel (ed.), *Ben Sira's God: Proceedings of the International Ben Sira Conference Durham-Ushaw College 2001* (BZAW, 321), Berlin 2002; G.G. Xeravits, J. Zsengellér (eds), *Studies in the Book of Ben Sira: Papers of the Third International Conference on Deuterocanonical Books, Shime'on Centre, Pápa, Hungary, 18–20 May, 2006* (JSJSup, 127), Leiden 2008; A. Passaro, G. Bellia (eds), *The Wisdom of Ben Sira: Studies on Tradition, Redaction, and Theology* (DCLS, 1), Berlin 2008; J.-S. Rey, J. Joosten (eds), *The Texts and Versions of the Book of Ben Sira: Transmission and Interpretation* (JSJSup, 150), Leiden 2011.

Festschriften: R. Egger-Wenzel, I. Krammer (eds), *Der Einzelne und seine Gemeinschaft bei Ben Sira. Fs F.V. Reiterer* (BZAW, 270), Berlin 1998; N. Calduch-Benages, J. Vermeylen (eds), *Treasures of Wisdom: Studies in Ben Sira and the Book of Wisdom. Fs M. Gilbert* (BETL, 143), Louvain 1999; I. Fischer, et al., *Auf den Spuren der schriftgelehrten Weisen. Fs J. Marböck* (BZAW, 331), Berlin 2003; J. Corley, V. Skemp (eds), *Intertextual Studies in Ben Sira and Tobit: Essays in Honor of A.A. Di Lella* (CBQMS, 38), Washington 2005; J. Corley, H. van Grol (eds), *Rewriting Biblical History: Essays on Chronicles and Ben Sira in Honor of P.C. Beentjes* (DCLS, 7), Berlin 2011.

Collected essays: J. Marböck, *Gottes Weisheit unter uns: Zur Theologie des Buches Sirach* (HBS, 6; Hg. I. Fischer), Freiburg 1995; J. Marböck, *Weisheit und Frömmigkeit. Studien zur alttestamentlichen Literatur der Spätzeit* (ÖBS, 29), Frankfurt a.M. 2006; P.C. Beentjes, *"Happy the One who Meditates on Wisdom" (Sir. 14,20). Collected Essays on the Book of Ben Sira* (CBET, 43), Louvain 2006; F.V. Reiterer, *"Alle Weisheit stammt vom Herrn…": Gesammelte Studien zu Ben Sira* (BZAW, 375), Berlin 2007; B.G. Wright,

Praise Israel for Wisdom and Instructions: Essays on Ben Sira and Wisdom, the Letter of Aristeas and the Septuagint (JSJSup, 131), Leiden 2008; G. Sauer, *Studien zu Ben Sira* (BZAW, 440), Berlin 2013; M. Gilbert, *Ben Sira: Recueil d'études—Collected Essays* (BETL, 264), Leuven 2014.

Doctoral theses: R. Hildesheim, *Bis daß ein Prophet aufstand wie Feuer: Untersuchungen zum Prophetenverständnis des Ben Sira* (TThS, 58), Trier 1996; U. Wicke-Reuter, *Göttliche Providenz und menschliche Verantwortung bei Ben Sira und in der Frühen Stoa* (BZAW, 298), Berlin 2000; M. Reitemeyer, *Weisheitslehre als Gotteslob: Psalmentheologie im Buch Jesus Sirach* (BBB, 127), Berlin 2000; J. Liesen, *Full of Praise: An Exegetical Study of Sir 39,12–35* (JSJSup, 64), Leiden 2003; O. Mulder, *Simon the High Priest in Sirach 50* (JSJSup, 78), Leiden 2003; F. Ueberschar, *Weisheit aus der Begegnung: Bildung nach dem Buch Ben Sira* (BZAW, 379), Berlin 2007; S.L. Adams, *Wisdom in Transition: Act and Consequence in Second Temple Instructions* (JSJSup, 125), Leiden 2008, 153–213; G. Schmidt Goering, *Wisdom's Root Revealed: Ben Sira and the Election of Israel* (JSJSup, 139), Leiden 2009; W. Urbanz, *Gebet im Sirachbuch: Zur Terminologie von Klage und Lob in der griechischen Texttradition* (HBS, 60), Freiburg 2009; B.C. Gregory, *Like an Everlasting Signet Ring: Generosity in the Book of Sirach* (DCLS, 2), Berlin 2010; I. Balla, *Ben Sira on Family, Gender, and Sexuality* (DCLS, 8), Berlin 2011; T.A. Ellis, *Gender in the Book of Ben Sira: Divine Wisdom, Erotic Poetry, and the Garden of Eden* (BZAW, 453), Berlin 2013.

The Place of Wisdom in the Formation of the Movement behind the Dead Sea Scrolls

George J. Brooke

1 Introduction

With a scene-setting Introduction that sets out some aspects of the research question behind this paper and a brief Conclusion this essay has three parts. In the first I argue that the recent study of the sapiential tradition has focussed on the texts themselves and their antecedents rather than on what they might signify through their use and reception by the communities that preserved them. In the second I consider three motifs which repay study in any attempt to link pre-sectarian wisdom compositions with later sectarian works. In the third I propose that the Teacher of Righteousness, whether in actuality as a Maskil or as remembered, was linked with wisdom traditions together with others.

Over the years it has been notoriously difficult for scholars to discern with any precision wherein lies the origin of the sectarian movement, commonly associated with the Essenes in various forms, some members of which eventually came to occupy the site of Qumran for some reason, probably in the first quarter of the first century BCE. Some scholars, from Frank Moore Cross to Florentino García Martínez, have proposed and argued that much in the sectarian writings is developed from a background in apocalyptic thinking of the late third and early second centuries.[1] Despite the transmission of works such as the Book of Watchers and other parts of the Enochic corpus, the overall absence of literary apocalypses, that is the narrations of auditions and visions, from the sectarian compositions proper suggests that if apocalyptic was at the heart of the origins of the movement, that movement very soon moved

---

1 See, e.g., F.M. Cross, *The Ancient Library of Qumran and Modern Biblical Studies*, Garden City, NY 1958, Sheffield ³1995; F. García Martínez, *Qumran and Apocalyptic: Studies on the Aramaic Texts from Qumran* (STDJ, 9) Leiden 1992; idem, 'Apocalypticism in the Dead Sea Scrolls', in: J.J. Collins (ed.), *The Encyclopedia of Apocalypticism*. Vol. 1 *The Origins of Apocalytpicism in Judaism and Christianity*, New York 1998, 162–92. See also the summary survey by J.J. Collins, *Apocalypticism in the* Dead *Sea Scrolls*, London 1997. See also L.G. Perdue, *The Sword and the Stylus: An Introduction to Wisdom in the Age of Empires*, Grand Rapids 2008, 372–87, who speaks somewhat imprecisely of 'Apocalyptic Wisdom in Qumran'.

away from such approaches and their realignments of authoritative traditions towards a concern with what has been and could still be revealed.[2]

The absence of sectarian visions or auditions, but the concern with the interpretation of the oracular has resulted in the association of the movement behind the sectarian compositions with prophecy of some kind.[3] There are no new oracles as such, but the prophetic insights of earlier generations are recast through both implicit and explicit interpretation so that they have a fresh oracular dynamism. Indeed, alongside the influence of the scriptural literary prophets, the prophetic status of Moses is recognized and built upon so that the halakhah of the movement develops as inspired interpretation of Torah materials: alongside the *nigleh*, what has been clearly revealed, the *nistarot*, what was hidden, can also be made known through correct interpretation.[4]

Apart from apocalyptic or prophecy, it is also entirely possible to latch on to the note in Pesher Psalms A (4Q171) that the Teacher was a priest to discuss the hieratical background of the movement. It is well known that the ideology in some of the sectarian rule texts, with their various attentions to Aaronide and Zadokite concerns, and in a composition like Miqṣat Ma'aśe Ha-Torah is explicitly priestly.[5] All that can very readily be developed into a retrojected notion that many of those who constituted the first generation of this sectarian movement, or at least its leadership, were priests. In its extreme form this kind of theorizing has led to the proposal that the Teacher of Righteousness

---

2   See, e.g., V. Triplet-Hitoto, *Mystères et connaissances cachées à Qumrân* (L'écriture de la Bible, 1), Paris 2011; Triplet-Hitoto studiously avoids using explicit apocalyptic language.

3   See, e.g., A.P. Jassen, *Mediating the Divine: Prophecy and Revelation in the Dead Sea Scrolls and Second Temple Judaism* (STDJ, 68), Leiden 2007; G.J. Brooke, 'La Prophétie de Qumrân', in: J.-D. Macchi, C. Nihan, T. Römer, and J. Rückl (eds), *Les recueils prophétiques de la Bible: Origines, milieux et contexte proche-oriental* (Le Monde de la Bible, 64), Geneva 2012, 480–510. See also for the link with wisdom, M. Nissinen, 'Transmitting Divine Mysteries: The Prophetic Role of Wisdom Teachers in the Dead Sea Scrolls', in: A. Voitila and J. Jokiranta (eds), *Scripture in Transition: Essays on Septuagint, Hebrew Bible, and Dead Sea Scrolls in Honour of Raija Sollamo* (JSJSup, 126), Leiden 2008, 513–33.

4   See, e.g., L.H. Schiffman, *The Halakhah at Qumran* (SJLA, 16), Leiden 1975, esp. pp. 22–32. For the purposes of this study see also W.A. Tooman, 'Wisdom and Torah at Qumran: Evidence from the Sapiential Texts', in: B.U. Schipper and A.D. Teeter (eds), *Wisdom and Torah: The Reception of 'Torah' in the Wisdom Literature of the Second Temple Period* (JSJSup, 163), Leiden 2013, 203–32.

5   See, e.g., H.-J. Fabry, 'Priests at Qumran: A Reassessment', in: C. Hempel (ed.), *The Dead Sea Scrolls: Texts and Context* (STDJ, 90), Leiden 2010, 243–62, who surveys various positions as well as offering his own.

had been the High Priest of the so-called intersacerdotum period prior to 152 BCE.[6]

My own preference has been to suggest that the ingenuity and genius of those responsible for articulating the identity of the new movement can be seen in their competence at combining streams of thought from several backgrounds, even some that might have been understood to be in competition with one another.[7] I suspect that one central figure, the Teacher of Righteousness, was able to articulate such recast traditions with a rhetorical flair, some of which could still be discernible in parts of the Hodayot. Along with his contemporaries he was engaged in the rewriting of tradition; he did this so as to inscribe his followers into a community that considered itself to be scriptural. Thus what emerged into full-blown sectarianism as expressed in some of the community's rule books and other compositions in the first century BCE is the heir to the interweaving of several traditions, all of which, if the historian is honest, were not themselves the various expressions of some kind of ideological purity, but were already composite and mixed. Several recent studies have helped articulate the intersecting boundaries in the third and second centuries of apocalyptic and prophecy, of priestly perspectives and visionary experience, and of other such combinations.

The purpose of the various parts of this short paper is to suggest that the pre-sectarian wisdom texts that survive from the eleven caves at or near Qumran strongly encourage the view that those responsible for their composition were also the direct forbears of at least some of the members of the movement, part of which eventually came to occupy the Qumran site. This suggestion is not new. It has been made over the years by several scholars who have been sensitive to the preservation in the Qumran caves of the writings of Ben Sira.[8] Indeed, one of the first scriptural scrolls from Cave 4 to be published was the large fragment of Qohelet (4QQoh^a), and although there are no reasons to think that it or any of the scriptural scrolls contain sectarian readings, its presence in the working library of the community at Qumran stands for the role of such materials in

---

6 Classically stated by H. Stegemann, *Die Enstehung der Qumrangemeinde*, Bonn 1971, 210–13, 218–21.

7 G.J. Brooke, 'The "Apocalyptic" Community, the Matrix of the Teacher and Rewriting Scripture', in: M. Popović, *Authoritative Scriptures in Ancient Judaism* (JSJSup, 141), Leiden 2010, 37–53.

8 D.J. Harrington, *Wisdom Texts from Qumran*, London 1996, 9–10, highlights three aspects of Ben Sira that recur in sectarian compositions: its interest in the figure of Wisdom, its cosmology and its theodicy expressed in a doctrine of pairs (Sir 33:15).

the thinking of the sectarians there.[9] But in addition to Ben Sira and Qohelet and indeed other texts, two factors in particular provoke a brief study such as this. The first we shall pass over swiftly but is nonetheless significant, namely some recent thinking about scribes and scribal schools and where and in what traditions they might have been trained. This is important since none other than Ben Sira himself suggests that the vocation of the scribe is above all other skills and concerns amongst other things the study of the Law, engagement with prophecies and proverbs, as well as petition and prayer (Sir 38:24; 39:1–3).[10] The second factor is the immediate core of what needs to be factored into the origins and identity of the sectarian movement, some members of which have ended up at Qumran. They preserved and collected together a surprising range of what can be broadly classified as wisdom compositions. The complete publication of the extant scrolls corpus, especially many previously unpublished items from Cave 4, permits a reconsideration of the place of wisdom traditions in the formation and ongoing self-understanding of the movement behind the Dead Sea Scrolls which were found in the eleven caves at and near Qumran.

2   Pre-Sectarian Wisdom Compositions and the Sectarian Movement

Several scholars, especially Daniel Harrington,[11] Matthew Goff,[12] and John Kampen,[13] have outlined the breadth and scope of what might be included amongst the sapiential literature of the Dead Sea Scrolls. Amongst compositions thus assigned are many with multiple functions, suggesting overlapping concerns with apocalyptic (as is Goff's reading of Instruction), with esoterica (Mysteries), with personified insight into the way things are (4Q184 and 4Q185), with Torah and halakhah (4Q420–421), with practical wisdom (4Q424), and with the cult (11QPs[a]). There are plenty of other fragments too which speak of the breadth of wisdom concerns as far as these can be perceived by scholars two millennia later: those fragments also hint at multiple interests, such

---

9   J. Muilenburg, 'A Qoheleth Scroll from Qumran', BASOR 135 (1954), 20–28.
10 See, notably, A. Lange, 'Sages and Scribes in the Qumran Literature', in: L.G. Perdue (ed.), *Scribes, Sages, and Seers: The Sage in the Eastern Mediterranean World* (FRLANT, 219), Göttingen 2008, 271–93.
11 Harrington, *Wisdom Texts from Qumran*, 23–80.
12 M.J. Goff, *Discerning Wisdom: The Sapiential Literature of the Dead Sea Scrolls* (VTSup, 116), Leiden 2007.
13 J. Kampen, *Wisdom Literature* (Eerdmans Commentaries on the Dead Sea Scrolls), Grand Rapids 2011.

as exegetical grappling with matters of creation (4Q303–305), the role of the divine in history (4Q413), priestly insight (4Q419), a concern to read eschatology into received traditions (4Q415–418), the juxtaposition of wisdom teaching with the Torah (4Q525), and the interplay of prayer, praise and poetry (4Q411, 4Q426, 4Q528). Indeed Goff finished his survey of the sapiential literature amongst the Dead Sea Scrolls by drawing out just these overlapping concerns with comments on wisdom and apocalypticism, wisdom and Torah, wisdom and piety, and so on.[14]

In addition to those helpful surveys some volumes of collected essays have been published, some of which have been based on conferences and symposia.[15] And there have been a few monographs, such as those by Torleif Elgvin,[16] Armin Lange,[17] Eibert Tigchelaar,[18] Matthew Goff,[19] Grant Macaskill,[20] Jean-Sébastien Rey,[21] and Valérie Triplet-Hitoto,[22] some of which have also been concerned to articulate the ways in which one or more of the wisdom compositions intersect with other traditions, particularly in circles where divination or priesthood or apocalyptic or eschatology was dominant.

---

14 Goff, *Discerning Wisdom*, 287–303.
15 C. Hempel, A. Lange, and H. Lichtenberger (eds), *The Wisdom Texts and the Development of Sapiential Thought* (BETL, 159), Leuven 2002; D.K. Falk, F. García Martínez, and E.M. Schuller (eds), *Sapiential, Liturgical and Poetical Texts from Qumran: Proceedings of the Third Meeting of the International Organization for Qumran Studies, Oslo 1998, Published in Memory of Maurice Baillet* (STDJ, 35), Leiden 2000; F. García Martínez (ed.), *Wisdom and Apocalypticism in the Dead Sea Scrolls and in the Biblical Tradition* (BETL, 168), Leuven 2003; J.J. Collins, G.E. Sterling, and R.A. Clements (eds), *Sapiential Perspectives: Wisdom Literature in Light of the Dead Sea Scrolls. Proceedings of the Sixth International Symposium of the Orion Center, 20–22 May, 2001* (STDJ, 51), Leiden 2004.
16 T. Elgvin, www.4reid.no/4QInstruction. On p. 182 he comments on the priestly elements in wisdom material from the Qumran caves.
17 A. Lange, *Weisheit und Prädestination: Weisheitliche Urordnung und Prädestination in den Textfunden von Qumran* (STDJ, 18), Leiden 1995.
18 E.J.C. Tigchelaar, *To Increase Learning for the Understanding Ones: Reading and Reconstructing the Fragmentary Early Jewish Sapiential Text 4QInstruction* (STDJ, 44), Leiden 2001.
19 M.J. Goff, *The Worldly and Heavenly Wisdom of 4QInstruction* (STDJ, 50), Leiden 2003; idem, *4QInstruction* (SBL Wisdom Literature from the Ancient World, 2); Atlanta 2013.
20 G. Macaskill, *Revealed Wisdom and Inaugurated Eschatology in Ancient Judaism and Early Christianity* (JSJSup, 115), Leiden 2007.
21 J.-S. Rey, *4QInstruction: Sagesse et eschatologie* (STDJ, 81), Leiden 2009.
22 Triplet-Hitoto, *Mystères et connaissances*; this study concentrates on the influence of Deut 29:28.

As a result, much in all the scholarly endeavour of the last two decades has been about the adequate description of certain manuscripts and the compositions they contain. The weight of descriptive and analytical work has been undertaken in ways that pay attention to the compositions in themselves or which trace the traditions that they seem to rework and represent in various ways. All that is well and good but the discussion has been dominated by reading those compositions with an eye to understanding where they came from, rather than with a concern as to how they might have been read and received by the movement that preserved them. Thus, in some ways the study of these wisdom compositions has seemed to imply a separation of the wisdom traditions from the core activity of the sectarian movement which preserved such compositions, and which probably was responsible for copying and disseminating them. As Adam van der Woude concluded in his essay of 1995: 'none of the wisdom texts discovered among the Dead Sea Scrolls originated in Qumran'.[23] But that conclusion does not mean that there was no place for an ongoing presence for wisdom traditions in the Qumran community and more importantly in the wider movement of which it was a part and from which it derived.

3   Three Wisdom Motifs

Several of the distinctive features of the pre-sectarian Wisdom compositions found in the eleven caves at and near Qumran belong to a time before the sect was fully fledged. The purpose of this section of this essay is to suggest that whilst these features are not necessarily sectarian in themselves, they are picked up, directly or indirectly, and echoed in some later compositions that are clearly sectarian such as the Rule of the Community. Three items might be particularly significant and can be briefly commented upon.

First is the term *rz nhyh*. The role of this term in Instruction (1Q26; 4Q415–418; 4Q423), has been the subject of extensive discussion.[24] The translation of the term is problematic. Perhaps it is best understood as polyvalent, carrying something of past, present and future: reflection of the principles of creation, foundations from the past; insight into the cosmic dimension of experience,

---

23   A.S. van der Woude, 'Wisdom at Qumran', in: J. Day (ed.), *Wisdom in Ancient Israel: Essays in Honour of J.A. Emerton*, Cambridge 1995, 244–56 at 256.

24   See, e.g., S.I. Thomas, *The "Mysteries" of Qumran: Mystery, Secrecy, and Esotericism in the Dead Sea Scrolls* (SBLEJL, 25), Atlanta 2009; Triplet-Hitoto, *Mystères et connaissances*, 148–73.

the way to live in the present; and a dimension that recognizes the combined roles of purpose, judgement and hope, eschatological perspectives. In Instruction the term *rz* appears predominantly in this idiom and *rz* is in the singular; apart from this idiom, *rz* can be either singular or plural (4Q416 2 II, 8; 4Q417 1 I, 2; 13; 25; 4Q418 177 7a). Although it is possible to discuss whether the appearance of *rz* in sectarian compositions, where it features predominantly in the plural, is a development of a separate or distinctive usage, it is important to notice the presence of the idiom *rz nhyh* in 1QS XI, 3–4: 'For from the source of his knowledge he has disclosed his light, and my eyes have observed his wonders, and the light of my heart the mystery of existence'.[25] Although 1QS IX–XI might contain the citation of an independent poem, it has been heavily edited with sectarian terminology and concerns, so much so that it is difficult to see the seams between earlier and later material. The *rz nhyh* is not widespread in purely sectarian compositions, but 1QS XI suggests that it has become an integral part of the sectarian outlook by the beginning of the first century BCE.[26] The extensive copying, largely in so-called Qumran scribal practice, of Instruction and the Mysteries text in which the term is ubiquitous also supports the view that it would have been well known in the sectarian movement.

Before moving to other terms it is worth highlighting two uses of *rz* in the Hodayot. Apart from a single use in a version of the Damascus Document, 4Q270 2 II, 13, 'one who reveals a secret of his people to the gentiles',[27] the only occurrences of *rz* in the singular in a sectarian composition are in the Hodayot. In 1QH[a] XIII, 27 the hymnist declares: 'With the secret you have hidden in me they go about with slander to the children of destruction'. The nature of that *rz*, 'secret', is associated with divine greatness, 'the spring (*m'yn*) of understanding and the foundation of truth' (XIII, 28).[28] It is as if the writer of the poem

---

25 Trans. F. García Martínez and E.J.C. Tigchelaar, *The Dead Sea Scrolls Study Edition*, Leiden, Grand Rapids 2000, 1.97.

26 Note that all that remains of 4QS[j] contains parts of this poem that closes the Rule of the Community in its Cave 1 version; perhaps 4QS[j] attests to the independent existence of the poem.

27 Trans. J.M. Baumgarten, *Qumran Cave 4.XIII: The Damascus Document (4Q266–273)* (DJD, 18), Oxford 1996, 145. Baumgarten commented (p. 146) that although the treasonable passing of information to a foreign nation is punishable by hanging according to 11QT[a] LXIV, 6–8, the phraseology of 4Q270 here is much closer to that found in an En Gedi inscription: 'He who reveals a secret of the city to the gentiles'.

28 Trans. C.A. Newsom in H. Stegemann and E.M. Schuller (eds), *Qumran Cave 1.III: 1QHodayot[a] with Incorporation of 1QHodayot[b] and 4QHodayot[a–f]* (DJD, 40), Oxford 2009, 180. The line numbers for 1QH[a] in references in the rest of this study follow that edition.

envisages that the fundamental basis of things has been embedded within him and it is this which allows him to be the conveyor and revealer of the greatness of God. The poet seems to have been given the singular mystery of existence, or insight into the way things will be, even if he does not name it as such. If the author of the hymn might be identified with the founding Teacher, or at least with a sectarian Maskil, his perception of bearing the *rz* within him as a divine gift might imply that he is claiming to be like one who has learnt from his father the mystery of existence as Instruction describes. A second use of *rz* in the Hodayot is also intriguing. In 1QH^a XX, 15–16 the Maskil declares: 'By your holy spirit you have [o]pened up knowledge within me through the mystery of your wisdom and the fountainhead of (*mʿyn*) [your] pow[er]'.[29] The poet is playing with the root *śkl* as in the label he gives himself (*mśkyl*) and the content and character of the mystery (*śklkh*). As in 1QH^a XIII, 28, the nature of this mystery is clarified through the association with a cosmic fountain or spring. These two singular uses of *rz*, both linked to what the hymnist or Instructor has implanted within him in terms of cosmic insight, make the poet a mediator of mystery to his community. However, although the members of that community can indeed read about the *rz nhyh* in compositions like Instruction, they themselves are more concerned with acknowledging externally the wonderful mysteries of God (CD III, 18).

A second significant term is *ʾbywn*, 'poor'. The relatively common use of this term and others, apparently as a self-designation, in some clearly sectarian compositions was one of the factors that initially caused Instruction and some other compositions to be understood by some as sectarian in origin. Further study has enabled greater nuance.[30] However, although it is now a consensus view that Instruction is not a sectarian composition, this should not mean that its terminology could not be picked up within the sectarian movement and used for particular purposes. The transmission of the term from the sapiential traditions to its use as a sectarian self-designation in Pesher Habakkuk but most explicitly in Pesher Psalms A, in the phrase *ʿdt hʾbywnym*, 'congregation of the poor', is intriguing. In Instruction *ʾbywn* is used in the singular, not least as the disciple or pupil is designated and addressed as such by the teacher: *ʾbywn ʾth*, 'poor you are'. In the Hodayot the term is likewise and commonly used in the singular, but this time as a self-designation of the poet as the poetic parallelism makes apparent: 'You have redeemed the soul of *the poor one* whom they

---

29 Trans. Newsom in *Qumran Cave 1.III: 1QHodayot^a*, 260.

30 See, e.g., E.J.C. Tigchelaar, 'The Addressees of 4QInstruction', in: *Sapiential, Liturgical and Poetical Texts from Qumran*, 62–75; B.G. Wright III, 'The Categories of Rich and Poor in the Qumran Sectarian Literature', in: *Sapiential Perspectives*, 101–23, esp. 109–23.

thought to destroy, pouring out his blood because of service to you. Yet they did [not] know that my steps come from you' (1QH^a X, 34–35); or again, 'the soul of *a poor person* dwells with tumults in abundance, and disastrous calamities dog my steps' (1QH^a XI, 26).[31] By the time of the pesharim in the second half of the first century BCE the term seems to have become a *terminus technicus*; its usage is intriguing. Its first extant occurrence is in the interpretation of Ps. 37:11 which speaks of the poor as *'nwym*; the interpretation carefully does not use the same word, a ready possibility, but *'dt h'bywnym*, 'congregation of the poor'. Later, in Ps. 37:14, the term *'bywn* is indeed used in the singular and it is interpreted as referring to 'the Priest'; the interpreter seems to be aware of the tradition in the Hodayot that the founding priest-Teacher or Maskil had designated himself as *'bywn*, 'poor'. In this way the community seems to adopt a self-designation that aligns it directly with its founder, but which also is a term that has a much wider scope of reference in the wisdom literature.

A third term worth brief comment is *mśkyl*, 'instructor' or 'sage'.[32] The verbal root to which the nominal form is related and also the segholate *śkl* are widespread in both non- or pre-sectarian compositions and in sectarian ones, not least the wisdom compositions and the Hodayot. As for *mśkyl* itself it occurs occasionally in the pre-sectarian wisdom compositions such as Instruction (4Q418 81+81a 17) and Ways of Righteousness (4Q421 1 12). It survives in both the Cave 1 and Cave 4 versions of the Hodayot, not least as a self-designation of the poet: 'And I, the Instructor, I know you, my God, by the spirit that you have placed in me' (1QH^a XX, 14–15).[33] Elsewhere, including in the Hodayot (1QH^a XXV, 34), it occurs most frequently with *lamed*: 'For the Maskil (instructor)'. For example, the idiom occurs in headings such as 'And these are the ordinances for the Instructor, so that he walks in them with every living thing' (CD XII, 20–21), 'For the Instructor, to help understanding and to teach all the sons of light' (1QS III, 13), and 'These are the regulations for the Instructor by which he shall walk with every living being' (1QS IX, 12). One of the Cave 4 versions of the Rule of the Community (4Q258) and possibly the Cave 1 version along with the Rule of Blessings seem to be compiled as guides for the Maskil, rather than as general constitutional rules. The use of the plural form for 'the wise' in Dan. 11:33–34 and 12:3, often traced to the use of the *hiph'il* form of the

---

31 Trans. Newsom in *Qumran Cave 1.III: 1QHodayot^a*, 143, 155.
32 See the notable study by C.A. Newsom, 'The Sage in the Literature of Qumran: The Functions of the Maskil', in: J.G. Gammie and L.G. Perdue (eds), *The Sage in Israel and the Ancient Near East*, Winona Lake 1990, 373–82.
33 Trans. Newsom in *Qumran Cave 1.III: 1QHodayot^a*, 259–60.

verb used with the servant as subject in Isa. 52:13, is commonly understood as the background to the technical individualised terminology of the sectarian compositions.[34] However, the use of the singular in compositions such as Instruction locates the language in a broader framework of sapiential traditions.

4 The Teacher of Righteousness

In the previous brief discussion of the use of some wisdom terminology in the sectarian compositions proper it has been noted that in all three case, for *rz*, *'bywn*, and *mśkyl*, the Hodayot are a significant set of poems for disclosing how such terms are moved from a broader sapiential literary context to more specific sectarian uses. Indeed, more than that, in all three cases the poet of the Hodayot sees himself in particular ways in relation to such terms: the mystery is embedded within him, he is the poor one par excellence, and he is the Maskil. It thus behoves us to consider briefly in this third part of the paper the poet himself, not least as he might be identified or constructed as the Teacher of Righteousness.

Some preliminary remarks are in order. Together with many scholars I am inclined to think three basic things about the Teacher of Righteousness. First, it seems to me most likely that he existed and that his title is not simply an office that anyone might fill. Second, I am strongly inclined to follow the majority and consensus view that the Teacher was active at some time in the middle of the second century BCE.[35] Despite wanting to affirm the existence of the Teacher as a significant individual of the second century BCE, I also want to assert, thirdly, that very little is known about him, much less than a simple reading of the surface of some texts might imply. That much has often been said, but it needs to be stressed again that, apart from a possibility in the case

---

34   J.J. Collins, *Daniel* (Hermeneia), Minneapolis 1993, 385; C. Hempel, '"*Maskil(im)*" and "*Rabbim*" from Daniel to Qumran', in: C. Hempel and J.M. Lieu (eds), *Biblical Traditions in Transmission: Essays in Honour of Michael A. Knibb* (JSJSup, 111), Leiden 2006, 133–56.

35   There have been a few voices wondering whether or even arguing strongly that the Teacher was a figure of the first century BCE: M.O. Wise, 'Dating the Teacher of Righteousness and the Floruit of his Movement', *JBL* 122 (2003), 53–87; J.J. Collins, 'The Time of the Teacher: An Old Debate Renewed', in: P.W. Flint, E. Tov, and J.C. VanderKam (eds), *Studies in the Hebrew Bible, Qumran, and the Septuagint Presented to Eugene Ulrich* (VTSup, 101), Leiden 2006, 212–29.

of the so-called Teacher Hymns (1QH^a X–XVII), little or nothing seems to come directly from his hand.[36] Rather, the construction of the Teacher as a figure arises out of how the movement with which he is associated chose to commemorate and talk about him. The depiction of the Teacher is in large part a matter of the collective memory of the movement.[37]

In a previous study concerning the circumstances of the middle of the second century BCE, I posed the question whether the large number of rewritings of authoritative traditions at that time might be associated with the Teacher in some way. In what ways might he have been able to take advantage of such rewriting practices to facilitate his leadership role within a movement that seems to have identified him as the one who brought focus to that movement. I argued that at least 'part of the matrix of scriptural interpretative rewriting which the Teacher exploits for a varied audience is priestly, scribal, mantic'.[38] priestly in terms of legal interpretation, scribal in terms of his teaching role, and mantic in the way that his oracular understanding of the mysteries of the prophets is represented in a quasi-divinatory fashion. All of these aspects could be appreciated further by paying attention to how they reflect issues commonly associated with or found in wisdom compositions.

Since the Hodayot may be the particular locus where the activity of the Teacher as Maskil can be identified, even if only as an ideal construct, it is worth making a few further comments about them. It has long been acknowledged that there are multiple wisdom elements in the Hodayot. Especially since the 1986 Harvard dissertation of Sarah Tanzer, 'The sages at Qumran: Wisdom in the "Hodayot"', which was never published, numerous features of the Hodayot have been understood as reflecting wisdom tradition. Even before

---

36 The most forceful voice against this possibility of seeing a historical Teacher behind the so-called Teacher Hymns is that of A. Kim Harkins, 'Who is the Teacher of the Teacher Hymns? Re-Examining the Teacher Hymns Hypothesis Fifty Years Later', in: E. Mason, S.I. Thomas, A. Schofield, E. Ulrich, K. Coblentz Bautch, A. Kim Harkins, and D. Machiela (eds), *A Teacher for All Generations: Essays in Honor of James C. VanderKam* (JSJSup, 153), Leiden 2012, 1.449–67: 'this is not a historical person. The vivid and dramatic references to the speaker's experiences in the Teacher Hymns do not point to a historical flesh and blood Teacher' (p. 467).

37 L.T. Stuckenbruck, 'The Teacher of Righteousness Remembered: From Fragmentary Sources to Collective Memory in the Dead Sea Scrolls', in: S.C. Barton, L.T. Stuckenbruck, and B.G. Wold (eds), *Memory in the Bible and Antiquity: The Fifth Durham-Tübingen Research Symposium (Durham, September 2004)* (WUNT, 212), Tübingen 2007, 75–94.

38 Brooke, 'The 'Apocalyptic' Community, the Matrix of the Teacher and Rewriting Scripture', 47.

that landmark work, some of the connections between the Hodayot and scriptural wisdom books, especially Job and Proverbs, had been noted.[39]

In a detailed study of the poem preserved in 1QH^a XII, 5–29, Alex Jassen has well argued that the description of the conflict between the poet and his enemies 'is couched in a much larger assessment of the competing claims to divine access by the hymnist (and by extension the sect) and the opponents'.[40] For Jassen while the enemies 'hold back the drink of knowledge' (XII, 12) and reject the 'vision of knowledge' (XII, 19), the hymnist asserts that God has given him understanding of the mysteries of his wonder and that he has been confirmed in his wondrous council (XII, 28–29). Jassen has concluded for the hymnist: 'His revelation is experienced neither through visions nor dreams; rather, for the hymnist the cultivation of divinely revealed wisdom characterizes his revelatory encounter'.[41] This kind of wisdom is closely akin to that which is to be found in Instruction or in the portrayal of the psalmist David in the 11QPs^a scroll: David is wise, 'a light like the light of the sun', a scribe with discernment who has received an enlightened and discerning spirit of prophecy from God.

And if the Maskil of the Hodayot, as Teacher, is constructed so as to claim to stand in a particular line of wisdom, so can the Teacher of the pesharim to whom is given knowledge (*d't*) of all the mysteries of God's servants the prophets. Amongst those who have written on the intellectual profile of the exegetical activity of the remembered Teacher, Marti Nissinen has clarified at least one major aspect of the context of such exegetical activity. It seems to be, at least from some perspectives, akin to the divination processes of omen interpretation. 'The idea and practice of the pesharim in general is related to the purpose of omen-based divination to acquire divine information on contemporary circumstances by systematic observation of god-given signs. In the case of the pesharim, the base-texts take the role of such signs'.[42] This is a kind

---

39   S. Holm-Nielsen, *Hodayot: Psalms from Qumran* (Acta Theologica Danica, 2), Aarhus 1960, considered there to be at least a dozen certain references to Job; J.A. Hughes, *Scriptural Allusions and Exegesis in the Hodayot* (STDJ, 59), Leiden 2006, in considering just some Hodayot passages, has noted strong allusions to Proverbs.

40   A. Jassen, 'Prophecy after "The Prophets": The Dead Sea Scrolls and the History of Prophecy in Judaism', in: A. Lange, E. Tov, and M. Weigold (eds), *The Dead Sea Scrolls in Context: Integrating the Dead Sea Scrolls in the Study of Ancient Texts, Languages, and Cultures* (VTSup, 140), Leiden 2011, 2.577–93 at 580.

41   Jassen, 'Prophecy after "The Prophets"', 590.

42   M. Nissinen, 'Pesharim as Divination. Qumran Exegesis, Omen Interpretation and Literary Prophecy', in: K. De Troyer and A. Lange with L.L. Schulte (eds), *Prophecy after the Prophets? The Contribution of the Dead Sea Scrolls to the Understanding of Biblical and Extra-Biblical Prophecy* (CBET, 52), Leuven 2009, 43–60 at 60.

of mantic wisdom as has been applied to the exegetical activities behind the pesharim by both Armin Lange and James VanderKam.[43]

The legal interpretation of the Teacher, perhaps of the Teacher as priest, as reflected in the correct understanding of legal matters also has wisdom dimensions in continuity with the kinds of revelation that are discernible in Instruction or in the Mysteries text. These are not based on dreams and visions but on divinely given insight into the way things are and the purposes of things as God intends them. Thus it is not sufficient to obey the law in its plain sense; it has to be correctly aligned with what is made known from the hidden things in terms of the cult and just stipulations (CD III, 12–20).

For van der Woude there is no doubt that in relation to all his activities 'the revelation imparted to the Teacher was considered as charismatic wisdom'. The term *ḥkmh* is not used of this insight but a range of technical wisdom language is used, some of which is set out in this study. 'Wisdom terminology also abounds in non-sapiential writings found among the Dead Sea Scrolls', states van der Woude correctly.[44] But more than that the extent of such terminology strongly suggests that in the second century BCE there were some who had long been associated with the scribal wisdom schools, such as are reflected in the text of Ben Sira, who were attracted along with apocalypticists and priests to join the movement that was brought into focus by the Teacher from a mixed range of dissenting people. The Teacher identified himself with various elements of wisdom traditions and spoke in such terms that those from that kind of background would readily have found his message appealing, if they had had any grounds to doubt where their allegiances lay. Wisdom traditions bring together both Teacher and community, as well as a range of legal, prophetic and scribal activities that both are engaged in: in some ways there may be diachronic continuity from pre-sectarian wisdom compositions through the nascent sectarianism of the second century BCE, but in other ways aspects of wisdom traditions are re-discovered at a later stage and form part of some layers of those compositions that fully deserve the label sectarian.

---

43 A. Lange, 'The Essene Position on Magic and Divination', in: M.J. Bernstein, F. García Martínez, and J. Kampen (eds), *Legal Texts and Legal Issues: Proceedings of the Second Meeting of the International Organization for Qumran Studies, Cambridge, 1995: Published in Honour of Joseph M. Baumgarten* (STDJ, 23), Leiden 1997, 377–435; J.C. VanderKam, 'Mantic Wisdom in the Dead Sea Scrolls', *DSD* 4 (1997), 336–53.

44 Van der Woude, 'Wisdom at Qumran', 256.

5 Conclusion

There are many overlapping concerns in attempting to put a picture together of how wisdom is transmitted into the sectarian movement. In this paper I have tried to argue that it is time for scholars to think yet more about continuities between the non-sectarian wisdom texts and traditions and the sectarian compositions and the activities they reflect. In the light of attention to some of those continuities it can be argued that at least part of the movement that talked about its Teacher had probably had some affiliation to scribal or wisdom schools of some sort. The persona of the poetic Maskil seems to have been well aware of wisdom texts and was given them both to describe himself and his exegetical and interpretative activities. Those who read and used the Hodayot found wisdom language so appealing that they variously applied it also to themselves and their ways of thinking. And as they continued to identify with the Teacher's apparent self-understanding, they also continued his interpretative activities, perhaps even retrojecting on him further dimensions of such activity, whether in legal or prophetic interpretation. Wisdom traditions and motifs play significant roles in being part of what binds together much of the priestly and prophetic interests of this group.

The Wisdom of Job's Conclusion (Job 42:1–6)

David J.A. Clines

In his response (40:3–5) to the first divine speech of Job 38–39, brief though it was, Job said that he stood by what he had previously argued in his speeches, but he will not reiterate his case: 'I have spoken once, but I shall not speak again, twice, but I shall say no more'. Now his response to the second divine speech of Job 40:6–41:34 goes one step further, in saying—not only that he has nothing to add, but—that he is abandoning his suit against Yahweh (which is how I will argue that we must read 42:6a). Just as in 40:3–5, he does not withdraw a word he has said, he does not admit that God is in the right or that he is in the wrong, he does not confess to any sins or apologize for what he has said.

In my translation, this second response of Job to Yahweh reads:

1   Then Job answered Yahweh, saying:
2   (A) I know that you can do anything,
    and that no purpose of yours can be thwarted.
3   (B) 'Who is this who obscures the Design[1] without knowledge?' [you ask].[2]
    To be sure, I made my depositions—without understanding—
    [concerning] things too wonderful for me—[things] I did not know.
4   (C) 'Listen, and I will speak', [you said];[3]
    'I will question you, and you shall let me know [your answers]'.
5   I have heard you with my ears,
    and my eye has now seen you.
6   So I submit—and I accept consolation [offered to me]
    for my dust and ashes.

---

1   The Hebrew, without the article, could mean 'counsel' in general, as RSV, NJPS. But it seems likely that the reference here is to the divine counsel or plan, which I understand to be Yahweh's design for the universe. Other translations that take the term in this sense include: NAB 'divine plans', NJB 'my intentions', NIV 'my counsel', and NEB, JB 'my design(s)'; similarly Robert Gordis has 'my plan' (*The Book of Job: Commentary, New Translation, and Special Notes*, New York 1978, 491). I give the term a capital letter because it is a grand design, of universal scope.
2   I add the phrase 'you ask' to make clear that Job is quoting Yahweh's previous words; a similar addition is made by NIV, TEV and REB.
3   'You said' is not in the Hebrew, but added also by NIV, TEV and REB to indicate that what precedes is a quotation of Yahweh's words.

It is an unprepossessing response, without a trace of the passion and rhetorical verve of his other speeches. But it is a crafty conclusion in that, while his speech appears quietly reasonable and even submissive, it amounts in reality to a cool dismissal of all that Yahweh has been saying. I don't think the commentators have really appreciated that, and this is the reason why I make a paper out of it.[4]

There are three elements in Job's speech. In the first, Job acknowledges the omnipotence of Yahweh (v. 2); in the second, he accepts that he has intruded into an area in which he has no competence (v. 3); and, in the third, having heard Yahweh's speeches, he abandons his case against God and determines to resume his normal life (vv. 4–6). Put like that, Job's intentions seem rather straightforward. But there is a subtlety in each of these responses.

1   You Can Do Anything

First, when Job acknowledges Yahweh's omnipotence, there is nothing new in that, for he has always done so, and there is none of his companions who would deny it. But this avowal of Yahweh's omnipotence stands here as a response to Yahweh's speeches, which have by no means had that as their central theme. If this is Job's response, it means that he has failed (perhaps, deliberately failed) to understand much of the divine speeches, whose purpose was rather to lay out the principles behind Yahweh's creation and maintenance of the world. Though Yahweh never mentioned justice, Job has not failed to notice its absence. Job declines to accept any worldview that does not prioritize justice, and so he effectively says, It is as I always said, Might is right with you!

There no doubt a concessive note here: he accepts that he is a mere mortal, unfitted by capacity or knowledge for the management of the universe; as he has said already, in comparison with Yahweh, he is of little account (40:4). And yet, if demands for justice and a questioning of God's manner of governing the universe are only ever to be answered by an invocation of the divine almightiness, it is a sorry state of affairs, and every bit as bad as Job had been complaining all along (cf. 23:13–14). In short, Job's words are both a capitulation and, in a way, a reiteration of his complaint.

There is yet more to this response by Job. However we state the purpose of the divine speeches, there are few who would argue that they intend only to

---

4   Much of what follows is to be found in one place or another in my commentary, *Job 38–42* (Word Biblical Commentary, 18B), Nashville 2011, esp. 1204–24. I thought it would be useful nevertheless to bring together my interpretation of these verses in a more manageable compass.

reassert the divine power. At the very least, they seem equally concerned to convey the divine wisdom, and they go far beyond that in sketching Yahweh's program for the whole universe. His created order is not a rule-bound mechanism, sustained by principles of balance and equity and retribution and equivalence. Yahweh's universe is a vast array of differences held together by the divine intimacy with its manifoldness and the divine delight in the quiddity and the contrariness of its parts that are exemplified by Behemoth and Leviathan.

This formal response by Job to the divine speeches ignores all that, and—as when Joseph says to his brothers after all their protestations of innocence, 'It is as I said to you, You are spies' (Gen. 42:14)—retorts in effect to Yahweh's subtle and engaging exposition of his vision for the cosmos, 'I know, it is as I said, you are only interested in power'. That ידעתי 'I know' is very revealing: whether it means 'I now know what I only guessed before, that you really are addicted to power' or 'You don't need to tell me, I've known all along that you only ever follow your own desires, which are never thwarted', Job can hear nothing that is not addressed to his single issue of concern: the question of justice. From Yahweh's point of view, Job is being recalcitrant, but Job's position is that, though he will have to submit and withdraw his case (v. 6), he is not going to accept that he has received the shadow of an answer.

2 Things Too Wonderful

Job's second remark consists of a quotation (with one minor change) of Yahweh's words in 38:2 as he began his first speech—'Who is this who obscures the Design by words without knowledge?'—followed by his own response to them.

Job's response is intriguing. He says that he spoke 'marvels' (נפלאות), things 'too wonderful for me' (ממנו נפלאות), which he did not 'understand' (בין) and did not 'know' (ידע). What, we may ask, in the Book of Job count as 'wonders'? They have always been the inscrutable deeds of God in creation, which Eliphaz speaks of in 5:9, Job himself in 9:10, and Elihu in 37:5, 14—except for 10:16, where Job speaks ironically of the heroic deeds of God in battle against puny Job. Outside the book of Job, God's 'wonders' tend to be acts of deliverance in history. So what 'wonders' has Job been speaking of, which have been 'too wonderful' for him, which he did not 'understand' (בין) or 'know' (ידע)? All Job has ever been speaking of are the principles on which the world is, or should be, governed; he thought they were pretty straightforward matters of justice and fairness, but the way Yahweh tells it, everything in the world is a marvel, and Job had better accept that justice and fairness too, like the structure of the physical universe, and the ways of Yahweh in rain and wind, are 'marvels' beyond his comprehension or understanding. Redefining cosmic justice as a 'marvel' puts it outside any realm that humans can access or have rights in. Job has to confess that he knows nothing, understands nothing, now that it is clear that justice is one of those 'marvels' or divine mysteries.

Now this is a capitulation indeed. If cosmic justice is God's business, then it is whatever he decides it is. It is not a principle to which he himself is subject, to which he gives his allegiance. It is not a rule, the knowledge of which is shared by Yahweh and humans. It is, rather, yet another sphere of divine might, another instance of the truth that Yahweh can 'do anything', as Job said in v. 2. And Job has come to know that such is in fact the truth about the universe through the divine speeches, which have—in his understanding—made Yahweh's power and Yahweh's knowledge the only issue, and have steadfastly suppressed Job's questions about justice. Calling Yahweh's manner of administering the universe a 'marvel' is not to praise it,[5] but Job's ultimate act of despair.

Job has no choice now but to accept that this is the way things are, but he cannot be at all happy about it—because he has now had his worst fears confirmed.[6] All along he had suspected that, for God, might meant right, and he had wanted that suspicion to be corrected. Too late; Yahweh has assured him that the creator of the universe is indeed subject to no law or principle. Such is the Design, and Job's demands for justice have been adjudicated out of order as an obscuring of it.

Job is not going to press the matter further. He has been defeated in his case against God, but he has won a victory of sorts, as Gordis puts it: 'God's admission that justice is not all-pervasive in the universe is a clear, if oblique, recognition of the truth of Job's position'.[7] As we saw on v. 2 above, Job's words of capitulation are not the end of the matter for the observant reader.

We should note the term Job uses of his speaking without understanding. נגד hiph is not the ordinary word for 'speak' or 'utter', but refers rather to informing or declaring; it is especially used of announcing things not previously known before (as in 1:15; 12:7; 36:9) or things kept secret (as in 11:6; 38:18),[8] and is thus almost like 'reveal'. One particular context is important for the present passage:

---

5 As Dale Patrick thought ('The Translation of Job xlii 6', VT 26 [1976], 369–71).
6 John Briggs Curtis, 'On Job's Response to Yahweh', JBL 98 (1979), 497–511 (509), sees this point very clearly.
7 Gordis, Book of Job, 491.
8 Cf. BDB, 616b §2.

31:37, where in the very last verse of Job's final speech (as we should probably emend the text[9]) Job says that if only he could encounter God face to face in a legal setting he would 'give him an account [נגד hiph] of [his] steps', i.e., he would set out in detail the evidence of his life that would prove him an innocent man. In using the same term here, he makes clear that the legal suit is still the framework of his thinking; what is different now is that he has come to a realization that the whole of that legal realm, with his self-defences and his accusations against Yahweh, were outside his scope. At the time, the lawsuit had seemed a reasonable step for a person to take who suffered an injustice; now it transpires that justice is not a value in its own right, but, if anything, a minor element in a huge divine plan consisting of 'wonders' (נפלאות). Though he did not understand it at the time, his 'depositions' (הגדתי) concerned matters that belonged to the realm, not of the prosecution of justice, but of the 'wondrous', a realm to which he recognizes himself an outsider, who knows nothing (ולא ידעתי 'and I did not know').

3 I Hear You

In v. 4, Job again quotes Yahweh. But unlike v. 3a, he does not quote a charge against himself that he must deal with here. It was a sentence of Yahweh's that dealt only with procedure and process, the matter of who will speak first, who will reply. It seems too trifling a matter to mention now, at the very climax of the interchanges between Job and Yahweh, does it not? And, more than that, it is all water under the bridge by now, is it not, now that the confrontation with Yahweh is drawing to a close? No, by no means; the function of Job's quotation of Yahweh's words is to declare, in the coolest manner possible, that the process of the dispute has now come to a close. What it means is that Yahweh has spoken, Job is giving his reply, and that will be that. The debate, the lawsuit, has nowhere else to go. I hear you, says Job to Yahweh, as people say, I hear you, when they mean, I understand you perfectly, but I don't agree.

But what does Job's reply amount to? He does not for a moment negate the words he has spoken, but he withdraws or abandons his case.[10] Why so?

---

9   For support for this view, see my *Job 21–37* (Word Biblical Commentary, 18A), Nashville 2006, 973.

10 So too Norman C. Habel, *The Book of Job* (OTL), London 1985, 582: '[Job] withdraws his case against Shaddai'; Norman Whybray, *Job* (Readings: A New Biblical Commentary), Sheffield 1998, 170: 'Job has capitulated'.

Habel thinks that 'Yahweh's appearance in person was sufficient vindication of Yahweh's integrity and clear evidence of his goodwill',[11] but the Job we have come to know in the course of the dialogues cannot have drawn such a conclusion from the divine speeches. It would seem rather that Job has come to the realization that his case is hopeless: Yahweh is determined not to answer questions about justice. Job will withdraw his suit not because he has lost his case but because, given the attitude of his opponent, he finally despairs totally of ever winning it—and even of having it heard.

In these sentences lies the dénouement of the whole Book of Job. It is a climax that has rarely (in my opinion) been properly understood. It is not an upbeat, 'comic', resolution, but it is not a tragedy either. Some may find it a deeply sad and cheerless outcome, but others may feel it rather a blessed release to recognize that there is no underlying principle of justice in the universe. However we may feel about the outcome of the book, in order to grasp the nature of that outcome there is much exegetical ground to cover.

A word about v. 5. It is usual to find a contrast between the two halves of this verse, between 'hearing' and 'seeing', between 'hearing about' and 'seeing (directly)', between 'then' and 'now', between (inferior) 'hearing' and (superior) 'seeing'. But all this is more than doubtful. First, Job has not actually seen Yahweh (there is no language of visual perception), but only heard him speak, so 'my eyes have seen you' can only be an idiom for a close or authentic encounter (and the view that seeing is a higher form of knowledge than hearing[12] is without foundation, and probably a Western intellectualization of the privileging of that particular sense). Secondly, Job does not say that he had previously heard 'about' Yahweh, as distinct from now seeing him directly; the Hebrew has 'I heard you with the hearing of the ears' (לשמע־אזן שמעתי). It would be strange if he were describing his imbibing of traditions about God or his listening to the friends' theological statements as 'hearing Yahweh'. All the sententious remarks of commentators about a contrast between mere hearsay in the past and immediate perception at the present moment are an irrelevance. Thirdly, though Job says that 'now' (עתה) his eyes have seen Yahweh, it is now also, just now, that he has heard Yahweh—for the first time;

---

11   Habel, *The Book of Job*, 582.
12   So, for example, A. de Wilde, *Das Buch Hiob eingeleitet, übersetzt und erläutert* (OTS, 22), Leiden 1981, 398; cf. also G. Gerald Harrop, '"But now my eye seeth thee"', *CJT* 12 (1966), 80–84.

so in effect the 'now' refers both to the hearing and the seeing.[13] Fourthly, seeing and hearing in the Hebrew Bible are usually parallel forms of perception and not contrasted with one another (cf., e.g., 13:1; 29:11; Gen. 24:30; Exod. 3:7; 2 Kgs 19:16; Prov. 20:12; Song 2:14; and Ps. 48:8 [9] 'as we have heard, so have we seen', where the hearing and the seeing are consonant).[14]

Finally, v. 6. This crucial verse forms the climax of the whole dispute between Job and Yahweh. But sadly it contains three major linguistic uncertainties: (1) the meaning of אמאס (is it 'I reject, despise' with perhaps 'myself' or 'my words' as the implied object, or 'I melt, submit'?), (2) the meaning of נחמתי (is it 'I repent' or 'I am consoled, I accept consolation'?), and (3) the meaning of 'dust and ashes' (is it a reference to the place and the situation of Job on the ashheap, or a reference to Job's status as a mourner, or to his human mortality?).

I cannot now argue my interpretation in detail.[15] In a nutshell, what I propose is that (1) in a legal sense, Job 'submits', i.e., he withdraws his lawsuit against Yahweh, (2) since he has done no wrong, he cannot 'repent', but having been in mourning, he now brings the period of mourning to an end by 'accepting consolation', for his lost children as well as for the loss of his honor, a consolation that is being offered to him both from the friends and (in his own way) from Yahweh, and (3) the consolation he accepts is 'for' the 'dust and ashes' that have been the visible expression of his state of mourning.

This sentence of Job's, as thus construed, contains one of the biggest surprises of the book. We have not been prepared by the course the book has taken to witness Job abandoning his case against God. His arguments have been so cogent, his passion so sincere, that it is almost unthinkable that at end of the day he should merely withdraw from the lawsuit. But he does; and we need to understand why he does. He has not been convinced by the divine speeches either that he is in the wrong—or that Yahweh's cosmic concerns truly outweigh his own call for justice. On the contrary, he has made it plain that he has heard the divine speeches as nothing more than a reaffirmation of divine power (v. 2)—which means inevitably a marginalization of the issues of

---

13   So too Edwin M. Good, *In Turns of Tempest: A Reading of Job, with a Translation*, Stanford, CA 1990, 374.

14   1 Kgs 10:7, where what the Queen of Sheba sees with her own eyes surpasses the reports she has heard of Solomon's wisdom and wealth, is only an apparent exception, for the contrast is not between hearing and seeing but between hearing a report and 'seeing' for oneself (a seeing that must include hearing, since she is more likely to be hearing than seeing Solomon's wisdom).

15   See my *Job 38–42*, 1207–11, 1218–23.

justice he cares about so passionately. And he has not admitted to any fault—apart from not recognizing that in the divine counsels justice is subsumed into supranatural 'wonders', which means that the discussion of cosmic justice is ultimately off limits to humans. Job will accept that he is not permitted to question the divine decisions—he has no choice—but his complaints are still not answered, and he knows it. Now he knows what he had always feared, that he would never get justice; now he can no longer hope that his champion will in the end rise to speak on his behalf (19:25), for the judge before whom his champion would prosecute Job's claim has now dismissed the claim out of hand.[16] And now the desire to 'behold Eloah while still in my flesh' (19:26), a desire so intense that it has been consuming his inmost being (19:27), has proved the ultimate disappointment of his existence: it was no beatific vision of the deity that Job wished for, but a face to face confrontation that would lead to his exculpation. What has happened now is the worst of outcomes, worse even than being judged guilty—it is Eloah's definitive decision that Job's case amounts to nothing, given the cosmic scope of the grand Design.

With one word, Job announces his withdrawal from his lawsuit: אמאס 'I submit'. And then, in words that have nothing to do with the processes of law or his grievance against the deity, and as if he had never raised the issue of justice, he declares that he will bring to an end his period of mourning and return to his usual life—as if it could ever be normal again: 'I accept consolation for my dust and ashes'. We readers may have somewhat lost sight of his dead children in the course of the great drama of his struggle with God, but that word נחמתי 'I accept consolation' is reminder enough that, in all his rage against heaven, he has also been a man in mourning. Now, in that word 'I submit', he has bidden farewell to theology, and, like Candide, will retire to cultivate his garden. He will not again say a single word (by the evidence of the Epilogue), he will conduct no more theological disputations with his friends or summon God again to defend himself; he will devote himself to his family and his farm.

But what he leaves unsaid is as important as what he says. What he does not say is that he is accepting consolation for his loss of standing and dignity, and for the traducing of his character, for he has had no consolation on that score. He is not 'content',[17] he is not convinced, he is not now possessed of a totally

---

16 I understand Job's champion (גאל) to be, not God, with whom he is in dispute and who therefore cannot be his advocate, but his own legal appeal, which he also refers to as his witness (עד, 16:19), his advocate (שהד, 16:19) and his 'spokesperson' (מליץ, 16:20); see my *Job 1–20* (Word Biblical Commentary, 17), Dallas, TX 1989, 459–60.

17 As Whybray, *Job*, 170.

new outlook on the world. He has submitted to the famous omnipotence of Yahweh (as in v. 2), that is all. His eyes have been opened by his encounter with God, to be sure, but what he has seen has not been his vindication but his ultimate humiliation.

Job's response, so modestly expressed, is a standing rejection of the principles by which God acts and governs the universe. Not a lot of people realize that, and therein lies the wisdom of Job's conclusion.

Ecclesiastes as Mainstream Wisdom (Without Job)

Katharine J. Dell

Job and Ecclesiastes have long been characterized together in the scholarship as representing a 'crisis' of wisdom, as 'wisdom in revolt',[1] or as protest literature.[2] They are seen either as a questioning sideline to the main business of practical wisdom as represented by Proverbs and later Ben Sira,[3] or they are acclaimed, over Proverbs, as a more profound exploration of wisdom's themes.[4] Sometimes the three canonical wisdom books have been described as a three stage 'ladder'—from humanism, to scepticism, to pessimism,[5] although the sceptical and pessimistic are seen to have more in common with each other than both have with the humanism of Proverbs. At other times, the term 'scepticism' is used of both Job and Ecclesiastes together.[6]

I have argued elsewhere[7] that the book of Job is very different to other 'wisdom literature' and outside a broad definition of that category. Although there are a few proverbs in Job (e.g. 6:5–6; 8:11–12; 12:12–13; 17:5) and a hymn to wisdom (28), the main wisdom genres are lacking in the book. There is little autobiographical narrative or didactic poetry, as found in Proverbs and Ecclesiastes, rather Job is characterized by prose narrative, debate and lament forms, and a lengthy dialogue. Recent studies in intertextuality have confirmed

---

1 The title of a book on Job by L.G. Perdue (*Wisdom in Revolt* [JSOTS, 112], Sheffield 1991), but also used generically of the two books.
2 R. Davidson, *The Courage to Doubt*, London 1983 and J.L. Crenshaw, *A Whirlpool of Torment* (OBT, 12), Philadelphia 1984.
3 An impression conveyed by G. von Rad's *Wisdom in Israel*, London 1972, in which the attention given to themes predominant in Proverbs and Ben Sira well outweighs attention to Job and Ecclesiastes.
4 W. Eichrodt, *Theology of the Old Testament*, vol. 2, London 1964 and D.J.A. Clines, 'The Wisdom Books', in: S. Bigger (ed.), *Creating the Old Testament: The Emergence of the Hebrew Bible*, Oxford 1989, 268–91 (272).
5 E.g. J.F. Priest, 'Humanism, Skepticism and Pessimism in Israel', *JAAR* 36 (1968), 311–26.
6 E.J. Dillon, *The Sceptics of the Old Testament: Job, Koheleth, Agur*, London 1895; J.L. Crenshaw, 'The Birth of Skepticism in Ancient Israel', in: J.L. Crenshaw, S. Sandmel (eds), *The Divine Helmsman: Studies on God's Control of Human Events*, New York 1980, 1–19. See also discussion in W.H.U. Anderson, *Scepticism and Ironic Correlations in the Statements of Qoheleth*, Piscataway, NJ 2010, 73–109, which also contains discussion of Job and of the sceptical tradition in general.
7 K.J. Dell, *The Book of Job as Sceptical Literature* (BZAW, 197), Berlin 1991.

this, with links between Job and the Psalms,[8] between Job and Deuteronomy[9] and further afield[10] drawing out those very genres of lament[11] and legal discourse[12] that have very little place in Proverbs and Ecclesiastes.

What I want to focus on in this paper however are the clear links between Proverbs and Ecclesiastes that indicate that they are on a continuum of forms and ideas that make up the central core of canonical 'wisdom literature' (however problematic that term may be, see below). The basic form of wisdom literature is, in my view, quite simply the proverb and the mainspring of the wisdom enterprise, the book of Proverbs.[13] The book of Ecclesiastes contains whole chapters of proverbs, sometimes just simply cited in clusters (7:1–12). The difference in Ecclesiastes is that they are often accompanied by an interpretation that qualifies the proverb in question, sometimes an additional comment (e.g. traditional proverbs in 7:1–6 are then relativized by v. 7's statement that 'this also is vanity'), and sometimes a refutation or contradiction (e.g. 2:24 refutes 2:18–19). It is not clear whether this technique is quotation of existing proverbs or whether, at times, the author makes them up in order to refute them. Indeed, Gordis found four methods of the use of quotations in Ecclesiastes. First is the straightforward use of proverbs to reinforce an argument with which the author agrees (e.g. 10:18; 11:1). Second, with only part of a proverb apposite to an argument the author wishes to promote, the rest is cited for the sake of completeness (e.g. 5:1–2; 11:3–4). Third, proverbial quotations are used as a text on which the author comments (e.g. 7:1–13; 4:9–12; 5:9–12; 8:2–4). Fourth, contrasting proverbs are used for the purposes of contradiction (e.g. Eccl. 4:5–6; 9:16, 18). Gordis kept open the question of whether the proverbs cited are genuine quotations or simply restatements of conventional wisdom by the author—he thought that those in which Qoheleth states his

---

8 See W. Kynes. *'My Psalm Has Turned into Weeping': Job's Dialogue with the Psalms* (BZAW, 437), Berlin 2012.

9 S. Ticciati, *Job and the Disruption of Identity: Reading beyond Barth*, London 2005. See also M. Weinfeld, *Deuteronomy and the Deuteronomistic School*, Oxford 1972.

10 See K. Dell and W. Kynes (eds), *Reading Job Intertextually* (LHBOTS, 574), London, New York 2013.

11 See C. Westermann, *The Structure of the Book of Job*, Philadelphia 1981 and correspondences with the Egyptian lament tradition.

12 H. Richter, *Studien zu Hiob* (Theologische Arbeiten, 11), Berlin 1959 writes, 'The all-pervasive basis of the drama of Job are the genres taken from law' (131).

13 As I wrote in 2000 of Proverbs that it is 'a book universally acknowledged as the supreme example of traditional Israelite wisdom' and of the proverb, 'the proverb is the basic form of all wisdom and in that sense is at the heart of the enterprise'. (K.J. Dell, *Get Wisdom, Get Insight: An Introduction to Israel's Wisdom Literature*, London 2000, 5).

own view were most likely to be his own composition. There is no doubt then that 'weighing, studying and arranging many proverbs', as Qoheleth's task is described by the epilogist (12:9), is a key part of his role.

The Instruction genre familiar from Proverbs 1–9 is also arguably found in a shortened form in Ecclesiastes.[14] Ecclesiastes 7:13–14 provides an example in which there is a command to reflect on the work of God (v. 13a) and commands to accept good and evil as it comes day by day (v. 14). This section provides comment upon the whole of chapter 7 with its predominance of wisdom sayings, so that 7:1–14 in its entirely could be regarded as an instruction. One could argue that 7:13–14 is simply an expanded didactic saying, comparable to some of the didactic points made by Job and his friends. However, there is a much less personal feel to this advice than the emotionally invested didacticism in the Job dialogue. The autobiographical narrative, found in short vignettes in Proverbs (e.g. 7:6–27; 24:30–34) is also found in Qoheleth in a longer narrative section 1:12–2:24 when the author appears to take on the persona of Solomon to describe his quest for pleasure and meaning in life, and in shorter descriptions such as the example story in 9:13–16. This is absent in Job with the exception perhaps of Eliphaz's experiential dream in Job 4–5 and Elihu's description of his youth in Job 32. Both Proverbs and Ecclesiastes contain what one might term 'didactic poetry', e.g. Prov. 1:10–19, 2:1–22, as also found in Eccl. 1:4–9; 3:2–8, a feature confined in Job to some of the friends' speeches (e.g. Elihu in 33:9–11; 34:5–9).[15]

The main distinctive genre of Ecclesiastes is the 'reflection', which is a broad genre designation that tends to contain other genres in its definition. Reflection (or interpretation, as above) contains observations from personal experience and often incorporates proverbs and rhetorical questions. Indeed it is on this smaller genre level that the distinctiveness of the authorial techniques used in the book start to emerge. My finding is that much of the distinctiveness of the book is the way the author 're-uses' familiar forms by placing them in a new context. The content remains the same, but the context, normally that of the author's own reflection, changes the meaning. Thus within the reflection genre it is predominantly wisdom forms that are used—proverbs, rhetorical questions and quotations. On this level of smaller forms it is clear that Ecclesiastes

---

14   Instruction has been suggested as an overall genre for Ecclesiastes, largely on the basis of cross-cultural comparison.

15   R.N. Whybray makes the point in *The Intellectual Tradition in the Old Testament* (BZAW, 135), Berlin 1974, 62, that the didacticism in the friends' speeches in Job is a deliberate imitation of that in Proverbs with the purpose of the refutation that Job himself will provide and so is of a different quality to that of Proverbs.

stays well within the wisdom orbit, whilst, in Job, wisdom is not the main smaller genre.[16]

In relation to the main ideas found in Proverbs and their continuation in Ecclesiastes, it is clear that Ecclesiastes often refutes or contradicts a 'given' of Proverbs. When it comes to the order found in the world through experience, for example, Ecclesiastes contradicts this idea with a resigned air that indicates that even if there is an order it cannot be known or understood by humankind (11:5, 7, 23–9). The God-given nature of that order is assumed by Proverbs but, ironically, emphasized more strongly in Ecclesiastes in the light of heightened uncertainty. Whilst Job too questions the order in the world, he never gives up on the idea, nor does the book with its happy ending. It is undeniable that events are ambiguous and Proverbs also acknowledges this with some contradictory proverbs. However there is a general confidence in human ability to understand not only the world, but also God, with 'the fear of the Lord' being the mainspring of wisdom. Interestingly the epilogue of Ecclesiastes brings us back to 'the fear of the Lord'[17] but the book itself questions the assumption, ie the possibility of understanding God or his activity (e.g. Eccl. 11:5). Job arguably relies too heavily on his 'fear of the Lord' to ensure his piety-prosperity nexus and the book airs the breakdown of that assumption. The appearance of God ostensibly to 'answer' Job is a unique feature of this book that takes us into the realms of theophany unknown in other 'wisdom' books.

The doctrine of retribution is at the heart of the wisdom literature and a straightforward system is at work in Proverbs, which is questioned in Ecclesiastes, where confidence in reward and punishment as meted out fairly has diminished. Although the author (Qoheleth) cites traditional ideas on this subject, they are often refuted to assert that the wicked prosper in every context (e.g. 3:16–17), and, deepening the idea further, that God is indifferent to human conduct. Of course Job airs this question in depth in the dialogue, but the happy ending confirms the point in traditional terms despite the profound questioning that precedes it. If life is supremely good and Wisdom a staff of life for Proverbs, then for Ecclesiastes life is empty and there is something to be said for being stillborn rather than living (e.g. 7:1). Contradiction abounds with the

---

16   See further discussion of examples in Dell, *Sceptical Literature*, 144–45.

17   T. Krüger, *Qoheleth* (Hermeneia), Minneapolis 2004 argues that what the fear of the Lord means for Proverbs and Qoheleth is rather different and that Qoheleth diverges here deliberately from Prov. 1–9, a contemporary text with which it engages on a number of levels.

'enjoyment' passages providing an antidote to more negative passages.[18] There is some question how 'good' life is for Job, except at the beginning and end of his life. Proverbs assumes that Wisdom is the goal of life—by contrast, the way of Folly is that of death. Ecclesiastes still believes Wisdom a prize to be gained, although the path to it is not straightforward or even knowable. Wisdom is not a goal for Job in and of itself, although its inaccessibility is described in chapter 28—rather it is a presupposition of his quest.

It is not just a matter, though, of characterizing Ecclesiastes, but also of the nature of Proverbs. The idea of a sharp divide between the two, one optimistic the other pessimistic, one definite, the other deeply contradictory has been open to some debate in recent scholarship. The work of P. Hatton is particularly key in this regard.[19] He draws out the point that Proverbs itself contains a number of contradictions. It has long been observed that there are proverbs that contradict one another, notably Prov. 26:4–5 where silence is both praised and criticized.[20] However, Hatton argues that this strain runs deeper in the book and shows Proverbs to be less simplistically optimistic than it is often perceived to be. He shows up oversimplistic oppositions made in the scholarship between Proverbs on the one hand and Job and Qoheleth on the other. He criticizes scholarship that has prioritized Job and Qoheleth as 'more interesting' over Proverbs.[21] However, whilst arguing for a 'fundamental kinship' of Proverbs with Job and Ecclesiastes in its 'challenging and provoking elements', he only in fact discusses parallels with Qoheleth in any detail and so falls into the trap of assuming Job and Ecclesiastes are a pair. Hatton uses the particular example of attitudes towards 'the powerful' to highlight similarities between Proverbs and Qoheleth. He highlights connections between Prov. 6:6–8 and 30:24–31, texts which are essentially animal proverbs. Hatton shows how reference to rulers and their practices are the hidden code within such imagery, how

---

18   See E.P. Lee, *The Vitality of Enjoyment in Qoheleth's Theological Rhetoric* (BZAW, 353), Berlin 2005, who somewhat overemphasizes the 'enjoyment' passages in the overall tone of the book.

19   P.T.H. Hatton, *Contradiction in the Book of Proverbs: The deep waters of counsel* (SOTS Monograph Series) London 2008.

20   See K.G. Hoglund, 'The Fool and the Wise in Dialogue', in: K.G. Hoglund et al. (eds), *The Listening Heart: Essays in Wisdom and the Psalms in Honor of Roland M Murphy, O. Carm.* (JSOTS, 58), Sheffield 1987, 161–80 (mainly on Prov. 26:4–5).

21   Hatton picks up my phrase 'easy optimism' (in K.J. Dell, 'Ecclesiastes as Wisdom: Consulting Early Interpreters', *VT* 44 (1994), 299–329 (302), as used of Proverbs in contrast to Ecclesiastes to suggest some denigration of the book (see discussion in Hatton, *Contradiction*, 17–20). I am not sure that such weight can be put on one phrase, but take the point that it could be interpreted in that way.

these texts frame the discussion of the theme of kings and rulers in Proverbs and how they offer veiled political comment to indicate in the main that kings are not really necessary.[22] This view is in tension with favourable views of monarchy such as 30:29–30 where the king is likened to three animals characterized by their leadership. Hatton writes, 'Proverbs handles this theme in a dialogic fashion, facilitating a clash between contrasting views about those who wield power; in this respect the book is not a smoothly flowing stream disrupted by the occasional stone, but one in which the ripples from several splashes interact with each other' (117). He shows parallels of these texts with Eccl. 10:16 in its criticism of an ignoble king and his neglectful courtiers (itself contradicted in 10:17 with the opposite scenario of a powerful king and proper behaviour from feasting courtiers) and in connection with a wider treatment of monarchy in the book, which is not without ambivalence. For example, is 10:20 a warning arising from respect of authority or does it describe a situation of informers spying either on or on behalf of their leaders? Both interpretations are possible. He also demonstrates that there is contradiction within Proverbs when in Prov. 19:12 and 16:14 the king's moods are likened to a lion—they are a powerful fact of life to be reckoned with if one is in his service. However in Prov. 16:32 and 20:2 it is stated that the king should control his anger. Hatton concludes, 'The general view of the relationships between ancient Hebrew wisdom texts needs to be modified. Proverbs and Qoheleth have more in common than is generally admitted' (135).

Other work on contradiction in Proverbs has been done, by, for example, van Leeuwen[23] and Yoder.[24] Van Leeuwen looks at contradiction in the relation of wealth and poverty to righteousness and wickedness.[25] Yoder argues that countering appeals are made throughout the book. So, wealth is good (10:15, 22; 14:20; 22:4, 7), but also a liability (11:4, 28). Similarly a wife is sometimes a good

---

22 Hatton, *Contradiction*, regards the example of the ant in Prov. 6:6–8 as making a point about unnecessary rulers. This might be a veiled reference to the forced labour and system of administrators thought to have characterized Solomon's reign (cf. 1 Sam. 8) and detracting 'the ant' from the main purpose of gathering food. In 30:27 'the locust has no king' but order and unity are achieved—no need then for the unnecessary military might of a monarch.

23 R.C. van Leeuwen, 'Wealth and Poverty: System and Contradiction in Proverbs', *Hebrew Studies* 33 (1992), 25–36.

24 Christine Yoder, 'Forming "fearers of Yahweh": Repetition and Contradiction as Pedagogy in Proverbs', in: R.L. Troxel et al. (eds), *Seeking out the Wisdom of the Ancients: Essays offered to honor Michael V. Fox on the occasion of his sixty-fifth birthday*, Winona Lake IN 2005, 167–83.

25 Cf. R.N. Whybray, *Wealth and Poverty in the Book of Proverbs* (JSOTS, 99) Sheffield 1990.

asset (18:22; 5:15–20), but sometimes not (2:9, 19; 27:15). She writes, 'Insofar as Proverbs preserves such divergent points of view, it ensures a certain ambiguity: wisdom does not afford only one perspective on wealth or poverty, wives, or, for that matter, most anything' (179). She argues that incongruities between proverbs draw attention to incongruities in the world, and to competing discourses. Moral points may be under discussion e.g. the attraction of the strange woman (7:14–20) or the 'language' of sinners (1:10–19). The father figure in Prov. 1–9 seeks to offer a path through competing moral claims (with authoritative links to Solomon, Wisdom and even God). By the time we get to Prov. 10:1 no such guide is provided and the young person seeking wisdom has to make their own choices in awareness of ambiguity and tension. Yoder acknowledges that some of the incongruity may have a sociological context in divergent social groups even amongst sages, whilst others, such as Hatton, regard the ambiguity as more of a literary phenomenon as the book of Proverbs received its final form. There is much discussion of contradiction in Ecclesiastes, itself a reason for the ambivalence of the rabbis towards the book when it came to canonization,[26] and it is a well-known feature of this author.

Thus there is a strong formal link between Proverbs and Ecclesiastes on the level of proverbial forms, and the way they are used to highlight contradictory points. The balancing of opposites is at the heart of the wisdom exercise and is featured in both texts. Maybe Ecclesiastes is to be characterized less as simply overturning and questioning the proverbial worldview, and rather as presenting further alternatives, highlighting existing contradiction and deepening different possibilities.

I wish briefly to highlight one more area in which I think that Proverbs and Ecclesiastes have more in common than generally thought and that is in the presentation of Wisdom and Folly as two different options. Ecclesiastes contains no overt mention of these 'characters' as in Proverbs, yet the idea of two options is an essential characteristic. It contains some discussion of the nature of wisdom in both positive and negative terms—and of folly in negative terms. Contradiction is ingrained in the presentation of wisdom's advantages and disadvantages. There is a certain ambivalence over wisdom's acquisition, e.g. in 8:16–17. On the one hand, one can spend all one's time trying to attain it (v. 16), but, on the other, it will always be out of reach when it comes to knowledge of God (v. 17). Wisdom provides no guarantees and whilst it generally guides

---

26   Yoder, 'Forming "fearers of Yahweh"', mentions, following Hoglund, that the Talmud thought the contradiction between Prov. 26:4 and 5 was a threat to this book's inclusion in the canon (b. Šabb. 20b). See discussion of contradiction and canonization in Ecclesiastes in Dell, 'Ecclesiastes as Wisdom'.

people in the direction of present satisfaction and taking life as it comes (see 9:1–12) it sometimes leads to knowing more than is actually helpful—'in much wisdom is much vexation' (1:18a). Wisdom is always countered by the possibility of Folly—e.g. 9:18: 'Wisdom is better than weapons of war, but one bungler destroys much good.' I wish to argue that the two paths represented by the two characters are if not overtly, at least implicitly there in the Ecclesiastes text. Notably, in the difficult chapter 7, I would argue that the Woman of v. 26, 'more bitter than death ... a trap, whose heart is snares and nets, whose hands are fetters', is clearly a reference to Woman Folly in Prov. 7. Whilst the one 'which my mind has sought repeatedly but I have not found' in v. 28 is Woman Wisdom.[27] Krüger, whilst he notes the Woman Folly link, sees 7:25–8 as a criticism of Woman Wisdom's dominance as found in Prov. 1–9. This is part of his theory that there is a 'crisis of wisdom' reflected in Prov. 1–9 and that Qoheleth is a reaction to it using the method of accentuating its relationship to personal experience.[28] I would however see it in terms of a continuum of ideas rather than an explicit critique. The implicit use of these two female opposites is an extension of the role of contradiction within Ecclesiastes as found in the more general approach to wisdom's ambivalence.

So if Proverbs and Ecclesiastes are on more of a 'wisdom continuum' than other books, what does that mean in the light of modern discussion of the definition and extent of wisdom? There has been recent questioning of the very category of wisdom as well as its extent, notably by Weeks in his *Introduction*.[29] Is it indeed an artificial category originating from the nineteenth century? Kynes[30] finds the origin of the modern category 'wisdom literature' in the work of J.C. Bruch (1851) under the influence of other commentators and of philosophical categories of the time.[31] Of course, other groupings are entirely possible. Kynes notes that the 'wisdom' category seems to have been a subsection of a larger poetry section that then was divided into 'lyrical' and 'didactic', the 'didactic' category evolving into 'wisdom'. The 'didactical books' was certainly an accepted way of referring to these books in the nineteenth

---

27 See K.J. Dell, *Interpreting Ecclesiastes, Readers Old and New* (Critical Studies in the Hebrew Bible, 3), Winona Lake, IN 2013, ch. 6.
28 Krüger, *Qoheleth*.
29 S. Weeks, An *Introduction to the Study of the Wisdom Literature*, New York 2010.
30 W. Kynes, 'The Nineteenth-Century Beginnings of "Wisdom Literature", and Its Twenty-first-Century End?' in: J. Jarick (ed.), *Perspectives on Israelite Wisdom: Proceedings of the Oxford Old Testament Seminar* (LHBOTS), London, New York 2015, 83–108.
31 J.C. Bruch, *Weisheits-Lehre der Hebräer: ein Beitrag zur Geschichte der Philosophie*, Strasbourg 1851.

century.[32] Ecclesiastes has tended to be divided off from Proverbs by another group—i.e. as part of the Megilloth, but has come together with it in the wider division of 'Writings'. 'Poetry', another widely accepted grouping from the nineteenth century, tends to range together Psalms, Song of Songs and Lamentations with Job, Proverbs and Ecclesiastes, but is itself a loose designation. Sometimes they were simply presented as individual books, eccentric and isolated within the canon. So W.M.L. de Wette (1807) combines some Psalms, Job and Ecclesiastes as characterized by 'misfortune' but not part of any group—although he does describe both Job and Ecclesiastes as works of sceptical philosophy, tending towards a joint grouping again.[33]

One helpful categorization, in my view, is to go back to the roots of this tradition in the Solomonic attribution. However literally one takes it, and not many do nowadays, certain of these books were from earliest times—as reflected in early rabbinic tradition—assigned to Solomon's pen. There are two attributions to Solomon in Proverbs—1:1 and 10:1 and then an ascription in 25:1 to the men of Hezekiah who 'copied' the proverbs of Solomon.[34] This is something else that Proverbs and Ecclesiastes have in common and Job has not—Solomonic attribution. However we interpret Eccl. 1:1, 12, an implicit attribution to Solomon as 'son of David' is there. This is supported by the 'royal testament' section in 1:12–2:24,[35] which some have argued is maintained throughout the book.[36] Another book linked to Solomon is the Song of Songs, which is also attributed to him and which contains five references to the king in its pages (1:5; 3:7, 9, 11; 8:11–12). This Solomonic sub-grouping held sway from early times[37] and continued to be the way groupings of commentaries fell—even in the nineteenth century.[38] Maybe we need to pay more attention to some of these alternative categories when arranging our material. Whilst Song of Songs is very different with regard to genre, consisting mainly of love poetry, I believe that it has a key link to the

---

32 See discussion in K.J. Dell, 'Studies in the Didactical Books of the Hebrew Bible/Old Testament', in: M. Saebø (ed.), *Hebrew Bible/Old Testament: The History of its Interpretation*, vol. 3, Göttingen 2013, 603–24.

33 W.M.L. de Wette, 'Beytrag zur Charakteristik des Hebraismus', in: C. Daub, F. Creuzer (eds), *Studien*, vol. 3.2, Heidelberg 1807, 261–312 (286–87).

34 Other attributions are found at the end of the book—to Agur (Prov. 30) and Lemuel (Prov. 31), but clearly tradition ascribed the bulk of the book to the wise king.

35 See Y.-V. Koh, *Royal Autobiography in the Book of Qoheleth* (BZAW, 369) Berlin 2006.

36 E.S. Christianson, *A Time to Tell: Narrative Strategies in Ecclesiastes* (JSOTS, 280) Sheffield 1998.

37 B. Baba Bathra 15a relates that Solomon composed Song of Songs in his youth, Proverbs in middle age and Ecclesiastes when he was old and disillusioned with life.

38 See Dell, 'Studies in the Didactical Books'.

wisdom worldview through the Solomonic connection.[39] Krüger makes a connection between the Song of Songs and Ecclesiastes when he writes, 'Canticles is the realization of the exhortation to enjoy life in the book of Qoheleth (esp. Qoh. 9:9, cf. Cant. 8:6–7; Qoh. 7:26).'[40] He emphasizes themes of seeking and finding (especially of Wisdom) in all three Solomonic books. There are even a couple of Psalms traditionally attributed to Solomon (e.g. 72, 127[41]), which makes a small connection with that book too, if not as extensive as a 'wisdom psalms' category. Such categorization cuts across usual groupings and gives us new lenses through which to view material even if ultimately we may be guilty of trying too hard to group essentially individual works.

So I argue that biblical wisdom has Proverbs as its mainspring and Ecclesiastes as its essential continuation and re-evaluation, but along similar lines of contradiction and alternative options found in both books. Chronologically speaking, this book emerges later than Proverbs on any dating scheme.[42] Ecclesiastes then, despite its critical elements, can be seen to stand closer to the already established mainstream and further away from the book of Job which is not to be viewed as a major part of the development of mainstream wisdom. There are links on from Ecclesiastes to Ben Sira (Ben Sira knew the Epilogue to Ecclesiastes and links thematically to its forerunner) and back to Proverbs in the dominance of the proverbial form, which might furnish further evidence for my wisdom continuum outside the Old Testament canon. But this discussion is for another day. In the meantime I rest my case concerning a Proverbs-Ecclesiastes continuum that may be called mainstream wisdom or could simply be designated 'Solomonic', but on any definition scheme still retain a close and 'contradictory' relationship.

---

39 See K.J. Dell, 'Does the Song of Songs Have Any Connections to Wisdom?' in: A.C. Hagedorn (ed.), *Perspectives on the Song of Songs* (BZAW, 346), Berlin 2005, 8–26

40 Krüger, *Qoheleth*, 28, n. 178 for textual references.

41 Ps. 72 has, in fact, closer thematic links than Ps. 127.

42 Of course majority opinion dates Ecclesiastes in the third century BC but C.L. Seow, *Ecclesiastes* (Anchor Bible, 18C), New York 1997, argued for the fifth century BCE. It is unlikely that Proverbs 1–9 was any later than fifth century and I would incline to an earlier dating.

Unity, Date, Authorship and the 'Wisdom' of the Song of Songs

J. Cheryl Exum

The time has come for scholars to look more closely at the evidence before repeating so-called established views about the unity and date of the Song of Songs, as if consensus exists. I refer to the views that the Song is an anthology or collection of love lyrics, and that on linguistic grounds (its affinities with Mishnaic Hebrew and the presence of late loanwords such as *pardes* and *'appiryon*) it can be dated to the Hellenistic period.[1] One can no longer speak of consensus at all with regard to the question of unity versus collection, and serious questions have been raised about our ability to date the Song, or any biblical book for that matter, on the basis of linguistic evidence alone. Reconsideration of these issues in Song of Songs study is therefore in order. Alongside them, I want to look briefly at the related question of authorship, and—because the theme of the 2012 SOTS/OTW meeting is 'Wisdom Traditions in the Hebrew Bible and Beyond'—to conclude with some observations on the Song's relation to Wisdom and wisdom literature.

1   Unity

With the rise of historical biblical criticism in the eighteenth century and its widespread practice in the following centuries, the Song of Songs, like other biblical books, fell victim to the atomizing tendencies of exegetes who were eager to identify multiple sources and signs of disunity everywhere[2]—a practice that, in the Song's case, has proved exceedingly popular. Since the latter part of the twentieth century, however, scholarly attention has increasingly

---

1   I heard these views most recently expressed in a paper, 'The Monarchy in Ancient Israel', delivered by J. Day at the Society for Old Testament Study Winter Meeting, 2012.
2   To mention only a few: P. Haupt, *The Book of Canticles*, Chicago 1902 (12 songs, not complete or in their proper order); M. Jastrow, *The Song of Songs*, Philadelphia 1921 (23, and some fragments); O. Eissfeldt, *The Old Testament: An Introduction*, translated from the 3rd German ed. by P.R. Ackroyd, New York 1965, 490 ('about 25'); F. Landsberger, 'Poetic Units within the Song of Songs', *JBL* 73 (1955), 203–16 ('far, far greater' than Eissfeldt's 25 [216]); R. Gordis, *The Song of Songs and Lamentations*, rev. and augmented ed., New York 1974 [1954] (28, and later, 29).

focused on the final form of biblical texts—even the unity of the Twelve[3]—and more and more interpreters are now arguing for the unity of the Song, or simply treating the Song as the present unity it is.[4] A number of studies since 2000 find evidence for the Song's unity in such features as its thematic coherence, the repetitions of larger and smaller units and the consistency of character portrayal, among them commentaries by Garrett (2004), Hess (2005), Barbiero (2011), and my own commentary (2005), and monographs by Assis (2009) and Landy (second edition, 2011).[5]

If the Song were an anthology of love poems, one might reasonably expect it to feature different protagonists and exhibit different attitudes toward love or describe different experiences of love, such as unrequited love, spurned love, secret love, fickle love. But this is not the case, and rare is the commentator who concentrates on discontinuity among the parts of the Song.[6] Even commentators who view the Song as a collection tend to discuss it in terms of its unity. For example, Bergant (2001) finds among the poems in the collection 'a kind of coherent plot of longing, searching, finding, losing, longing, etc.' and 'consistency in the characters' behavior'.[7] Longman, in his 2001 commentary, views the Song as an anthology of twenty-three poems with no 'overarching narrative or plot', but nevertheless finds 'progression' in the Song and observes that consistency of character portrayal and repetition of scenes and refrains

---

3   See J.T. LeCureux, *The Thematic Unity of the Book of the Twelve* (HBM, 41), Sheffield 2012.

4   Among those who simply get on with interpreting the Song as it stands without concern for debates about unity, see C.E. Walsh, *Exquisite Desire: Religion, the Erotic, and the Song of Songs*, Minneapolis 2000; F.C. Black, *The Artifice of Love: Grotesque Bodies in the Song of Songs* (LHBOTS, 392), London 2009; C. Meredith, *Journeys in the Songscape: Space and the Song of Songs* (HBM, 53), Sheffield: Sheffield Phoenix Press, 2013).

5   For a more detailed discussion of the question of unity, see J.C. Exum, *Song of Songs: A Commentary* (OTL), Louisville 2005, 33–45; see also D. Garrett, *Song of Songs* (WBC, 23B), Nashville 2004, 27–35; R.S. Hess, *Song of Songs*, Grand Rapids 2005, 27–34; G. Barbiero, *Song of Songs: A Close Reading* (trans. Michael Tait), Leiden 2011, 18–24 (rev. ed. of his *Il Cantico dei Cantici* [Milan 2004]); E. Assis, *Flashes of Fire: A Literary Analysis of the Song of Songs* (LHBOTS, 503), New York 2009; F. Landy, *Paradoxes of Paradise: Identity and Difference in the Song of Songs*, 2nd ed., Sheffield 2011, 29–54.

6   Of recent commentators, Zakovitch offers the strongest case, in my view; Y. Zakovitch, *Das Hohelied* (HThKat), Freiburg 2004. He sees the Song as a 'sorgfältig getroffene Auswahl' of 27 songs and four fragments, 'die langsam und allmählich gewachsen ist' (30–31); moreover, 'Gelegentlich ist beim Übergang von einem Lied zum nächsten auch eine Entwicklung im Verhältnis der beiden Liebenden zueinander zu beobachten' (68).

7   D. Bergant, *The Song of Songs* (Berit Olam), Colllegeville 2001, xv.

gives it a certain unity.[8] More recently, he would describe it as an anthology by a single poet, and possibly therefore a unity.[9]

The main objection to unity is the absence of any demonstrable logical sequence or an obvious structural organization or perceptible narrative development.[10] The Song, however, is a lyric poem, not a dramatic one, and lyric poetry is a discontinuous form. We should therefore not expect it to display the kind of narrative development that produces, say, a plot, or even any progression at all.[11] Moreover, the number of proposals that have been put forward for structural organization in the Song suggests that, as Francis Landy observes, far from being structureless the Song offers a superabundance of structural clues.[12] It is not just repetitions and stylistic and literary coherence that argue for unity but also the consistency with which the lovers speak about love along gender-determined lines (she is lovesick, he is awestruck; she tells stories about their relationship in which she and he are both characters, he looks at her and tells her what he sees and how it affects him).[13] Another sign of unity is the way the poet *shows* as well as *says* (8:6) that love is strong as death by means of poetic strategies, or techniques, employed across the space of the poem. They include creating an illusion of immediacy (the impression that, far from being simply reported, the action is taking place in the present, unfolding before the reader); conjuring the lovers up and letting them disappear in an endless deferral of presence;[14] inviting readers to identify with the lovers by presenting them as types of lovers rather than specific lovers of the past; providing an audience within the poem, the women of Jerusalem, whose

---

8   T. Longman, III, *The Song of Songs* (NICOT), Grand Rapids 2001, 15–17, 55–56.

9   Personal communication.

10   Cf. Landy, *Paradoxes*, 30: '[T]he only irrefutable ground for rejecting the unity of the Song, that it lacks logical sequence, rests on a false premise, namely that logical sequence is an indispensable requirement of lyric poetry'. There is, in fact, narrative development in the Song, but only in the speeches of the woman; see Exum, *Song of Songs*, 44 *et passim*.

11   Are the lovers not, at the end, in the same position they were at the beginning? The sense one might get of 'progression' comes more from the fact that the lovers seem to take on distinct personalities as we get to know them than from any plot development; see Exum, *Song of Songs*, 8–9, 11–13, 262–63.

12   F. Landy, Review of M. Timothea Elliott, *The Literary Unity of the Canticle*, Biblica 72 (1991), 571.

13   Exum, *Song of Songs*, 15–17.

14   Note, for example, the similarities between the description of the man in 2:8–9 and the palanquin in 3:6–11: both are acts of conjury on the part of the woman in which the man (as himself, then in Solomonic guise) approaches from afar and gradually comes closer and closer to the speaker; see Exum, *Song of Songs*, 123–25, 142–43.

presence encourages the reader's entry into the lover's seemingly private world of eroticism; blurring distinctions between anticipation, enjoyment of love's delights, and satisfaction (and so between past, present, and future); and, in an effort to make love appear on-going and never-ending, refusing to bring the poem to closure, so that the Song, in effect, circles back upon itself to begin ever again with desire *in medias res* ('let him kiss me...').[15]

New approaches to the text could also shed incidental light on the question of unity. Christopher Meredith's application of spatial theory to the Song reveals that units often thought to be quite distinct are linked through spatial continuity. For example, Song 3:1–5 and 3:6–11 both display a concentric pattern, with an enclosed centre (the chamber within the mother's house, the enclosed litter) surrounded at its outer edges by a male circle whose function is defence. And spatial continuity also exists between 4:1–5:1 and 5:2–6:3:

> While the controlling *imagery* has changed in the text—from garden to city—the underlying spatiality that structures ch. 4 rolls into ch. 5. The description of a locked garden/lover (4:12–5:1) has made way for a locked house/lover. The focus of the text is still a fairly unelaborated enclosed space... inhabited by the female. It must again stand in for the female body as the double entendres build up. The domestic space unfolds as a loose replication of the garden and the configuration of the lovers' world forms a point of relative continuity as the poem moves into a new symbolic world. If these sections are to be read as entirely different, why reuse the same notions—of locking, of enclosure, of the female-as-container? Why has the basic spatial supposition of the text, the supposition of entry, exclusion and access, not changed too?[16]

Debate on the question of unity will no doubt continue (old theories die hard), but the burden of proof, as Michael Fox already compellingly argued in 1985, now rests with those who would claim that the Song is a collection.[17]

---

15 On these techniques, see Exum, *Song of Songs*, 3–13; see also, on voice, mode of presentation and major themes, M.V. Fox, *The Song of Songs and the Ancient Egyptian Love Songs*, Madison 1985, 253–94.
16 Meredith, *Journeys in the Songscape*, 51.
17 Fox, *Song of Songs*, 202–26.

2 Date

There is little evidence from the poem itself to help us date it.[18] A reassessment of the view that the Song was composed in the late post-exilic or Hellenistic period is particularly in order in view of the difficulty—if not impossibility in the view of some—of dating texts on linguistic grounds alone.[19] It is frequently pointed out that the Song contains Aramaisms and stylistic features typical of late biblical and Mishnaic Hebrew. But as Ian Young, in particular, has argued, these linguistic features could already have existed in the pre-exilic period;[20]

---

18   Clearly it was composed after the time of Solomon, and the appearance of Tirzah in parallelism with Jerusalem in 6:4 would seem to indicate that the Song was written after the division of the monarchy—though some would not see Tirzah as a proper noun (see, e.g., M.H. Pope, *Song of Songs* [AB, 7C], Garden City 1977, 558–60), and it could be argued that this is one of the scribal changes the text underwent after it was composed. The parallelism cannot be used to prove that the Song was written during the time that Tirzah was the capital of the Northern Kingdom, for, by the time of composition, Tirzah could have had simply a legendary status (e.g. Fox, *Song of Songs*, 187), but it is an attractive argument in view of recent arguments for the Song's early date and Northern connections. David Carr, e.g., observes that taking references to places associated with Israel's early history as no more than literary allusions to past times 'is only demanded if other factors require a later dating' (*The Formation of the Hebrew Bible: A New Reconstruction*, Oxford 2011, 441).

19   Ian Young has made a strong case for reassessing common assumptions about 'Early' Biblical Hebrew and 'Late' Biblical Hebrew, and for seeing EBH and LBH not as representing different chronological periods in the development of Hebrew but rather as co-existing styles of literary Hebrew throughout the biblical period, with EBH representing a conservative tendency among scribes and LBH a non-conservative one; see I. Young, *Diversity in Pre-exilic Hebrew* (FAT, 5), Tübingen 1993); I. Young and R. Rezetko, with the assistance of M. Ehrensvärd, *Linguistic Dating of Biblical Texts*, 2 vols., London 2008. See also A. Hurvitz, 'The Chronological Significance of "Aramaisms" in Biblical Hebrew', *IEJ* 18 (1968), 234–40; Hurvitz, 'Can Biblical Texts Be Dated Linguistically? Chronological Perspectives in the Historical Study of Biblical Hebrew', in: A. Lemaire and M. Sæbø (eds), *Congress Volume Oslo 1998* (VTSup, 80), Leiden 2000, 143–60; and the articles in I. Young (ed.), *Biblical Hebrew: Studies in Chronology and Typology* (JSOTSup, 369), London 2003.

20   I. Young, 'Biblical Texts Cannot Be Dated Linguistically', *Hebrew Studies* 46 (2005), 341–51. Young's argument that late biblical Hebrew or proto-late biblical Hebrew already existed in the pre-exilic period and that no linguistic features, not even Persian loanwords (if there are Persian loanwords), can be connected to only one chronological phase of biblical Hebrew has particular relevance for the Song of Songs. Hurvitz observes that the numerous Aramaisms in the Song may be vestiges of Northern dialect and not necessarily late biblical Hebrew ('The Chronological Significance of "Aramaisms" in Biblical Hebrew', 236; Hurvitz, 'Hebrew and Aramaic in the Biblical Period: The Problem of "Aramaisms" in Linguistic Research on the Hebrew Bible', in: Young [ed.], *Biblical Hebrew*, 24–37 [31 and

they could be dialectic (specifically, a northern literary dialect);[21] and some (if not many) of them could also be the result of scribal changes in the course of an early text's transmission.[22]

One cannot appeal to the presence of loanwords from Persian (*pardes*, 4:13) and Greek (*'appiryon*, 3:9) as prima facie evidence of a late date. Not only do we have to reckon with scribal changes in the course of the text's apparently fluid transmission history[23] but also the origin of these words is debatable, as is the question of how and when they might have entered the Hebrew language. It is by no means certain that *'appiryon* comes from Greek,[24] and *pardes*, widely but not unanimously agreed to be of Persian (or, better, Iranian or Indo-European)

---

n. 15]). Some time ago W.F. Albright noted the use of archaic language and signs of Northern dialect, as well as the dominance of northern geographical terms, and posited a fifth to fourth century BCE date for the final form of the Song ('Archaic Survivals in the Text of Canticles', in: D. Winton Thomas and W.D. McHardy [eds], *Hebrew and Semitic Studies Presented to Godfrey Rolles Driver in Celebration of His Seventieth Birthday*, Oxford 1963, 1–7 [1]).

21 Young, *Diversity*, 165–66, where he proposes that the author was from the North but probably lived in Jerusalem.

22 See Young, 'Biblical Texts Cannot Be Dated Linguistically', 350. Based on his comparison of the MT Song with 4QCant[b], where he notes numerous linguistic variants, Young concludes that language was subject to constant revision by the scribes who transmitted the texts over time; I. Young, 'Notes on the Language of 4QCant[b]', *JJS* 52 (2001), 122–31 (130). See also Young et al., *Linguistic Dating*, vol. 1, 359: 'Textual stability is a fundamental premise of the linguistic dating of biblical texts ... yet the extant evidence shows that ancient texts of the Bible were characterized by textual *instability*' (italics theirs). See, too, the discussion of all three of the points mentioned above in Carr, *Formation*, 442–47, and the sources cited there.

23 See Carr, *Formation*, 432–33. Carr observes that this fluidity works against Dobbs-Allsopp's arguments (F.W. Dobbs-Allsopp, 'Late Linguistic Features in the Song of Songs', in: A.C. Hagedorn [ed.], *Perspectives on the Song of Songs/Perspektiven der Hoheliedauslegung* [BZAW, 356], Berlin 2005, 27–77) for dating the Song based on its orthography (*Formation*, 433 n. 3). He also notes that, as a love poem, the Song may have a more colloquial profile than other texts to which it is compared (432, 442–45).

24 Albright, 'Archaic Survivals', 1 and n. 2; Young, *Diversity*, 162; Dobbs-Allsopp, 'Late Linguistic Features,' 67–71; cf. Scott B. Noegel and Gary A. Rendsburg, *Solomon's Vineyard: Literary and Linguistic Studies in the Song of Songs*, Atlanta 2009, 179–80. Dolls-Allsopp concludes, '[T]he linguistic profile of Cant, while compatible with a Hellenistic dating, does not require it, and therefore, the supposition that Cant is a Hellenistic work will need to be funded [*sic*, founded?] and moved on other than linguistic grounds' ('Late Linguistic Features', 71).

origin, could have come into Hebrew before the Persian period through early trade contacts.[25]

The argument that the Song is written in a northern dialect, proposed over a century ago by S.R. Driver,[26] has been championed recently by Scott Noegel and Gary Rendsburg, who conclude that the Song was written around 900 BCE in a northern dialect of ancient Hebrew.[27] At the other end of the spectrum, the late dating has recently been defended by F.W. Dobbs-Allsopp, whose analysis

---

25   Young et al., *Linguistic Dating*, vol. 1, 286–311; vol. 2, 61. See also Young, *Diversity*, 161–62; Noegel and Rendsburg, *Solomon's Vineyard*, 174–84; S.R. Driver, *An Introduction to the Literature of the Old Testament* (7th ed.; Edinburgh 1898), 449. The fact that Greek *paradeisos* (which LXX uses to translate Hebrew *pardes* in 4.:3) refers to the pleasure parks of Persian kings in earlier sources but in the third century BCE came to mean 'garden' or 'orchard' (Noegel and Rendsburg, *Solomon's Vineyard*, 178; J.A.L. Lee, *A Lexical Study of the Septuagint Version of the Pentateuch* [Septuagint and Cognate Studies, 14], Chico 1983, 53–55) does not mean that *pardes* could not have meant 'garden, orchard' in Hebrew at an earlier date. Moreover, whether we are to think of the garden of Song 4:12–15, with its exotic, imported plants and spices, as an orchard or garden of fruit-bearing trees and other plants, or as something on a grander scale, along the lines of the famed gardens of Assyrian and Egyptian royalty, is debatable; on such gardens and their cultivation, see Meredith, 'Locked Gardens and the City as Labyrinth', Chapter 3 in *Journeys in the Songscape*, esp. 73–78. On the question of Persian or other origins of foreign names for aromatics, see Dobbs-Allsopp, 'Late Linguistic Features', 65–66; A. Brenner, 'Aromatics and Perfumes in the Song of Songs', *JSOT* 25 (1983), 75–81.

26   Driver, *Introduction*, 449.

27   *Solomon's Vineyard*, 3–62, 174–84. See also G.A. Rendsburg, 'Israelian Hebrew in the Song of Songs', in: S.E. Fassberg and A. Hurvitz (eds), *Biblical Hebrew in Its Northwest Semitic Setting: Typological and Historical Perspectives*, Jerusalem 2006, 315–23. A number of northern place names are mentioned, and, if the poem is written in a northern dialect, these features might suggest a northern origin (so Driver, Noegel and Rendsburg, among others; but see the caveat of Dolls-Allsopp ['Late Linguistic Features', 72 n. 259] that large portions of the North and Samaria were well populated during the Persian period, and so could easily appear in a poem composed in the post-exilic period). Locating the place of composition from geographical references in the poem is problematic because of the lack of connections with specific historical events; most of the references appear in metaphors (e.g., Tirzah, Carmel, Sharon, Damascus, Lebanon, Engedi, Heshbon, Gilead). These places could have been chosen because they were famous—Lebanon for its cedars, Engedi for its oasis, etc.—or for their associations and ability to evoke a magical time and place. The principal setting of the poem seems to be Jerusalem—the women of Jerusalem are the audience—but the lovers traverse the whole countryside, including remote Lebanon, Senir, Amana, and Hermon. There is nothing to stop a poet from writing about far-away or legendary places, nor does the poet have to live where the characters in the poem seem to live.

of the linguistic evidence leads him to posit a date between 530 and 323 BCE.[28] In his monumental study of the growth and development of the Hebrew Bible, David Carr provides a judicious survey of the evidence and concludes that it points to an early pre-exilic date 'at least of major portions of the Song', though its present form is Hellenistic.[29]

Scholars continue to repeat the arguments for the traditional late dating of the Song, but there now exists a serious and substantial body of evidence to challenge this position, and continuing investigation of the linguistic evidence is needed.[30] Further study of cultural contacts and cross-cultural influences could shed light on the question of date. The similarities between the Song and ancient Egyptian and Mesopotamian love poems are so strong that we can assume their general influence on the poet.[31] Under what historical and social circumstances would a poet writing in Hebrew have been influenced by Egyptian and Mesopotamian love poetry?[32] Can we find the influence of

---

28 Dobbs-Allsopp, 'Late Linguistic Features'; for a critique of a number of Dobbs-Allsopp's arguments, see Carr, *Formation*, 444–45 nn. 41, 43, 445–46 nn. 50, 51.

29 Carr, *Formation*, 432–48 (447). Zakovitch suggests the influence of the Song or a work like it on such texts as Jer. 6:2–5; Gen. 30:14–18; Hos. 14:6–8; Isa. 5:1–7 and Prov. 31:10–31 (*Das Hohelied*, 54–56).

30 To illustrate the importance of on-going assessment of the evidence, I might note that Carr is not the only one to have reassessed his views on the date of the Song; Young has changed his position from advocating an early date (*Diversity*, 165) to 'complete agnosticism' on the subject ('Notes on the Language of 4QCant^b', 130 n. 50), and Rendsburg, who was prepared to accept a late date for the Song ('Israelian Hebrew', 318), now advocates an early one (Noegel and Rendsburg, *Solomon's Vineyard*, 184). The conclusion of Young, Rezetko, and Ehrensvärd merits repeating here: 'Song of Songs fits nowhere in a linear history of BH. Whatever period we date it to, we must explain its language as evidence of another variety of Hebrew than that of the rest of the Hebrew Bible. Once we realise that Song of Songs' Hebrew was, according to our current knowledge, never the normal sort of literary Hebrew in any age, we no longer have any firm peg to date its composition. If this language reflects a colloquial or regional dialect, for example, there is no reason why it is necessarily late or early—it is just different' (*Linguistic Dating*, vol. 1, 197).

31 It is not a question of direct borrowing but rather of a cultural milieu in which such poetry was available. Throughout his commentary, Pope notes numerous Ugaritic parallels, and concludes, '[T]he antiquity of at least parts of the Songs [read 'Song'] cannot be doubted in light of the Ugaritic parallels' (*Song of Songs*, 27).

32 Fox considers the Ramesside period (the only period from which Egyptian love songs have survived) to be the most likely time for the importation and influence of Egyptian love poetry in Palestine, but notes as well contact in the reign of Solomon and in the time of Hezekiah (*Song of Songs*, 191–93); G. Gerleman attributes the strong Egyptian influence on the Song to the political and cultural contacts between Egypt and Israel in the Solomonic era (*Das Hohelied* [BKAT, 18], Neukirchen 1965, 68–77). Antonio Loprieno attri-

Hellenistic literature as well? This question is especially relevant for the dating of the Song, for, if it could be shown that the poet was familiar with Hellenistic love poetry, the argument for a late date would be confirmed. Some scholars have argued for Hellenistic influence on the Song, but to date we lack the kind of thoroughgoing study needed to demonstrate it—something along the lines of Michael Fox's *The Song of Songs and the Ancient Egyptian Love Songs*—that looks not only at selected or isolated themes and motifs but at the larger picture, at point of view, voice and mode of presentation, poetic technique, major themes, attitudes to love, similarities and, importantly, differences.[33] Although they are not strong enough to suggest direct influence, some scholars have noted similarities between the Song of Songs and the *Idylls* of Theocritus.[34] Joan Burton posits a third-century BCE date for the Song, noting similarities to Theocritus and other early Greek poetry, such as themes of mutual desire,

butes the similarities to a common festive background of the genre in Egypt and Israel ('Searching for a Common Background: Egyptian Love Poetry and the Biblical Song of Songs', in: Hagedorn [ed.], *Perspectives*, 105–35). A seventh-century BCE Akkadian text, The Love Lyrics of Nabu and Tashmetu, is considered by Martti Nissinen to be the closest Mesopotamian parallel to the Song ('Love Lyrics of Nabû and Tašmetu: An Assyrian Song of Songs?', in: M. Dietrich and I. Kottsieper [eds], *'Und Mose schrieb dieses Lied auf': Studien zum Alten Testament und zum Alten Orient* [Fs O. Loretz], Münster 1998, 585–634 [624]), and its date raises the question of possible Neo-Assyrian influence on the Song, though of course both texts could be influenced by similar, and perhaps long-established poetic traditions.

33 A recent contribution in this area can be found in: Hagedorn (ed.), *Perspectives*, which includes a section on ancient Near Eastern and ancient Greek parallels. In his contribution to the volume, Hagedorn, who assumes a Hellenistic date for the Song and the 'strong possibility' of the poet's knowledge of Greek literature, compares the Song to the *Fragmentum Grenfellianum* (174/3 BCE), but wisely observes 'one should not disregard the differences'; A.C. Hagedorn, 'Jealousy and Desire at Night: *Fragmentum Grenfellianum* and Song of Songs', in: Hagedorn (ed.) *Perspectives*, 206–27 (225). In my view, the similarities are too general to be meaningful, and herein lies the problem: love poetry the world over, ancient and modern, displays many shared features. Indeed, Hagedorn is hard pressed to find jealousy of a rival/rivals, the key theme of the *Fragmentum*, in the Song. One wonders if meaningful connections between the Song and Greek literature exist, since they are so difficult to establish; for other attempts, see A. Hagedorn, 'Of Foxes and Vineyards: Greek Perspectives on the Song of Songs', *VT* 53 (2003), 337–52; H.-P. Müller, 'Eine Parallele zur Weingartenmetapher des Hohenliedes aus der frühgriechischen Lyrik', in: Dietrich and Kottsieper (eds), *'Und Mose schrieb dieses Lied auf'*, 569–84.

34 J. Burton, 'Themes of Female Desire and Self-assertion in the Song of Songs and Hellenistic Poetry', in: Hagedorn (ed.), *Perspectives*, 180–205; R. Hunter, '"Sweet Talk": *Song of Songs* and the Traditions of Greek Poetry', in: Hagedorn (ed.), *Perspectives*, 228–44 (240–41); Hagedorn, 'Of Foxes and Vineyards'.

female self-assertion, a female erotic gaze, and a challenge to traditional gender roles—but these are themes that appear in ancient Near Eastern love poems as well.[35] In the search for a provenance, Burton's conclusion nevertheless merits consideration: 'the multi-cultural context of a [third-century] Hellenistic kingdom centered in Egypt and extending to Palestine would have offered Jewish writers a multiplicity of literary traditions—including not only Greek poetry but also Egyptian love songs—as possible background for the Song'.[36]

Need we assume Hellenistic influence (and thus a late date) to explain similarities between the Song of Songs and early Greek love poetry? It is not difficult, after all, to find similarities between love poems from completely different times and cultures, without any likelihood of dependence.[37] Are the poet of the Song of Songs and the Greek poets simply writing within a broad shared Mediterranean poetic tradition?[38] The similarities between the Song

---

[35] Along with the themes of female desire and self-assertion, Burton notes the prominent theme of male helplessness and erotic passivity, a theme lacking in the Song ('Themes', 201 *et passim*) The Song's male lover does, however, feel the loss of control ('*you* have captured my heart', 4:9; 'turn your eyes away from me, for *they* overwhelm me', 6:5); see Exum, *Song of Songs*, 15–17.

[36] Burton, 'Themes', 183.

[37] C. Rabin proposed similarities to Tamil poetry, though his examples are limited ('The Song of Songs and Tamil Poetry', *Studies in Religion/Sciences religieuses* 3 [1973/4], 205–19); there are arresting similarities to the Gita Govinda of Jayadeva (twelfth century CE), which F. Edgerton refers to as 'The Hindu Song of Songs', in: W.H. Schiff (ed.) *The Song of Songs: A Symposium*, Philadelphia 1924, 43–47, as well as in the Bengali Vaishnava love lyrics (sixteenth century CE), which show the influence of the Gita Govinda (see the translation of E.C. Dimock, Jr and D. Levertov, *In Praise of Krishna: Songs from the Bengali*, Garden City 1967). F.X. Clooney finds points of comparison between the Song and the *Holy Word of Mouth* (*Tiruvaymoli*), a ninth-century CE Hindu text (Clooney, *His Hiding Place Is Darkness: An Exercise in Interreligious Theopoetics*, Stanford 2013; see also Clooney, 'By the Power of Her Word: Absence, Memory, and Speech in the Song of Songs and a Hindu Mystical Text', *Exchange* 41 [2012], 213–44). For years one of my essay assignments for my Song of Songs class was to compare the Song of Songs to a love poem of the student's choice; the many, varied results revealed remarkable similarities (as well as differences) across cultures and historical periods.

[38] As R. Hunter cautions: 'Early Greek poetry cannot in fact offer clear parallels to the type of semi-dramatic exchanges between young lovers familiar from the Hebrew poems. Certain motifs and images are, of course, shared between the poetic traditions (for example, the association of fruitfulness and gardens with love), but … claims of transmission from one culture to another are always vulnerable to assertions that such ideas might easily arise independently in many places and/or that we should rather be thinking of a broad Mediterranean *Gemeingut* of images, motifs, and poetic structures (such as the *paraklausithyron*), which have their basis in shared cultural features' ('"Sweet Talk"', 229–30).

and the poetic traditions of Egypt and Mesopotamia are much greater than those between the Song and parallels so far adduced to ancient Greek love poetry. Is the poet consciously archaizing, looking to the past for models? Or is the poet unfamiliar with, or uninspired by, Greek love poems?

Like Young, I remain agnostic on the question of date. Although I find the question fascinating, I suspect that knowing its date would have little effect on interpretation of the Song. Attempts to posit a historical or political background—such as a polemic against Solomon or the excesses of his reign[39]—simply do not find support from the poem itself. The Song is a love poem; it universalizes love by not limiting itself to a particular time and place.[40]

3   Authorship

The Song offers no clue to the circumstances of its composition or the identity of its author.[41] If the Song is a collection, then we are dealing with multiple authors, or perhaps a combination of smaller collections or even the common authorship of many of the individual poems. Unless one concludes that the editing is haphazard[42] or extremely loose (e.g., simply connecting poems on the basis of catchwords),[43] one may recognize either some general principles of arrangement that lend coherence to the Song or a plan so thoroughgoing that the editor or redactor deserves to be considered the author of the final

---

39 Noegel and Rendsburg, for example, identify the genre of the Song as akin to the medieval Arabic *hijā'* and *tašbīb*, which emphasize blame through what resembles praise, and conclude that the Song is a love poem on a surface reading, but the subtext is one of ridicule and invective, aimed at censuring Solomon in particular and the Judean monarchy in general (*Solomon's Vineyard*, 133–68).

40 One could say it reflects the attitudes of its time to social and gender roles (as Burton, 'Themes', observes; see also Exum, *Song of Songs*, 25–28), even though it may entertain alternative visions.

41 It is, in fact, the poet's success in creating lovers who are universal figures and in depicting love as not bound by time or place that makes identifying the historical context of the Song so difficult. Solomon is not the lover of the poem, but the mention of Solomon in the superscription and six times in the poem (1:5; 3:7, 9, 11; 8:11, 12), the sense of leisure and luxury, the interest in flora and fauna, and the important role played by Jerusalem, all bring to mind some of the descriptions of Solomon's reign (1 Kings 4:20, 24–25, 33; 10:22–29), and lend the Song a Solomonic ambiance.

42 E.g., Pope, *Song of Songs*, 54.

43 E.g., W. Rudolph, *Das Buch Ruth, Das Hohe Lied, Die Klagelieder* (KAT XVII, 1–3), Gütersloh 1962, 97–100; O. Keel, *The Song of Songs*, trans. F.J. Gaiser, Minneapolis 1994, 17 (German original: *Das Hohelied* [ZBAT, 18], Zurich 1986).

product.[44] If the Song exhibits cohesiveness, homogeneity, consistency of character portrayal, and a distinctive vision of love—and I believe it does—is there any need to posit an editor at all? No literature is created in a vacuum; poets work within poetic traditions, and the author of the Song clearly draws upon a rich cultural heritage of love poetry, as the Mesopotamian and Egyptian examples that have come down to us reveal. Nor would the literary influences on the poet have been limited to love poetry, and the poet could have drawn on oral as well as written sources—traditional material such as folk songs, for example.

The Song is the work of an educated poet, a poet familiar with ancient Near Eastern erotica and accomplished in the art of composition. Its lyric beauty and sophisticated style are frequently hailed by commentators, and its rich, sensuous imagery and dense metaphorical language bear ample testimony to the poet's literary skill. Moreover, it is surely an artistically sophisticated poem that can be read, as the Song has been, as both delicately erotic and sexually overt at the same time. As evidence that the poet moved in educated circles, we should also note the poet's knowledge of the world of nature, of exotic plants and exotic places, of spices and other luxury items, as well as the poet's sensitivity to both a woman's and man's point of view.[45] Does this suggest that the poet was—to use the unfortunate term—a 'sage', and that the poem was part of Israel's so-called intellectual tradition?

4   Is the Song a 'Wisdom' Book?

The Song *can* be connected to 'wisdom'. In a recent article Katharine Dell has shown this in an assessment of the evidence that is both far-ranging

---

44   Fox, *Song of Songs*, 218–226; Exum, *Song of Songs*, 33–45.
45   The sex of the poet is also impossible to ascertain, though perhaps future research will shed some light on this question. Men were more likely than women to have been educated, but this does not rule out the possibility of an educated woman having composed the Song; on literacy, see A.R. Millard, 'Literacy (Israel)', *ABD* IV, 337–40; I.M. Young, 'Israelite Literacy: Interpreting the Evidence: Part I', *VT* 48 (1998), 239–53; Young, 'Israelite Literacy: Interpreting the Evidence: Part II', *VT* 48 (1998), 408–22; S. Niditch, *Oral World and Written Word: Ancient Israelite Literature*, Louisville, 1996, 39–77. Love poetry, given its emphasis on a woman's point of view and its association with the domestic sphere, may have been a genre to which women made a special contribution; see S.D. Goitein, 'Women as Creators of Biblical Genres', *Prooftexts* 8 (1988), 1–33; F. van Dijk-Hemmes, 'Traces of Women's Texts in the Hebrew Bible', in: A. Brenner and F. van Dijk-Hemmes, *On Gendering Texts: Female and Male Voices in the Hebrew Bible*, Leiden 1993, 71–81.

and cautious in its conclusions.[46] But to my mind the connections adduced between the Song and 'wisdom' by Dell and others remain speculative and tenuous. My problem is that I do not know what 'wisdom' is, and I do not believe an 'intellectual tradition'—if we prefer to use that more general term[47]—was the domain of one group, the so-called sages.[48] But even if we accept the argument that there was an intellectual tradition and a group that shaped and transmitted it,[49] does the Song belong to this tradition? Perhaps the Song was used in education,[50] though we know little about this subject, but does that make it a 'wisdom book'?

The Song is not usually included in discussions of wisdom literature. In his classic study, *Wisdom in Israel*, von Rad mentions it only once, in a footnote, and that note is not even about the Song as related to 'wisdom'.[51] And no less a wisdom authority than Roland Murphy can assert, in his Preface to the volume on wisdom literature for the Forms of the Old Testament Literature series, in which the Song of Songs is included, that 'It will be clear to the careful reader

---

46   K. Dell, 'Does the Song of Songs Have Any Connections to Wisdom?', in: Hagedorn (ed.), *Perspectives*, 8–26; see also the briefer, more general comments of M. Sadgrove, 'The Song of Songs as Wisdom Literature', *Studia Biblica 1978*, I. *Papers on Old Testament and Related Themes* (JSOTSup, 11), Sheffield 1979, 245–48.

47   See R.N. Whybray, *The Intellectual Tradition in the Old Testament* (BZAW, 135), Berlin 1974; J. Blenkinsopp, *Sage, Priest, Prophet: Religious and Intellectual Leadership in Ancient Israel*, Louisville 1995, 9–65.

48   Cf. R.E. Murphy, 'Wisdom in the OT', *ABD* VI, 928: 'A common culture and world of ideas was shared by all classes in Israelite society. The sapiential understanding of reality (descried above in "thought world") was not a mode of thinking cultivated exclusively by a small group... [W]isdom motifs could have circulated and would not be the exclusive possession of a given class. The wisdom heritage must have constituted a common fund of knowledge experience for each Israelite.'

49   Blenkinsopp criticizes Whybray for supposing that a tradition can be sustained and transmitted without institutional grounding, and he locates this activity in an upper-class, educated type of intellectual leadership (e.g., teachers, scribes) within that tradition (*Sage, Priest, Prophet*, 10–20 *et passim*). I mention above that the Song is the work of an educated poet, but that is not enough to place the Song in Israel's intellectual tradition as Blenkinsopp describes it (and Blenkinsopp does not include the Song in his discussion). Whybray discusses the Song briefly, concluding that there is 'no reason to suppose a connection between the author(s) of the book and the intellectual tradition' (*The Intellectual Tradition*, 119–20 [120]).

50   Carr considers it likely that ancient Israel included love poems in its educational corpus, both in Northern and early Judean education (*Formation*, 433, 439).

51   G. von Rad, *Wisdom in Israel*, Abingdon 1972, 168 n. 29: 'The loved one is also called "sister", S. of S. 4.9f., 12; 5.1; etc.'

that only three (Proverbs, Job, Ecclesiastes) of the six books treated here are technically "wisdom literature".[52] He does not include the Song in his discussion of 'Wisdom in the OT' for the *Anchor Bible Dictionary*, apart from one paragraph, in which he observes that the only wisdom element in the Song may be the lines about love as strong as death in 8:6, but this, he avers, does not change the Song's genre (love poetry).[53] Even Dell, in her discussion of the Song's connections to wisdom, observes, 'Clearly the Song is not to be characterized as wisdom literature in the same way as Proverbs or Ecclesiastes on a narrow, form-critical definition',[54] and '... even on a wider definition of the genre of wisdom, which might arguably include works influenced strongly by wisdom forms or ideas, the Song tends to stay off the list. The reason is because "love songs" are a clearly defined genre in their own right...'[55] And Joseph Blenkinsopp, who makes a plausible case for a lay intellectual tradition in biblical Israel—one that 'presuppose[s] a more or less coherent, if seldom articulated, worldview'—includes Proverbs, Job and Ecclesiastes but finds it 'unclear whether [the Song] relates in any way to the tradition of the sages, apart from the formal attribution to Solomon'.[56]

What about the possibility of such a thing as 'wisdom influence' on the Song? Dell cites numerous examples of links between the Song and 'wisdom'. But should we think of direct influence, whose direction is hard to ascertain,

---

52 *Wisdom Literature: Job, Proverbs, Ruth, Canticles, Ecclesiastes, and Esther* (FOTL, 13), Grand Rapids 1981, xiii. He does go on to state, 'As a whole, the Song emphasizes values which are primary in wisdom thought (cf. Proverbs 1–9)'. What values would that be, one wonders.

53 Murphy, 'Wisdom in the OT', 928. He adds, 'Nevertheless, it may be that the sages were responsible for the transmission and editing of the Song (and its attribution to the wise Solomon), because it was in line with the societal values (fidelity, etc., of Prov 5:15ff.) which the sages treasured'—a statement that is vague at best; see also Murphy's brief remarks in *The Song of Songs* (Hermeneia), Minneapolis 1990, 99; and Murphy, *The Tree of Life: An Exploration of Biblical Wisdom Literature*, 2nd ed., Grand Rapids 1996, 106–7. On 'wisdom editing', see also Dell, who abandons her normally cautious stance when she concludes, 'It seems then that the argument for a wisdom redaction or stage of literary transmission is quite convincing...', before continuing, 'and yet it is hard to know at precisely what stage the wisdom editors would have made their mark' ('Connections', 17). Who were these editors and why should they be connected with wisdom?

54 Dell, 'Connections', 8; elsewhere she argues that on such a narrow definition even Job does not fit (*The Book of Job as Sceptical Literature* [BZAW, 197], Berlin 1991, 87). She does not include the Song in her contribution to *The Blackwell Companion to the Hebrew Bible* on 'Wisdom Literature' (ed. L.G. Perdue; Oxford 2005, 418–31).

55 Dell, 'Connections', 9.

56 Blenkinsopp, *Sage, Priest, Prophet*, 14, 48.

or of common ideas, motifs and topoi that circulated, perhaps for centuries, in the wider culture? If connections can be found between the Song and sapiential literature such as Proverbs, Job (?), and Ecclesiastes, it may mean no more than a familiarity with love poetry on the part of 'the sages'.[57] In some cases a direct influence may exist, as, for example, Prov. 31:10–31, which Yair Zakovitch sees as a polemic against the Song of Songs.[58] But in others, the use of motifs from love poetry in 'wisdom' contexts, either consciously or unconsciously, and either from the Song of Songs or a work like it, cannot be used to argue that the Song of Songs is wisdom literature.

If the Song is a 'wisdom book', wherein would its 'wisdom' lie? In recommending that one fall head over heels in love because it is so wonderful, and in urging readers to pass their time enjoying sexual pleasures and romantic trysts *al fresco*? In encouraging the love-struck among its readership to flout social conventions, and to give no thought to their personal safety (like the woman in 3:2–3 and 5:6–7)? The Song does not teach or preach or offer advice to its audience, except to tell the women of Jerusalem not awaken love before it wishes (and the meaning of this exhortation is debated).[59] Its one didactic statement, in 8:6–7, would not be out of place in Proverbs,[60] but one aphorism does not a wisdom book make. If 'love is strong as death' is the Song's teaching, its wisdom, I would say that as a Wisdom Book the Song of Songs is not very successful, for, although the sentiment may be profound, the four couplets about love are rather banal:

---

57   Dell mentions links to all three books, and suggests that Proverbs reflects the influence of the Song ('Connections', 17–24).

58   Y. Zakovitch, '"A Woman of Valor, *'eshet hayil*" (Proverbs 31.10–31): A Conservative Response to the Song of Songs', in: D.J.A. Clines and E. van Wolde (eds), *A Critical Engagement: Essays on the Hebrew Bible in Honour of J. Cheryl Exum* (HBM, 38), Sheffield 2011, 401–13.

59   See Fox, *Song of Songs*, 109; Exum, *Song of Songs*, 117–18; Brian P. Gault, 'A "Do Not Disturb" Sign? Reexamining the Adjuration Refrain in Song of Songs', *JSOT* 36 (2011), 93–104.

60   J.C. Exum, 'The Poetic Genius of the Song of Songs', in: Hagedorn (ed.), *Perspectives*, 78–79. I see these verses as central to the Song, but the medium, the poem itself, is the message ('Poetic Genius'; Exum, *Song of Songs*, 2–13 *et passim*). Note too, that these verses appear in the mouth of one of the characters in the poem, and in a subordinate clause, not as a description of love in and of itself. To suggest that an editor added 8:6–7 (and perhaps other references) to bring the Song into wisdom's ambit is pure speculation. If an editor had wanted to make the Song a 'wisdom book', putting these verses in the author's voice and placing them at the end, like the editorial conclusion to Qoheleth, would have been easier and more effective.

> ...for love is strong as death,
>   jealousy as adamant as Sheol.
> Its flames are flames of fire,
>   an almighty flame.
> Floods cannot quench love,
>   nor rivers sweep it away.
> Should a man offer all his wealth for love,
>   it would be utterly disdained.

Apart from these verses, the Song does not describe the meaning of love or the nature of love. Rather than pontificating about love, it shows its readers how delicious and thrilling erotic love is by allowing us to overhear what lovers say about it. The Song of Songs is a love poem, and it is as a love poem that it certainly belongs among *The Best of Songs*, as its title boasts.

The Song of Songs is not Torah and not Prophets. 'Writings' is a good all-purpose category. Dell speaks of 'wisdom literature' as describing 'a certain corpus of closely defined books in the Bible'.[61] The advantage I see in including the Song in a corpus of so-called Wisdom Books is that it gives us a larger context, if we need one, in which to place the Bible's only love poem in some kind of relation to other books of the Bible rather than isolating it from them.

To summarize: Evidence points to the Song as a unity. Scholars who choose to describe it as a collection need to be prepared to demonstrate it. The date of the Song remains an open question, but an increasing body of evidence suggests it may be earlier than previously thought, and a Hellenistic date cannot be assumed simply on the basis of linguistic evidence. Its authorship remains a mystery, and its connections to wisdom are tenuous at best.

---

61   Dell, 'Connections', 8. In introductions to the Song for a general audience, I have found myself writing, for lack of a better alternative, 'In the Christian canon it is among the Poetical and Wisdom books' (J.C. Exum, 'Introduction and Annotations to the Song of Solomon', in: M.D. Coogan [ed.], *The New Oxford Annotated Bible* [NRSV], Oxford 2010, 950), or 'In the Christian canon it is last among the wisdom books (Job, Psalms, Proverbs, Ecclesiastes, Song of Songs) and precedes the Prophets (J.C. Exum, 'Song of Songs', in: C.A. Newsom, S.H. Ringe, and J.E. Lapsley [eds], *The Women's Bible Commentary*, 3rd ed., Louisville 2012, 247).

The Substance of Job: Beginnings and Endings

Jan Fokkelman

The book of Job contains a huge debate between Job and his three friends, plus one. They try to assess the meaning of the events that are covered by the narrative of chapter 1—three disasters plus one. The fourth disaster is the climax of the series, for it is obviously the worst, Job loses all his children.[1]

Before we meet more instances of the literary pattern 3 + 1, I want to look at the start of the first chapter. For the time being the writer takes on the posture of the omniscient narrator. His very first verse is remarkable because it introduces the hero right away and immediately continues with a string of four qualifications. Job is *tām*, the first one says, 'perfect', and if we were God, we would be perfectly happy with this adjective: what more could we want? Nevertheless, three more forms of praise follow. Why so abundant? Or shouldn't we call this string redundant?

The sense of these forms of characterization appears when we study their order. Up front are the single terms *tām wəyāšār*. Next, we find double terms, the phrases 'fearing God' and 'shunning evil' (*yərē' 'elōhîm wəsār mērā'*). In this way, the foursome is articulated in two pairs. Their validity and truth are backed by the authority of their creator, the writer.

A bit later, the writer introduces a new creature, God. In the heavenly council, this narrative character speaks to the Prosecutor (*haśśāṭān*, indicating a profession), points to Job and proudly calls him 'incomparable'. He proves it by exactly repeating the four qualities of the man; he parrots the writer. In Job 2:3 he does so once more, literally. The final count is three times four terms of praise, a sum of twelve.

Why did the writer decide to be almost unbearably emphatic? Because the rest of his work feeds on it. The real weight of the foursome appears in various ways when we detect their follow-up. The pair of double terms anticipates the punchline of a brilliant poem on wisdom, spoken by Job himself, chapter 28. His 28th verse is a quotation of God which defines 'fearing God' as wisdom and 'shunning evil' as insight. The connection with 1:1 can be assessed as follows.

---

1 For detailed structural and prosodic studies of the Book of Job see J.P. Fokkelman, *Major Poems of the Hebrew Bible at the Interface of Prosody and Structural Analysis*, 4 volumes (SSN, 37, 41, 43 and 47), Assen 1998–2004. Job 3 is discussed in vol. 1, Job 4–14 in vol. 2 and Job 15–42 in vol. 4. See also Jan P. Fokkelman, *The Book of Job in Form: A Literary Translation with Commentary* (SSN, 58), Leiden 2012, and the website www.janfokkelman.nl.

The man who quotes the divine instruction of moral perfection in 28:28 lives in the epical world evoked by the narrative envelope and in the lyrical world of the versified debate. The world of reader and writer is beyond that. Job cannot be aware of the exchanges of meaning happening between the book and us. We know that 28:28 exactly matches the second half of 1:1, and at the same time we are aware that Job cannot know this connection. A weird consequence of this is that God's instruction of moral perfection is authorized by Job's qualities, while Job's qualities were authorized earlier on by the writer.

1 From Keyword to Pattern

Back to the string of terms in 1:1, and searching for more echoes in the body of poetry. The fourfold characterization is an excessive case of synonymy that needs more study. This time I turn to the head and the tail. Could this fourfold chain be another case of the literary pattern 3 + 1? I think so, because the fourth part is a case of litotes. This figure is based on the operation 'minus times minus makes plus'. We are familiar with it, in the sense that words like blame-less and in-nocent do the same. 'Shunning evil' is one more case and as such anticipates the largest and most important poem of the book. It is deviant because the three terms before it are straightaway positive.

How does one do this, shunning evil? Later on, Job himself gives an enormous exposition of all the ways shunning evil can and should be practised, in chapter 31. That poem is a gigantic case of litotes, as it is a comprehensive enumeration of crimes and sins which, says Job, I never have committed. In this way Job offers the deity exhaustive proof of his innocence. The writer underscores his argument and celebrates the moral perfection of his hero by turning the poem into a spectacular and many-levelled example of numerical perfection.

The first term of the fourfold chain reads *tām* and is the shortest conceivable form of the root *t-m-m*. This monosyllabic word leads the way because it is the most important keyword of the book of Job, together with the longer form *tāmîm* and the substantive noun *tummâh*. When we consult the concordance we discover that the use of these forms is special in terms of statistics, so that I need to appreciate them in context. The short form does not often occur in the Bible, only fifteen times; but Job alone has seven of them. The long form shows the opposite. The form *tāmîm* occurs no fewer than 91 times in the Bible, but Job has only three of them, with peculiar effects to boot. Elihu calls himself 'perfect of knowledge' in chapter 36 but in the next chapter says the same about God. The combination of the two passages drowns him in ridicule;

he has deconstructed himself with his own words.[2] The only other instance of *tāmîm* is quite special for two reasons; it is part of a rare asyndeton (in 12:4), and this figure, *ṣaddîq tāmîm*, occurs elsewhere only once: in Gen. 6:9 where another luminary from primeval times is introduced: Noah, and just like Job is immediately characterized by this couple of adjectives. Which is no surprise for the reader of Ezekiel 14.

The use of *tummâh* is even more special. This substantive form of the keyword occurs only five times in Tanakh, and four of these are here in the book of Job.[3] Moreover, this group has the order 3 + 1—again the literary pattern! The series of three refers to Job himself, applies the neat series of suffixes for the 3rd, 2nd and 1st person singular that refer to the hero, and testifies that Job 'is still holding fast to his/your/my integrity (*tummâh*)'. Its importance is enhanced by several kinds of variation. The speakers differ, and their addressees too, each time. Each time the tone differs dramatically: first God, who praises; next, Job's wife, who scoffs at her better half; then the man himself, who lends definitive gravity to the words by turning them into an oath. These three occurrences of *tummâh* are all part of a dialogue; they are spoken directly to another person. Then comes the fourth instance, in 31:6. It stands apart, because its context is special.

Chapter 31 is unique on the grounds of sheer length, content, structure, numerical perfection and purpose. This poem is Job's ultimate challenge to his cruel lord, the silent God. *Tummâh* is part of the strophe in which Job asks to be weighed with fair scales, so that God finally has no other choice than to make himself known and recognize Job's innocence:

yišqəlēnî bəmōʾzənê ṣedeq / wəyēdaʿ ʾElōah tummātî.[4]

Let him weigh me on the scales of righteousness, then God will know my integrity.

---

2   Elihu says *təmîm dēʿôt* first, 36:4, and then *təmîm dēʿîm*, in 37:16; is there an additional shade of meaning, conveyed by the change in the plural ending?

3   The occurrences of *tummâh* in Job: in 2:3 (God proudly speaking, *ʿōdennû maḥăzîq*...), in 2:9 (Job's wife scorning, *ʿōdəkā maḥăzîq*...), in 27:5–6 (Job himself, swearing an oath). Note how in chapter 27 the words *ḥ-z-q* and *tummâh* are expanded and their colon is doubled, through the use of synonyms (*lōʾ ʾāsîr* and *ṣidqātî*).

4   Note how the word pair *ṣ-d-q* // *tummâh* of 27:5–6 is kept working and chiastically mirrored in the crucial verse 31:6.

The narrative which provides the start of the book seems to go underground after chapter 2, but its power to carry on should not be underestimated. A good narratology can show that. Soon after the introduction of the hero we meet an intriguing word that will become the fountainhead of the plot: *ḥinnām*. The word sounds pleasant, but it is treacherous. Guess how many times it occurs. Well, three times, plus one,[5] and each time the speaker is a different one—again a good variety of voices.

2   The Nature of the Argument

The question whether Job is pious 'for nothing' leads to a bet. The wager accepted by God launches the plot and propels it throughout the entire book, because it implies the unabated tension of two questions: will Job break under the terrible blows the Prosecutor is allowed to deal to him? And ultimately the breath-taking question: will God win or lose the wager?

The arch of tension spanning over the entire book is supported unexpectedly by an element we easily overlook during the hundreds of hours we spend in studying the difficult poems; an element that is so familiar to us that we take it for granted. It is the sentence which appears up front in many chapters and says: *wayyaʿan* + PN (= personal name) + *wayyōʾmar*. It is the simple quotation formula we meet so often elsewhere. In the Book of Job there are some thirty cases, and from chapter 3 up to 26 the change of speaker is introduced by this couple *wayyaʿan... wayyōʾmar* twenty times. What is its contribution, actually?

I prefer to give a semiotic answer. Each time the writer uses these words that seem so subservient or even trite; he continues to leave his footprint, so to speak. He delivers a signal that says: 'Here I am again. I am the boss! I am the one who gives the floor to a new speaker; the decision how to distribute the speeches is still mine!' In this way the reader is repeatedly reminded that narration is going on, that the arch of tension may have gone underground but is still alive, and that an outcome of the plot is still in the offing. Moreover, this repetition of the unassuming formula has an impact on the body of poetry. The chain of clauses with *wayyaʿan... wayyōʾmar* changes the condition and the status of the poems. They assume their real mode of being: embedded text,

---

5   *Ḥinnām* occurs in the initial prose section in 1:9 (the Prosecutor asks his dangerous question about Job's sincerity), in 2:3 (God reproaches him to have incited Him), in 9:17 (Job complains God has wounded him) and in 22:6 Eliphaz attacks his friend viciously with the term. Note that the voices change each time.

that is, direct speech offered to us in a narrative. Narration appears to be the ultimate provider of the forty poems, and the speakers cannot escape from their status as narrative characters.

All this leads to a new question. What is the nature of this book? What would be an appropriate name for its genre? Some time ago, I came across the term artificial. Marvin Pope wrote it in his Anchor Bible commentary.[6] It took me a minute before I decided that artificiality is not an insult. In fact, I think it can guide us in a search for the right genre indication. Here is my list of the things that seem artificial in the book of Job: (1) The writer picks up his hero from primeval times. The suspicion that he found him in Ezekiel 14 can be corroborated by new data that amount to full proof. (2) Job reaches an old age that is patriarchal. (3) The terms that characterize him in 1:1 are not only redundant, they are ostentatious. (4) The writer shows off his omniscience when he looks into the heavenly council and reports its deliberations. (5) The experiment with Job, held with God's openly permission, is cruel. (6) It is inconceivable that no less than four disasters in a row hit somebody within the compass of one day. And (7), the report of these events in four tight and extremely schematic sequences is so unnatural that we understand: this is a case of surrealism. 'Surreal' does not mean less real; on the contrary, it means more real, pointing at the intensifying of reality throughout the book. That is the spirit of the poet.

I take all this to mean that the writer coquets with the message: this may be narration, but it is not history-writing. The quality of the surreal guides us to the conclusion that the genre of this book can be called 'a thought experiment'. The entire debate is in its service. All the time the participants are busy to find out what their values and theology are, and when they defend their concepts and arguments, their strife is mostly heated. The traditional theodicy is quickly demolished—the doctrine of symmetrical retribution is in shatters. The conclusion in chapter 28 offers us a well-articulated exercise in epistemology. But the bewilderment over Job's predicament keeps stinging.

3 Two Central Triads

The end of the debate comes in sight when Bildad has spoken for the third time. Job answers him in chapter 26 and closes the debate proper for the time being with some afterthoughts in chapter 27; in the detached argument of

---

6 Marvin H. Pope, *Job: A New Translation with Introduction and Commentary* (AB 15,1), New York 1973, xxiii, xxx.

chapter 28 he presents his final judgment on Wisdom, with a special twist at the end.

Bildad's poem is very short, but unlike many commentators I don't think his text is truncated. It consists of two strophes (25:2–3 and 25:4–6) which due to a systematic opposition cooperate to form a meaningful whole—one stanza. The short strophe wants to present an impressive image of God, but it is Bildad's hidden purpose to intimidate his friend with it, so that he can deal him an awful blow in the next verses. The long strophe uses generalizing words to present an ugly image of man. It is almost a copy of two passages spoken earlier by Eliphaz, in 4:17–18 and 15:15–16. The very negative view of man offered by the friends can be taken as an unpleasant projection.

Job answers Bildad's curt proposal with subtle corrections. Picking up the cosmic terms, he widens them into a much more beautiful panorama of creation, and this view then serves as the ground for quite a different view of man. In 26:14 Job implicitly rejects Bildad's conclusion (man is a filthy maggot) and substitutes his own conclusion (26:14) for it. No pretentious ontological description, but a word on the right attitude or behaviour: humankind should just be humble, because our understanding of God's wonders is very shallow, 'how small a whisper we hear of him! And the thunder of his might who can comprehend?' This line of argument and the rhetorical *mî yitbônān* are anticipations of his final statements on Wisdom in chapter 28.

The start of chapter 27 has a binding, definitive ring, as Job turns to the language of swearing. He puts in two oaths. The first one (27:2–4) is positive with a negative content (against uttering deceit), the second one (27:5–6) is negative (*ḥalîlâh lî*) with a positive content (pro integrity). Note how Job begins: *ḥay 'Ēl* sounds good, but in the same colon he adds *hēsîr mišpāṭî*—a sarcasm which becomes clear when we read the contrast introduced in 27:6, *lō' 'āsîr tummātî*. In the competition for justice God is overtaken...

The philosophical chapter 28 explores three fields: the mining industry, the market and the universe. The composition covers them by three long stanzas which are marked by the two nearly identical verses 12 and 20. Both contain two questions and have a great impact. They are signs of an implicit but powerful quest which underlies the entire poem. The ambitious and successful miner, a striking image of *homo faber*, enters the market with his precious finds to purchase wisdom, but to no avail. The poet then calls in former gods like Yam and Mot, but these authorities fail: they confess they do not possess Wisdom, 'what we heard of her is hearsay', words that link up with 26:14 and 42:5a. As the quest seems to end in failure, the third stanza (28:20–28) comes to the rescue and ends with another quotation, this time from the true God. He does not teach Job all the mysteries of his creation, but limits his instruction to the practical and the ethical. Verse 28 is the punchline, recommends decent living, and is a reminder of Job 1:1.

The Book of Job has, as I see it, two large climaxes. The last one presents God's answer from the storm plus Job's final words. The first one consists of the three poems in chapters 29–30–31. In July 2006 I gave a lecture in Heidelberg in which I explained how dialectical their mutual relations are. They are truly a Hegelian triad. What I said at the time is available in print, and today it will be sufficient to summarize it.[7] In chapter 29, the thesis, the hero speaks of the past, which brought happiness, richness and great prestige in the community. Job was the active and exemplary defender of justice. In chapter 30, the antithesis, Job speaks of the present, his horrible and unexpected suffering. In chapter 31, however, he offers a synthesis. He manages to re-assume his principled stance and proves his innocence by presenting a catalogue of crimes and sins he never committed. It is, as stated above, a gigantic case of litotes. Job touches rock-bottom: he will not budge and reaffirms his ethical and religious positions.

Actually, Job has remained the loyal person he was. In 2:21 we find a true verse (a full poetic line, bicolic) in which he gives his very first response to God's scourge: two short and asyndetic clauses that represent thesis plus antithesis, *yhwh nātan wəyhwh lāqaḥ*, crowned by the B-colon that reveals Job's unflinching faith, *yəhî šēm yhwh məbōrāk*. This passage anticipates the triadic construction of the first Climax.

What is happening there in a Hegelian sense? Chapters 29 and 30 stand for the stages of being and becoming. Enjoying the good life brings the temptation of taking happiness, health and fortune for granted. It is the stage of naiveté and the situation is static. Then catastrophe breaks in and shatters all which is good. Everything has to be reassessed, nothing is certain anymore. This situation of radical crisis however is dynamic, and Job is forced to move and above all to reflect. He is forced to reinvent himself. And that is exactly what he is doing in chapter 31. With a truly Hegelian term, we can say that he is overcoming the shocking opposition between fortune and catastrophe. The achievement of chapter 31 may be called a case of sublimation. Expounding the many forms of his integrity, Job reaffirms the roots of solidarity, justice and religion. He stubbornly refuses to let go of them, and once more his wife's advice to curse God has no chance. Job has his own ideas about relating to the deity. His long enumeration is a message to God who up till now kept an embarrassing silence.

---

7 Jan Fokkelman, 'Job 28 and the Climax in Chapters 29–31: Crisis and Identity', in: Hanna Liss and Manfred Oeming (eds), *Literary Construction of Identity in the Ancient World*, Winona Lake, IN 2010, 301–22.

It is important to understand what the function of this climactic section is. Therefore I would like to define the nature and the claim of these poems. Chapter 29 is the comprehensive and authoritative summary of the past, chapter 30 is the comprehensive and authoritative summary of the present, and chapter 31 is the comprehensive and authoritative summary of Job's life and inspiration.

All this is the work of a writer. Where does *he* stand? He stands by his man. He gives evidence of this in a radical operation. Chapter 31 is the inner climax of Climax I and the poet has turned it into a pinnacle of numerical perfection. If we give the sof pasuq of 31:11 a little push, without changing any letter of the poem, we find a beautiful tricolon. Each colon is a short nominal clause with the pronoun of the 3rd person singular and two long i-vowels. Now, the poem has 84 (read 7 times 12) cola, and when we divide 672, the total number of premasoretic syllables, by 84, we find the central normative figure eight. I read 84 as seven times twelve, and 672 multiplies these sacred numbers with eight.

With its forty verses chapter 31 is the longest poem of the book. The number of stanzas is seven. Strophes are either short or long. The two groups work in Job 31 as follows:

- 8 S-strophes (280 syllables in 35 cola: the average per colon is exactly eight) and
- 8 L-strophes (392 syllables in 49 cola: the same exact eight).

The manifold contribution of the central normative figure eight is decisive for this chapter. However, what clinches the matter is a measure that hitherto remained undetected as well, and sheds new light on the purpose of the poem. When we look at the eighth colon from the start and the eighth colon from the end, we find a chiasm that points at the heart of the matter. God should 'count all my steps', Job says in 31:4b: *kol ṣəʿāday yispōr*. That is how He can finally 'recognize my integrity' (*tummâh*). In 31:37a Job proudly says *mispar ṣəʿāday ʾaggîdennû*; in a wonderful wordplay he feels 'like a prince', *kəmô nāgîd*.

This figure of inversion offers us a good label for the entire poem, and does so in the nick of time, in strophe 15.[8] Chapter 31, this huge catalogue, is itself 'the number of my steps'. In this same strophe, Job uses the word *sēfer* (we recognize the root!) and says with a sigh that he wishes to see the indictment written by his legal opponent: *sēfer kātab ʾîš rîbî* (31:35). In the same breath, he

---

8 The majority of commentators consider the final strophe (31:38–40) to be a later addition, because they find 31:35–37 a worthier ending. The location of the chiasm (*m*)*spr* + 'my steps' refutes it.

counters with his own document, *hēn tāwî*, and this mark or signature coincides completely with the *mispar ṣəʿāday*.

This unit is audacious. Job has found his last strength and challenges God to make his position clear. Moreover, he wants to make sure that it is impossible to ignore or eliminate his counterclaims. His target is to have a fixed text, an indelible statement which cannot possibly be ignored. He has made his preparations as early as chapter 19. Let us listen to 19:23–24:

> Oh, if only my words were written down!
> Oh, if only they were engraved in a sefer!
> Would that with an iron stylus and lead
> they were incised on a rock forever!

In a way, this wish has found fulfilment—on a different plane. It was the writer of this book who took care of it. On behalf of his hero, he wrote a list which is part of what we call a *sēfer*, and his testimony has defied the ages. I pass on that he applied the verbal form of the root (Qal and Piʿel) exactly eight times, and he used the noun *mispār* twelve times in his poetry. The two passages from chapters 19 and 31 are crucial stations on the long trajectory of the hero. Note how they are connected through another device: the specific phrase for a strong wish, *mî yittēn*, appears in 19:23 and in 31:35.

Let us pursue our way towards the second and final Climax. Job has appealed many times to God, longing for an answer. The first signal that his hope may not have been in vain appears in 38:1, the threshold to God's answer from the storm. From chapter 3 on, the narrator has used the quotation formula twenty times *wayyaʿan . . . wayyōʾmar* without adding an addressee. The form *wayyaʿan* never got an object. The start of chapter 38, however, is the first of five instances which explicitly mention the person who literally gets an answer. Is this a first sign that a true dialogue between the hero and the deity is possible and will come about? God will speak two plus two poems, but in between, at the start of chapter 40, there is even a short, but very real discussion between the two.

We now enter the last chapter. Here, all the official Bible versions succeed in completely ruining the portrait of the hero. They have mistranslated three phrases. Let us see what happened.

4   The Final Poem

The writer has decided to give the last word (in poetry) to his hero and that is suggestive of a close relationship. Job's poem in 42:2–6 is short. This text consists of two strophes, just like chapter 25, Bildad's last instalment. The first strophe, the 42:2–3, is delineated by a remarkable inclusion. Job starts with *yādaʿtî kî kōl tūkal* and ends with *lōʾ ʾēdaʿ*. That is a paradox, connecting all to nothing: 'all' goes to God, nothing goes to me. The last word is an effective case of ellipsis. There is no object, so the transitive verb 'to know' is used absolutely, which means that knowing is not limited to an object. And that is to say: my ignorance is all-sided. With these words, mortal man determines and admits precisely where he stands with respect to his Maker.

This short poem has more than ten verbal forms that are transitive. Nevertheless there are at least four more cases of ellipsis. Ellipsis appears to be the main feature of style here, and that is what we should be aware of when we approach the first pitfall for Bible translators: 42:6a, *ʿal-kēn ʾemʾas*.[9]

I skip all the variants of misunderstanding the verb and prefer to offer a clear reading. One: the verb is well-known, in Job as well as in Samuel and elsewhere, and its meaning is unequivocal, 'to reject'. Nearly all the modern Bible versions went astray because the translators got deeply embarrassed by the ellipsis and didn't understand what to do. An ellipsis is a poetic device, and as such it represents a challenge to stand it, to endure it; it is an invitation to respect it.[10] Next comes the interpreter who has the right and the task to suggest the right filling-in. In our case, we could follow Habel and others. Then the verb and the left-out object say: I reject my present approach of the matter; I reject my demand of a fair trial, or something like that.

In 42:5 the foundation for this decision was laid, when Job said: 'By the hearing of the ear I had heard of you, but now my eye has seen you.' The two main senses are a popular source for the poets who want to create a word pair that in its turn warrants parallelismus membrorum. Seeing and hearing (or eye and ear) are a well-known pair with the poets. They can be used in a synonymous vein, but sometimes they convey a contrast. In Job 42:5 there is a 'but' between their half-verses. Job has not a high opinion of hearing as a source of knowledge; it is superseded by the immediacy of seeing. In 26:14b he spoke of 'glimpses of His ways, / how small a whisper we hear of Him!' And the question 'who can comprehend?' prepared us for the difficult and disappointing quest for wisdom/insight in chapter 28. Yam and Mot had to admit their embarrassing ignorance, in verses 14 and 22. Just like 42:5a the colon 28:22b, 'what we

---

9   The misery begins with the King James Version, which said: 'Wherefore I abhor *myself*, and repent in dust and ashes'. This rendering combines four mistakes, and most of them still survive.

10 The verb *m-ʾ-s* is also an ellipsis in 7:16a (in view of dying); compare 9:21 with *ʾemʾas ḥayyāy*, and especially 36:5 (cf. 8:20).

heard of her is only hearsay' is completely filled with three auditive terms that all denote a downsizing.

So the B-colon of 42:5 is the winner. Its clause is the perfect successor of the passage by the end of chapter 19 which represents the core and the glow of Job's hope. Job awaits what he wants, a meeting with the one who is 'my redeemer', and the intensity of the encounter can only be expressed by choosing the visual: 'Yet in my flesh I will behold God' (19:26b), 'and it will be my eyes that see, and no other' (19:27b).[11] To Job, God's answer from the storm means seeing God; his final strophe establishes that his hope is realized.

It is time to turn to the right understanding of the second clause of 42:6, *wənihamtî 'al 'āfār wā'efer*. Regret, relent and repentance should be thrown into the dustbin as quickly as possible. For Job, there is nothing to repent of. Two super-authorities have unequivocally, explicitly and repeatedly assured to us that the man is blameless. The maker of the book was the first to say so, and God has parroted him twice. As a consequence, we do not need to foster any doubts when a third super-authority steps in with the same message. This person is Job himself and the writer gives his protagonist many poems to posit and reiterate his complete innocence.

What, then, does verse 6b mean? The complement *'al 'āfār wā'efer* is not a complement of space, but a kind of prepositional object. This eloquent double denotes Job's terrible condition, it refers to his suffering. With it, Job quotes himself. In 30:19 he defined his predicament with the words *wā'etmaššēl kā'āfār wā'efer*. That was in the midst of his dialectical triad, which (by the way) was called a *māšāl* by the writer.

Nice to see how *'āfār* and *'efer* are split in the prose section with which the book opened: Job sits *bətôk hā'efer* in 2:8, and his friends throw *'āfār* upon them, 2:12. What is more important, however, is the fact that the graphical combination *'āfār wā'efer* occurs nowhere else in the Bible, except in Genesis. In Gen. 18:27 Abraham uses the phrase in order to denote his own state vis-à-vis God, and there are three more details which link him with Job. Like Noah, he receives the label *tāmîm* (Gen. 17:1, a passage in which God calls himself El Shadday—compare Job 27:2), and in Genesis 18, being in a true dialogue with God, Abraham constantly makes *mišpaṭ* the subject and uses the strong expression *ḥalîlâh lî* (cf. Job 27:5, the very verse in which Job defends his *tummâh*).

---

11 The combination of the verb 'to see' with the word 'eye' occurs eleven times in Job. Ten times they are from the lips of Job: in 7:7, 8; 10:4, 18; 13:1; 19:27; 21:20; 28:10; 29:11 and 42:5.

The form *niḥamtî* is a Nif'al and speaks of comfort.[12] Here is Clines' rendering: 'I accept consolation for my dust and ashes.' The importance of this very last clause from the hero is crucial. With it, Job gives a sober and correct interpretation of God's intervention. He has understood that the primary meaning of the divine speech is the main meaning: God has said 98 times 'you' and 'your' to him, in the chapters 38–40. So God finally has spoken directly to him, God has turned to him in a very personal way. This raises the intuition or the surmise in Job that he is or will be vindicated. And that is exactly what happens.

It is time to mention Ezechiel 14, the chapter that reminds the reader of the primeval luminaries Noah, Job and Daniel. There are more points of contact with the prophet than is commonly thought. In Job 42:11, the Nif'al form of the verb *niḥam* is followed up by a Pi'el form. Family and friends give comfort to the hero, which is the opposite of 2:11, where comfort was impossible 'because the pain was too great'. Now 42:11 says 'they consoled him' and then adds: 'for all the evil Yahweh had brought on him.' The surprise of Ezekiel 14 is fourfold: we find the very same words in this chapter, it has the same succession of Nif'al and Pi'el for the verb *niḥam*, and a second later we meet the full anagram *ḥinnām*—the very adverb that is so essential for the plot in the book of Job. The prophet started his passage with four disasters in quick succession—just like the second half of Job 1. All this supports the idea that the writer of Job knew the text of the prophet.

5   The Prose Conclusion

In the final prose section Job receives full vindication. A look on the handout shows that the narrator repeats some sentences, but does so in a balanced structure A-B-X-B'-A' around 42:8:

vs. 7	וַיְהִי אַחַר דִּבֶּר יְהוָה אֶת־הַדְּבָרִים הָאֵלֶּה אֶל־אִיּוֹב
	לֹא דִבַּרְתֶּם אֵלַי נְכוֹנָה כְּעַבְדִּי אִיּוֹב
vs. 8	וְאִיּוֹב עַבְדִּי יִתְפַּלֵּל עֲלֵיכֶם
	לֹא דִבַּרְתֶּם אֵלַי נְכוֹנָה כְּעַבְדִּי אִיּוֹב
vs. 9	וַיַּעֲשׂוּ כַּאֲשֶׁר דִּבֶּר אֲלֵיהֶם יְהוָה

---

12   The verb *niḥam* occurs eight (!) times in Job, and these occurrences obey a well-ordered symmetry, abcd-d'c'b'a'. The verses of 2:11 and 42:11 are an oppositional pair in the prose envelope. The other occurrences are all spoken by Job: n-ḥ-m in 6:10 and 42:6 (another opposition: death or life, received from God). Job 7:13 and 29:25 (inconsolable versus bringing comfort) and 16:2 and 21:34 (Job's criticism of his friends' contribution) are synonymous.

In 42:7a and at the end of 42:9a we find the phrase *yhwh dibbēr* plus the preposition *'el*. Nobody ever wasted a minute in thinking that this says anything else than God's speaking *to* somebody. It is absolutely stunning and absurd that the phrase *dibbartem 'ēlāy nəkōnâh*, which also occurs twice (in 42:7b as well as in 42:8b, the elements B-B' of the concentric structure), suddenly is rendered as speaking *about* God. The combination *dibbēr 'el* occurs seven times in Job and always denotes a direct 'speaking to'.[13]

God appreciates the fact that Job, unlike his friends, has spoken to Him directly, and that his speeches were 'well-founded'—whether we think *nəkônâh* is an adverb or a direct object in the clauses of 42:7b and 8b is of no consequence in this context. Job did speak directly to God, as a full scan throughout the book confirms. In the entire debate his friends never speak *to* God. They are theologians who always speak *about* God and think they are in the know. Job is different. In the first round of the debate alone he speaks twenty-four strophes directly to God, and he is not gentle.

The plot of the book ('let us test Job', since chapter 1) and the quest which made the heavenly court wonder ('will God win the bet?') have covered a long trajectory. To Job, it was a nightmare, but at the end of his predicament he has met and seen God. I appreciate this as an allusion to the patriarch Jacob, who could only transcend the boundaries of his over-ambitious ego by a nocturnal and numinous fight (Genesis 32). When he came through, he had to figure out what happened and put into words what he understood. His conclusion read 'I have seen God face to face and I am saved'. The positive outcome in the 42th chapter of Job is a close parallel.

---

13   The phrase *dibbēr 'el* occurs seven times, in 2:13, 13:3, 40:27, 42:7a, 7b, 8 and 9. Compare the noun *dābār* plus *'el* in 4:2 and 5:8. In 9:14 *dābār 'im*. The preposition *'el* occurs 78 times and nearly always implies direction. Also compare *dibbēr 'el* with phrases like *pānâh 'el, ha'tîr 'el, bô' 'el, šûb 'el*. The preposition *'al* occurs 202 times in Job, and can hardly ever be substituted by *'el*. P. Van Hecke, *From Linguistics to Hermeneutics: A Functional and Cognitive Approach to Job 12–14* (SSN, 55), Leiden 2011, 379–90, has an accurate discussion on the phrase *dibbēr 'el*. I myself endorsed 'speaking *to*' already in vol. 4 of my *Major Poems of the Hebrew Bible* (2004).

An Awfully Beastly Business: Some Thoughts on *behēmāh* in Jonah and Qoheleth

Alastair G. Hunter

1   Context

Many years ago Elias Bickerman described Jonah, Daniel, Qoheleth and Esther as *Four Strange Books of the Bible*. His declared intention was to explore what they revealed of 'the mentality of men of [the Hellenistic] period in the ancient Near East'.[1] While one response might be to wonder why he only found *four* strange books in Tanakh, I want rather to propose that two of them—Jonah and Qoheleth—share specific features which are not just strange, but suggest a shared eccentricity. Firstly, the fact that both present anti-heroes whose words and actions specifically deny the calling which they are supposed to exemplify: the traditional pious *ḥākām* and the Yahwistic prophet; and secondly, the presence in both of a dramatic deployment of animals (literally, *behēmāh*) at highly sensitive turns. It is the latter that I want to explore in this brief essay.

We are accustomed in the modern world to a variety of attitudes to animals which range from that of the full-blooded carnivore whose intent is to 'kill-em-and-eat-em' (the rarer the better) to their bitter opponents, the regiment of self-styled animal lovers who police the planet's supposedly dwindling supply of bio-diversity while seemingly failing to notice—or perhaps to acknowledge— the complicity of pet cats in the catastrophic decline of European song-birds.[2] Contemporary movements to recognise the rights of animals and the ethical problems of human consumption of non-vegetable life have grown particularly strongly amongst the most secularised and post-Christian sections of Western society. That is not to say that Christian and Jewish scholars have been silent on this theme, nor that it is a matter of unconcern to devout people; however it does appear as one of the moralities which fulfil a quasi-religious role in the modern world.

Nevertheless, there are important strands in Tanakh which support some of the key principles of the concern for animal welfare and ethical human

---

1   E. Bickerman, *Four Strange Books of the Bible*, New York 1968, iii.
2   This is a controversial claim, as a Google search will confirm. Equal numbers of confident and seemingly authoritative statements are made on both sides, with little sign (to the inexpert searcher) of any independent consensus.

regard for them. Indeed, as this paper argues, in important respects the ancient world was *more* in tune with the shared nature of human- and animal-kind than we are today. This observation prompts a further observation: that it is in a world where the Darwinian truth about the common origins of *all* life should by rights have nurtured a more empathetic attitude to animals, that we have brought to the status of a fine art factory processes for the production, slaughtering and distribution of all kinds of meat and fish protein. The Genesis injunction on Adam to take responsibility for creation (Gen. 1:28–30) has given way to the implications of the later permission to consume animal flesh and its consequent—and perfectly rational—response of fear of humankind on the part of animals (Gen. 9:1–3).

It is with these contradictory principles and emotions in mind that I turn to this review of the Biblical understanding of animals, with particular reference to my 'two strange books'.

2 Survey: Beasts and Living Things in Tanakh

The two principal terms relevant to this review are *behēmāh* and *ḥayyāh*, both of which refer almost exclusively to four-footed creatures.[3] *Behēmāh* seems to refer to larger, possibly domesticated animals, and that seems to be implied in Jonah. It should be noted, however, that the famous discussion in Qoh. 3:18–21 does not necessitate that restriction. *Ḥayyāh* has an obvious etymology in the root *ḥāyāh* 'to be alive', and includes both wild animals ('the beasts of the fields') and domesticated herds. There is no known etymology for *behēmāh*, though BDB (and so presumably Gesenius) postulates an 'unused root' **bhm* with the supposed meaning 'to be mute'.[4]

---

[3] It is clear that there are many other life-forms named in Tanakh, things that creep, crawl and slither, and things that fly or swim. These belong to separate categories, and are not part of the present discussion. Indeed, some of the dietary and purity rules make it clear that they occupy a separate cultural niche.

[4] The only plausibility this has seems to be a questionable association with the common phrase 'dumb animals', the only biblical support for which is the well-known declaration in Isa. 53:7:

... yet he did not open his mouth;
like a lamb that is led to the slaughter,
and like a sheep that before its shearers is silent,
so he did not open his mouth.

Whatever this metaphor means, it cannot surely be literal dumbness; more likely the sense is that, just as animals cannot articulate their feelings (having no language we as humans can

Since it is *behēmāh* that is found in Jonah and Qoheleth, my primary concern is to elucidate further its use and meaning in the wider Hebrew Bible. The first possibility to dispose of is the natural hypothesis that the latter term is more general—that the class of *behēmāh* forms a subset of all *ḥayyōt*, specifically referring to domestic animals. There are undoubtedly places where this is so, and Modern Hebrew usage follows this line. But it is by no means the only, or the most dominant, usage in Tanakh, and it is important to examine these others more closely. The results are rather surprising.

2.1   Semantic equivalence between the two. The most striking instances are Gen. 3:14, where they are in parallel, and 1 Sam. 17:44 and 46 where very similar phrases are repeated using first *behēmāh* and then *ḥayyāh*.[5] While the Samuel passage is a simple equation of terms, the Genesis case raises other intriguing possibilities. The fact that the serpent is to 'eat dust' is not unrelated to the 'dusty' conclusion of all life, and the fact that Eve, whose name in Hebrew can be connected to the same root as *ḥayyāh*, is the mother of all life (Gen. 3:20), both serve to strengthen the already strong likelihood that there are links between Gen. 3:19 and Qoheleth. They suggest two things: that Adam is one of the animals, and that the use of *behēmāh* in Qoheleth is not restricted to cattle.

A related pairing is found in Gen. 8:19 and 20. In v. 19 *ḥayyāh* is used of all animals, while in v. 20 *behēmāh* is used in an equally general sense to refer to all *clean animals*; a similar pairing is found in Lev. 11:26–27, this time regarding *unclean* animals. It should be noted further that there are a good many texts in which the paired categories of *clean* and *unclean* are discussed with reference to *behēmāh* (Gen. 7:2, 8; Lev. 7:21; 20:25; 27:11; Deut. 14:6; Ezek. 8:10; 44:31). Isa. 46:1 seems to suggest that both are beasts of burden.

---

understand), so the servant chose (?) to suffer without protest. While on the subject of spurious etymology, I cannot resist pointing out the rare form *bāhēmmāh* ('with *or* by means of them': Exod. 30:4; 36:1; Hab. 1:16) and suggesting, mischievously, that the animals are named *behēmāh* because they are our close companions.

5 Gen. 3:14: 'The Lord God said to the serpent, "Because you have done this, cursed are you among all animals [*behēmāh*] and among all wild creatures [*ḥayyat*]; upon your belly you shall go, and dust you shall eat all the days of your life"'. 1 Sam. 17:44 and 46: 'The Philistine said to David, "Come to me, and I will give your flesh to the birds of the air and to the wild animals of the field [*behēmāh*]"' ... 'This very day the Lord will deliver you into my hand, and I will strike you down and cut off your head; and I will give the dead bodies of the Philistine army this very day to the birds of the air and to the wild animals of the earth [*ḥayyāh*], so that all the earth may know that there is a God in Israel.'

2.2   These observations lead neatly to the next category: examples of the use of *behēmāh simpliciter* to refer to animals in general. Loosely associated with the creation and flood themes we find Gen. 6:7, 20; 7:23; 1 Kgs 5:13 [4:33]; Ps. 8:8. References to *behēmāh* as 'wild animals' are found in Deut. 28:26; Job 35:11; Prov. 30:30; Isa. 18:6; Jer. 7:33; 15:3; 15:4; 19:7; 34:20; and Mic. 5:7.

2.3   References to *behēmāh* in cultic contexts include some quite suggestive parallels. Thus they are included in the ban on working on Sabbath (Exod. 20:10; Deut. 5:14); they can be stoned for encroaching on the sacred mountain (Exod. 19:13); and they are found praising God, with *ḥayyīm* and other created life, in Ps. 148:10.[6] All of these imply a oneness of essence not unlike that which I shall argue is presupposed by both Qoheleth and Jonah. Add to these verses like Ps. 36:6[7] 'you save (*yāšaʻ*) humans and animals alike, O Lord' or 50:10 and 104:14 which express God's care for both humans and animals; in this regard, Joel 2:21–24 is particularly striking:

> Do not fear, O soil;
> be glad and rejoice,
> for the Lord has done great things!
> Do not fear, you animals of the field,
> for the pastures of the wilderness are green;
> the tree bears its fruit,
> the fig tree and vine give their full yield.
> O children of Zion, be glad
> and rejoice in the Lord your God;
> for he has given the early rain for your vindication,
> he has poured down for you abundant rain,
> the early and the later rain, as before.
> The threshing-floors shall be full of grain,
> the vats shall overflow with wine and oil.

The theme of animals apparently in mourning, which is such a striking feature of Jon. 3:7–8, can be found also in Judith (4:10), where the mistaken information

---

[6] The ban on bestiality (Exod. 22:18 and parallels) suggests a primitive concept of similar forms of being consonant with widespread cultural myths about the possibility of offspring of the miscegenation of humans and animals.

that Nebuchadnezzar was king of Assyria (Jdt. 4:1) might hint at an allusion to Jonah. See also Joel 1:18–20 for a similar motif.[7]

Less directly, but still carrying something of the same implication, we find parallels between the treatment of the firstborn of both humans and animals;[8] further, the ban on likenesses (Deut. 4:17) could be interpreted on the same lines, as could the assumption that they are suitable for substitutionary sacrifice.[9] There is also the inclusion of *behēmāh* in the plagues in Exod. 8–13 *passim* (also Ps. 135:8: 'He it was who struck down the firstborn of Egypt, both human beings (*'ādām*) and animals'), and as victims of God's punishment of Israel in many prophetic texts.

2.4   Jer. 27:5–6 (with a parallel in 28:14 which uses *ḥayyāh*) affords a curious link to the association of subject animals in the kingdoms of Mesopotamia. No doubt this is a coincidence—but it is a tempting one. It refers to Babylon under Nebuchadnezzar, but that scarcely affects the general point, that this affords yet another plausible connection to the book of Jonah.

> It is I who by my great power and my outstretched arm have made the earth, with the people and animals that are on the earth, and I give it to whomsoever I please. Now I have given all these lands into the hand of King Nebuchadnezzar of Babylon, my servant, and I have given him even the wild animals of the field to serve him.

2.5   Job 12:7–10 is an intriguing passage. Whether it pertains to our subject is moot—but it is worth reproducing to illustrate the kind of ambiguity which

---

7 Jonah and Joel 2:12–14 is are of course connected through their shared reference to Exod. 34:6–7. These further links are accordingly the more suggestive; see further T.A. Perry, *The Honeymoon is Over: Jonah's Argument with God*, Peabody, MA 2006, 44–48. In this important passage Perry notes a number of the points raised in this section, though his final note is somewhat pessimistic: 'If the Ninevites have quite correctly appealed to the principle of solidarity between humans and animals, however, their general imposition of penance upon the general populace … has a sinister side. For one might ask: even if the general public is guilty of "evil", what about the innocent? What about children, who have not reached the age of responsibility, and animals, who may not be even capable of evil?' (47–48) An Augustinian approach to 'original sin' might deal with the former objection, while Perry's citing of Montaigne's discussion of animals in his 'Apology for Raymond Sebond' (*The Complete Essays of Montaigne*, transl. Donald Frame, Stanford 1976, 330–58) addresses the latter at least to the extent that Montaigne (*Essays*, 353) famously attributes to animals the powers of repentance, acknowledgement of faults, and clemency amongst other moral values!

8 Lev. 27:26–27; Num. 3:13; 8:17; 18:15; Neh. 10:37; and note also the tenth plague.

9 E.g. Lev. 7:25–26; 27:9–11, 26–28.

surrounds the subject of the boundaries and distinctions between the animal and human realms.

> But ask the animals, and they will teach you;
> the birds of the air, and they will tell you;
> ask the plants of the earth, and they will teach you;
> and the fish of the sea will declare to you.
> Who among all these does not know
> that the hand of the Lord has done this?
> In his hand is the life of every living thing
> and the breath of every human being.

No doubt this passage is metaphorical—certainly the idea of birds, plants and fish literally 'teaching' is not one I would wish to pursue; nevertheless the conclusion, that everything living knows that *nephesh* and *ruach* are ultimately in God's power is clearly a *shared* knowledge. Incidentally, the use of the verb *yādaᶜ* in the context of animals is rare: apart from this instance, Qoh. 3:21 and Jon. 4:11, it is only found in Pss. 50:10–11 and 73:22.

2.6   Lastly in this survey I submit a verse which is beloved of animal rights campaigners: Prov. 12:10, which seems to come some way towards expressing a contemporary sensitivity to animals. Since it is isolated, not too much weight should be placed on it; nonetheless it is intriguing:

> The righteous know the needs of their animals,
> but the mercy of the wicked is cruel.

In fact the Hebrew is even more surprising, for the English 'know the needs of their animals' renders the Hebrew phrase *yōdēaᶜ... nefeš behemtō* which might signify an understanding of a beast's appetite, but could equally mean 'understand the very life of their animals', indicating empathy rather than 'mere' sympathy.

I conclude that there is much more to *behēmāh* in Tanakh than our modern clear-cut species distinctions allow for, and that, in short, there is plenty of evidence for the possibility that Jonah is in fact very far from satire in his incorporation of animals into the salvation story of Nineveh and the reluctant prophet.[10] Clearly, as Perry (see footnote 10) observes, there is no actual equality; indeed, on some readings human attitudes to *behēmāh* are more abusive because of the

---

10   Perry, *Honeymoon*, takes a similar view (pp. 45–48), citing several of the passages I have referred to.

closeness (their use for sacrifice, for instance). I hope this does not disappoint: it is a shame, I suppose, to lose Jonah's wonderfully bizarre conclusion. By way of consolation, I remind you that in a world of plural readings I have not displaced one with another, merely added to the rich stock of available interpretations.

This is perhaps the place to record a seemingly dissonant voice. Thomas Bolin argues, in an article from 2010,[11] that contrary to modern thought (which sees the end of Jonah as evidence of God's universal concern) the proper ancient context is that of ritual sacrifice. Thus the links between *'ādām* and *behēmāh* in Jonah (twice in 3:7–8 and again in 4:11) belong to a deliberate authorial attack on sacrifice. References to sacrifice in Jon. 1:17, 2:10 and Gen. 8:20 are designed to emphasise that God does *not* need them, for 'they are not demanded by God, nor is their efficacy automatic or guaranteed'.[12] Bolin's case seems to be that we should understand the *behēmāh* as objects of sacrifice, mimetically clothed in sackcloth[13] in preparation for their substitutionary sacrifice. All this is no doubt to the point, but it remains arguable that their suitability for sacrifice lies precisely in their being perceived to be rather close to *'ādām* in nature. Indeed, in his conclusion Bolin seems to admit this when he observes:

> As domestic beasts, the animals of Nineveh are not under Yahweh's control and indeed, they are the only non-human living thing in the book of Jonah that is not the object of the verb מנה with God as its subject.[14]

Bolin makes this comment in the context of a note to the effect that Yahweh cannot control, but can only coerce his human subjects; it seems the same is true of his beastly subjects.

3 Application: Understanding the Beasts in Jonah

Armed with the information gleaned above, we can now approach the heart of the matter. Jon. 4:11 is my starting point:

---

11   T.M. Bolin, 'Jonah 4,11 and the Problem of Exegetical Anachronism', *SJOT* 24 (2010), 99–109.
12   Ibid., 105–6. Note that the reference here to Gen. 8:20 reflects the clear evidence that Jonah makes use of the primitive Genesis material as part of its complex intertextual programme.
13   He refers here (ibid., 106) to Jdt. 4:10 which also speaks of animals in mourning, suggesting that Judith may in this instance be following Jonah: Nebuchadnezzar is King of Nineveh!
14   Ibid., 108.

> And should I not be concerned about Nineveh, that great city, in which there are more than a hundred and twenty thousand people who do not know their right hand from their left, and also many animals?

The subordinate clause in this verse contains two tantalising statements and poses a syntactic puzzle. What is the significance of the claim that such a large number of people 'do not know their right hand from their left'? Why are 'many animals' listed? And finally, are the animals an afterthought or should they be included in the class of ignorant beings? There is a putative chiastic structure to the clause which might support the latter contention:

מִשְׁתֵּים־עֶשְׂרֵה רִבּוֹ אָדָם
אֲשֶׁר לֹא־יָדַע בֵּין־יְמִינוֹ לִשְׂמֹאלוֹ
וּבְהֵמָה רַבָּה

> More than a hundred and twenty thousand <u>people</u>
> who do not know their right hand from their left
> <u>and animals</u> *in great number.*

Given the care with which the language of Jonah has been crafted—something on which all who have examined the text closely agree—it is not unreasonable to interpret this chiasmus as part of an intentional coda to the book, a deliberate extension of the inclusion of *behēmāh* in the ritual mourning instructed by the king of Nineveh in the previous chapter.

That said, there are aspects to this verse which challenge our ability to read it by appealing to other biblical texts. For one thing, nowhere else is there a challenge to distinguish between right and left—the middle term of the chiasmus is wholly unique. Secondly, the phrase 'many animals' has no specific parallels, apart from one or two places where people are described as owning large flocks or herds (without the use of the word *behēmāh*). And thirdly, this is the only occasion where the inhabitants of a city are specifically numbered.[15] The importance of the final phrase in its setting is precisely not that it identifies the people of Nineveh as being cattle-rich; what it identifies is the presence of an equally important population of animals—specifically *behēmāh*—in the city.

---

15   Three other cities are described as 'large': Calah, in Gen. 10:12; Gibeah in Josh. 10:2; and Jerusalem in Neh. 7:4 where it is described as 'wide and large' but with few people and no houses. Apart from these, I can find no significant parallels to the enumeration of the population of Nineveh.

A consideration of the pairing of 'right and left' in Tanakh shows that by far the most common uses are (a) to make it clear that some thing or some effect is present[16] either on two sides or, in some cases, to the north and the south, and (b) to express either literal or metaphorical deviation (including a choice between options). The second of these has some bearing, since it usually refers to disobedience or moral vacillation,[17] which might be thought to be the point of Jon. 4:11. In two places the reference is to a source of blessing—Isaac's contrary blessing of Ephraim and Manasseh in Gen. 48:13–14, and Wisdom holding long life in her right hand and riches in her left (Prov. 3:16). The residue consists of two passages which I want to look at more closely: Isa. 30:20–21, where the idea of moral choice is reinforced by means of a figure described as 'your Teacher' (*mōrekha*), and Qoh. 10:2, where the wise choose the right and the foolish the left. Isa. 30:20–21 is tempting, but in the end it is more likely to belong with those passages which guard against deviation to the left or the right:

> Though the Lord may give you the bread of adversity and the water of affliction, yet your Teacher will not hide himself any more, but your eyes shall see your Teacher. And when you turn to the right or when you turn to the left, your ears shall hear a word behind you, saying, 'This is the way; walk in it.'

The figure of the Teacher is somewhat mysterious—is he someone different from Yahweh? (cf. the 'man of God' in Judg. 13:8 and other similar instances)—but in the end his purpose is to keep the people of Zion on the right path. The reference to not hiding himself bears comparison with Job 23:9; interestingly, the only other instance of the title 'teacher' for God is also in Job, at 36:22.[18]

Having identified these preliminary data, let me turn to a closer examination of the final chiasmus of Jonah. I shall adopt as a working hypothesis the proposal that we should take seriously the claim that 120,000 *'ādām* and many *behēmāh* share a failure to know the difference between right and left. In the setting of Jonah, what does this failure imply? I think we can at once rule out

---

16 In Job 23:9 God *cannot* be found either on the left or the right.
17 Thus Deut. 5:32; 17:11, 20; 28:14; Josh. 1:7; 23:6; 2 Sam. 14:19; 2 Kgs 22:2; 2 Chron. 34:2; Prov. 4:27.
18 The other occasions where God teaches, using the verb *yrh*, are in Exod. 4:12, 15 (God teaching Moses and Aaron what to say), 24:12 (the stone tablets 'for teaching them'); 1 Kgs 8:36 (= 2 Chron. 6:27) (Solomon refers to God's teaching Israel 'the good way in which they should walk'); Isa. 2:3 (= Mic. 4:2); 28:9, 26; Pss. 25:8, 12; 27:11; 32:8; 86:11; 119:33, 102; Job 6:24; 34:22.

literal uses: the author of Jonah is not interested in literal wandering from a path, or in the precise placement of things. On the other hand, it seems certain that the element of choice is central to Jonah—the prophet's choice whether to obey Yahweh or not, the Ninevites' choice whether to repent or not, even God's choice about what to do with recalcitrant humans, whether prophets or Ninevites. It follows that even those passages which imply a moral deviation (listed in note 17) are only of incidental interest. While they confirm that 'right and left' is regularly used in the realm of ethics, the predominant reference is the unacceptable nature of deviation in either direction from a strict code. Of the remaining passages, the only one which provides in the end a helpful parallel is Qoh. 10:2. But what an interesting passage it is—particularly given the other connection to be made between Qoh. 3:18–21 and Jonah:

לֵב חָכָם לִימִינוֹ וְלֵב כְּסִיל לִשְׂמֹאלוֹ:

'The wise man's mind is of the right hand, the fool's of the left.' A very clear moral distinction, and one that is (surprisingly) unique in Tanakh: only here are right and left invested with specific moral values, so that it matters that a person should be able to tell the difference. Of course, wisdom literature and Psalms are replete with references to wisdom and the wise, and folly and the fool; to cite just one striking example, Proverbs 9 dramatizes the competing attractions of the Goddesses Folly and Wisdom, inviting the reader by implication to make his or her choice. Qoheleth, notoriously, challenges himself to investigate the relative merits of the two and seems—at times—to conclude that there is little advantage in the long run (2:12–26). Despite this, he never quite abandons his belief that it is, all things being equal, preferable to be wise (and, of course, to eat, drink and be merry).

Can this understanding of Qoh. 10:2 be applied to Jonah? To answer that question we need to take seriously the question of some kind of relationship between the two books. There is admittedly little or nothing in the way of direct citation of Qoheleth in Jonah, an awkward fact that stands in contrast with the undoubtedly extensive evidence of intertextual connections between Jonah and many other books—Genesis, 1 Kings, Ezekiel, Joel and Psalms, to list just a few. A further obvious difficulty is the late date of Qoheleth, something agreed upon by the great majority of commentators. While Jonah itself is surely post-exilic, it may at first sight seem improbable that it belongs in some kind of literary ensemble with Qoheleth.[19] Nevertheless I find the proposal

---

19   Bickerman places Jonah in the fifth century BCE on the grounds that Tobit cites Jonah and was written in the fourth century; others however place the latter in the third or second century, which would allow the kind of interaction I am positing. Moreover the possible

interesting enough to pursue a little further. In favour of some kind of intersection I note the following:

i. Both are pseudonymous on the basis of a character from Kings, though admittedly the fame of Solomon is vastly superior to that of the obscure prophet from Gath-hepher.
ii. Both undermine the credibility of their eponymous authors: Qoheleth by his radical questioning of the value of wisdom; Jonah by his undermining of the authority of the prophet.
iii. Both address the problem of trust in God: Qoheleth by proposing a remote, arbitrary and inscrutable deity kept emphatically at arm's length, and the resulting ethical dilemmas; Jonah in his encounter with an all-too-predictable God whose direct interference in the affairs of individuals and empires poses intractable ethical dilemmas.
iv. Both introduce animals, using the specific term *behēmāh* in surprising ways: Qoheleth by insisting on the essential similarities of humans and animals; Jonah by seemingly including them as part of the repentant population of Nineveh.
v. Both introduce a moral dimension to the choice between right and left, and are in fact the only two biblical books to do this.
vi. While Jonah notoriously makes extensive use of the adjective 'great' (*gādōl*), Qoheleth's use of it is restricted to two places. 10:4 is not of interest, but the three occurrences in 9:13–14 are found in a curious little parable which has strong echoes of Jonah. The core of the parable is as follows: 'There was a little city with few people in it. A great king came against it and besieged it, building great siege-works against it. Now there was found in it a poor, wise man, and he by his wisdom delivered the city. Yet no-one remembered that poor man.' There are intriguing verbal similarities between this mini-saga and Jonah which hint at some kind of intertextuality—especially since they are pretty much unique to these two sources.[20]

---

reference to Jonah in Tob. 14:4 is only found in certain manuscripts; the preferred reading is Nahum.

20 Specifically: (a) 'Siege-works' is *meṣōdīm* from same root as *ṣayid*, the 'mighty hunter', Nimrod, the founder (according to Gen. 10:8–12) of the cities of Mesopotamia where Jonah is set; (b) The same word is used for the 'cruel (*rā'āh*) net (*meṣōdāh*)' in which fish (*dāgīm*) are caught in 9:12, a verse which offers metaphors for the unpredictability of calamity ('*ēt rā'āh*) when it falls (*nāpal*—cf the lots cast in Jon. 1:7 which led to his fate in the whale); (c) The 'little city' prompts instances of the 'great city', and these

vii. Note also the intriguing use of *hebel* in Jon. 2:9 with reference to 'vain idols'.

Did Qoheleth and Jonah know each other? I suspect that there is some crossover—and if I were to hazard a guess it would be that Qoheleth, already familiar with Jonah's deconstruction of the high claims of prophets and prophecy, took on as a parallel endeavour a similar undermining of the unquestioned authority of kings and the received wisdom of the sages. In doing so he did not copy Jonah, but emulated him, planting for our pleasure the odd incident in 9:12–16 and extending to its logical conclusion his understanding of the nature of animals.

Returning to the main argument of this essay, I submit that there is the basis of a case for linking how animals are regarded in Jonah and Qoheleth, and that this reinforces the proposal that they are to be understood as having a form of existence which is not wholly other than that of humankind. This means that they can indeed be understood to experience innocence and guilt, that they can be faced with moral choice, and that it therefore makes sense for the king of Nineveh to include them in the rites of repentance, bizarre though it may appear to our modern sensibilities. This also suggests that whatever we mean by the 'spirit' (*ruaḥ*) of humankind it is the same as that of the animals, and suffers the same fate.

Qoheleth's position is reinforced by his deliberate citation of Gen. 3:19 which by implication extends the rubric 'dust to dust' to animals as well as humans.[21]

---

are surprisingly rare: one in Gen. 10:12, referring to Reseth, between Nineveh and Caleh; Gibeon in Josh. 10:2; an intriguing description of Jerusalem in Neh. 7:4 ('The city was wide and large, but the people within it were few…'); Lam. 1:1 bemoans the fate of the once-great city of Jerusalem, but here it is importance (*rav*) rather than size that is referred to; and of course the references to Nineveh in Jonah; (d) The lack of inhabitants ('few *me'aṭ* people: cf Neh. 7:4) contrasts with the great numbers given in Jon. 4:11.

21 There is, incidentally, considerable reluctance in some circles to recognise this connection. Despite the fact that it is the closest parallel to the Genesis saying anywhere in Tanakh, the cross-reference edition of the NRSV allows no link at all. It offers Job 10:9 and Ps. 103:14 as parallels to Gen. 3:19. Qoh. 12:7 (a much less radical statement of the same theme) is allowed as a parallel to Ps. 103:14 and to Gen. 2:7—but not, incidentally, to 3:20! The only direct parallel indicated is to Sir. 16:30—and there, at last, the assiduous explorer will find the following list of parallels: Gen. 3:19; Job 34:15; Ps. 104:29; and Qoh. 3:20 and 12:7. The whole process reminds me of childhood game in which you start with a word, look up its definition in the dictionary, and then repeat the process with that definition as starting point to see where you end up—either in a circle, back at the word of origin, or (preferably) at some quite unexpected conclusion! I confess that the principles

Incidentally, this association suggests that the use of *behēmāh* in Gen. 3:14, which we noted earlier, might for Qoheleth have been more inclusive than we normally take it to be. The serpent—who, after all, has the gift of speech—is counted amongst all behēmāh; Eve is 'the mother of all that live' (3:20) in a self-conscious pun on Eve's name and *ḥāyāh*; and *behēmāh* and *ḥayyāh* amount to the same thing. (See above, 2.1).

4 'Behold Behemot'

The proposition which these various observations lead to is that there is a case for taking Jonah's references to animals literally, rather than (or in addition to) modern sensibilities which are inevitably drawn to explanations such as hyperbola, satire, or irony. There is an interesting precedent in Greek thinking, which the writers of Jonah and Qoheleth may well have been aware of: namely, the Pythagorean concept of transmigration of souls and the one-ness of human and animal souls. The date and cultural milieu of both books renders this at least possible, suggesting that the chiasmus in Jon. 4:11 is not simply a throw-away parting shot, but a reminder that in the eyes of God the king of Nineveh (and the prophet of Yahweh) belong to the same moral universe as the lowly *behēmāh*.

If, then, Qoheleth and Jonah between them have succeed in reducing human pretensions by emphasising their oneness with animals, perhaps there is comfort to be drawn from the magnificent presence of the semi-divine *Behemot* of Job 40:15–24. The first of God's great acts (v. 19), just like Wisdom herself (Prov. 8:22), this mighty creature challenges our own pretensions to supremacy, and reminds us that Jonah's conclusion is not after all so odd: there is a commonality to life, both in its everyday needs and in its divine aspects, that we do well to remember.

underlying the process of cross-referencing seem at best unclear, and at worst to exemplify (at least in this instance) a theologically influenced choice. NIV isn't much better—though it does allow a link between Qoh. 3:20 and Gen. 2:7. (Another interesting example of interpretative cross-referencing from the same context is the linking of Gen. 3:15 with Rom. 16:21, which succeeds in introducing Satan to Eden by a sleight of hand.)

Ecclesiastes Among the Tragedians

John Jarick

1   Introduction

It has long been noted that certain affinities can be detected between the ideas presented in the biblical book of Ecclesiastes and the wider Hellenistic culture within which or over against which the book may well have emerged. Many commentators on Ecclesiastes have made remarks on this matter, pointing to the writings of various sceptics, stoics, or epicureans for similarities in thought, and there have also been a number of studies focused on such aspects.[1]

As a further contribution to this discussion, I wish to consider some affinities between Ecclesiastes, especially as transmitted in its Septuagintal guise, and the concerns and phrasings of the fifth-century Athenian dramatists Aeschylus, Sophocles, and Euripides.[2] I am not claiming that the writer of the Hebrew book of Qohelet was necessarily familiar with any of the plays of those three writers, nor even that the translator of the Greek book of Ecclesiastes was necessarily a connoisseur of classical tragedy; I am simply noting that the musings of the sage of Jerusalem bear interesting comparisons with various utterances placed in the mouths of the tragic characters in the Athenian theatre.[3]

---

[1] Among the commentaries, mention might be made particularly of A.H. McNeile, *An Introduction to Ecclesiastes*, Cambridge 1904, 39–55; G.A. Barton, *A Critical and Exegetical Commentary on the Book of Ecclesiastes*, Edinburgh 1912, 32–43; and R. Gordis, *Koheleth—The Man and His World: A Study of Ecclesiastes*, New York ³1968, 51–58. For other treatments, see H. Ranston, *Ecclesiastes and the Early Greek Wisdom Literature*, London 1925; R. Braun, *Kohelet und die frühhellenistische Popularphilosophie* (BZAW, 130), Berlin 1973; C.F. Whitley, *Koheleth: His Language and Thought* (BZAW, 148), Berlin 1979, 158–75; L. Schwienhorst-Schönberger, *'Nicht im Menschen gründet das Glück' (Koh 2,24): Kohelet im Spannungsfeld jüdischer Weisheit und hellenistischer Philosophie* (HBS, 2), Freiberg 1994; and S. Weeks, *Ecclesiastes and Scepticism* (LHBOTS, 541), New York 2012, 134–52.

[2] The translations deployed in this study are those of the Loeb Classical Library (Harvard University Press): for Aeschylus, the translations of Alan Sommerstein (vols. 145, 146, and 505); for Sophocles, those of Hugh Lloyd-Jones (vols. 20, 21, and 483); and for Euripides, those of David Kovacs (the extant plays: vols. 9, 10, 11, 12, 481, 484, and 495) and of Christopher Collard and Martin Cropp (the fragments: vols. 504 and 506).

[3] I make similar observations concerning tragedy's dramatic companion, comedy, in my essay 'Ecclesiastes Among the Comedians', in Reading Ecclesiastes Intertextually, ed. K. Dell and W. Kynes (LHBOTS, 587), London 2014, 176-88 [[OR 176–188]], where I investigate Aristophanes, Menander and other comic poets.

Such an observation should presumably come as no surprise. After all, declamations on the instability of human life and the fragility of human happiness, themes writ large upon the pages of Ecclesiastes, are the very stuff of tragedy. Little wonder, then, if something rather akin to the view of life taken by Qohelet should also be heard on the lips of protagonists within the dramatic presentations of the three great classic tragedians. To borrow a phrase from the Jerusalemite work, we might say that 'a threefold cord is not quickly broken' (Eccl. 4:12)—that is to say, if the tragic vision deployed by the three prominent winners of the drama prizes in Athens carries affinities with the viewpoint of the Hebrew Bible's most prominent gadfly, then Qohelet's perspective stands in solid company.

2   General Themes in Common

2.1   *Aeschylus*

'Farewell to you, old friends,' intones the ghost of Darius in Aeschylus' *Persians* (840–842), 'and even amid these troubles, see you give your hearts pleasure day by day: wealth is of no benefit to the dead.' So does the great Persian king echo, as it were, the words of the so-called 'king in Jerusalem' (Eccl. 1:1) who was said to 'commend enjoyment, for there is nothing better for people under the sun than to eat and drink and enjoy themselves, for this will go with them in their toil through the days of life that God gives them under the sun' (8:15), whereas after death 'they have no more reward' (9:5) and 'never again will they have any share in all that happens under the sun' (9:6).

Meanwhile the Chorus of Persian elders had lamented the human condition in the following words:

> What mortal man can escape the guileful destruction of a god? Who is so light of foot that he has power to leap easily away? For Ruin begins by fawning on a man in a friendly way and leads him astray into her net, from which it is impossible for a mortal to escape and flee. (*Persians* 93–100)

Such ruminations call to mind Qohelet's gripping observation:

> I saw that under the sun the race is not to the swift, nor the battle to the strong, nor bread to the wise, nor riches to the intelligent, nor favour to the skilful; but time and chance happen to them all. For no one can anticipate the time of disaster. Like fish taken in a cruel net, and like birds caught in a snare, so mortals are snared at a time of calamity, when it suddenly falls upon them. (Eccl. 9:11–12)

The book of Ecclesiastes includes the memorable summary that 'all is futility' (τὰ πάντα ματαιότης, Eccl. 1:2 and 12:8), everything is unsatisfying and insubstantial. For his *Prometheus Bound*, Aeschylus crafts a saying, which he places on the lips of Kratos, that bears a certain affinity with that expression of thoroughgoing exasperation with the way of the world: 'Everything is burdensome' (ἅπαντ' ἐπαχθῆ, *Prometheus Bound* 49), all is grievous and annoying. Kratos and Qohelet appear to be singing from a similar tune-sheet.

Mention should also be made of an evocative fragment from Aeschylus' work—'The race of mortals has thought only for the day, and is no more to be relied on than the shadow of smoke' (Aeschylus frag. 399)—which suggests a particular rhetorical question in Ecclesiastes, namely 'Who knows what is good for mortals while they live the few days of their vain life, which they pass like a shadow?' (Eccl. 6:12).

2.2 *Sophocles*

'Ah, generations of mortals,' laments the Chorus in Sophocles' *Oedipus Tyrannus* (1186–1196), 'how close to nothingness I estimate your life to be!... I say that nothing pertaining to humankind is enviable.' In Qohelet's frequent lament, 'all is futility and a chasing after wind' (Eccl. 1:14; 2:11, 17); moreover, mortals 'shall take nothing for their toil' (5: 15) and 'besides, all their days they eat in darkness, in much vexation and sickness and resentment' (5:17).

We might note too the words of the Oedipus character himself in *Oedipus at Colonus*, where he offers these observations to the Athenian king Theseus:

> Dearest son of Aegeus, for the gods alone there is no old age and no death ever, but all other things are submerged by all-powerful time! The strength of the country perishes, so does the strength of the body, loyalty dies and disloyalty comes into being, and the same spirit never remains between friends or between cities, since for some people now and for others in the future happy relations turn bitter, and again friendship is restored. And if now all is sunny weather between Thebes and you, time as it passes brings forth countless nights and days in which they shall shatter with the spear the present harmonious pledges for a petty reason. (*Oedipus at Colonus* 607–620)

A particularly evocative depiction of that notion of 'the strength of the country' and concomitantly 'the strength of the body' both perishing is to be found in chapter 12 of Ecclesiastes, where a poetic description of an estate falling into ruin suggests also the ageing of the human body and indeed the undoing of all individual and collective enterprise (Eccl. 12:1–7).

In Sophocles' *Philoctetes* the Chorus laments, 'O contrivances of the gods! O unhappy race of mortals to whom life is unkind!' (177–179). And the hero Philoctetes bitterly muses:

> Nothing evil has ever perished, but the gods carefully protect it, and somehow they delight in turning back from Hades cunning and villainy, while righteousness and valour they are forever sending away. How can we account for this, and how can we approve it, when, if we survey the actions of the gods, we find that the gods are evil? (*Philoctetes* 446–452)

Ecclesiastes, too, was unable to account for the observable fact that 'there are righteous people who perish in their righteousness, and there are wicked people who prolong their life in their evil-doing' (Eccl. 7:15). 'All this I laid to heart,' he says, 'examining it all, how the righteous and the wise and their deeds are in the hand of God, [but] whether it is love or hate [on the part of God] one does not know' (9:1).

But meanwhile, back with Philoctetes, our hero follows his earlier earth-shattering deductions with the further conviction that

> for mortals all things are full of fear and of the danger that after good fortune may come evil. While free from trouble one must look on what is to be feared, and while prosperous, then most of all one must look to one's life in case ruin should come upon one unawares. (*Philoctetes* 502–506)

We may recall Ecclesiastes' formulation, already quoted above, that 'mortals are snared at a time of calamity, when it suddenly falls upon them' (Eccl. 9:12).

2.3 Euripides

Euripides provides our largest store of treasures from the Athenian theatre, so it is no surprise to find many examples of lines from that preeminent dramatist which resonate over against the observations of the Jerusalemite sage. Consider, for example, the words that Euripides places on the lips of Heracles in *Alcestis*:

> Death is a debt all mortals must pay, and no one knows for certain whether he will still be living on the morrow. The outcome of our fortune is hidden from our eyes, and it lies beyond the scope of any teaching or craft. So now that you have learned this from me, cheer your heart, drink, regard this day's life as yours but all else as Fortune's! (*Alcestis* 780–789)

We might almost be reading from chapter 8 of Ecclesiastes:

> No one knows what is to be ... and no one has power over the day of death ... So I commend enjoyment, for there is nothing better for people

under the sun than to eat and drink and enjoy themselves... I saw that no one can find out what is happening under the sun... Even though those who are wise claim to know, they cannot find it out. (Eccl. 8:7–17)

In the *Children of Heracles*, Euripides has his Chorus sing:

> One fortune after another pursues us. It takes one man from his loftiness and settles him in low estate, and moves another from misery to blessedness. It is not possible to flee from fate, no one by skill can ward it off, and the man who is eager to do so shall always toil in vain. (*Children of Heracles* 611–617)

This sentiment too puts one in mind of certain words in Ecclesiastes, namely that 'no one has power over the wind to restrain the wind, or power over the day of death; there is no discharge from the battle, nor does wickedness deliver those who practise it' (Eccl. 8:8).

In the *Suppliant Women*, Euripides' audience hears Theseus proclaim:

> Now let the dead be buried in the earth, and let each element return to the place from whence it came into the light of day, the spirit to the upper air, the body to the earth. We do not possess our bodies as our own: we live our lives in them, and thereafter the earth, our nourisher, must take them back. (*Suppliant Women* 531–536)

Or as Ecclesiastes would put it, 'The dust returns to the earth as it was, and the spirit returns to God who gave it' (Eccl. 12:7).

In his *Heracles*, Euripides crafts the following final thoughts from Amphitryon:

> My labour is fruitless: our death, it seems, is fated. Well then, old sirs, our life is but a trifle: pass through it as pleasantly as you can, feeling no distress as day gives way to night. Time does not know how to preserve our hopes intact but worries about its own affairs and flies on. (*Heracles* 503–507)

And then in due course the Chorus intones:

> Youth is the thing I love. But age is a burden that always lies heavier than the crags of Aetna upon the head, and over my eye it casts a veil of darkness... Youth is the fairest thing... but grim and deadly old age I hate. (*Heracles* 637–650)

We might recall the advice of Ecclesiastes:

> Rejoice, young man, while you are young, and let your heart cheer you in the days of your youth… Remember your creator in the days of your youth, before the days of trouble come, and the years draw near when you will say, 'I have no pleasure in them.' (Eccl. 11:9; 12:1)

Within the midst of the *Bacchae*, Teiresias concludes that

> it is this [i.e. wine] that frees trouble-laden mortals from their pain—when they fill themselves with the juice of the vine—this that gives sleep to make one forget the day's troubles: there is no other treatment for misery. (*Bacchae* 280–283)

And meanwhile the Chorus offers the sage observation that 'our life is short: this being so, the one who pursues great things may miss what lies at hand' (*Bacchae* 397–399).

Amidst such sentiments, one might think of Ecclesiastes' depiction of himself as having pursued such greatness as to surpass all who were before him in Jerusalem, and his conclusion that in this fleeting life we should rather be content with the simple pleasures that lie at hand: eating, drinking, and finding enjoyment in our toil (Eccl. 1:12–2:26).

In *Iphigenia at Aulis*, we hear the mighty Achilles confide:

> I know how to be moderate in grieving at misfortune or rejoicing in lofty successes. Mortals like that have a reasoned hope of living their whole lives through intelligently. To be sure, there are times when it is pleasant not to be too wise, but also times when it is useful to have intelligence. (*Iphigenia at Aulis* 920–925)

Such a path of moderation is also to be found in Ecclesiastes, where the advice is given, 'Do not be too righteous, and do not be too wise; why should you destroy yourself? Do not be too wicked, and do not be a fool; why should you die before your time?' (Eccl. 7:16–17).

3   Two Particular Perspectives

The sage of Jerusalem and the tragedians of Athens evidently express comparable ideas on the vicissitudes of human life in general. But it is also worthy of note that two specific opinions of a certain notoriety that are expressed in Ecclesiastes—namely 'it is better not to have been born than to have been born' and 'woman is more bitter than death'—are not infrequently echoed by characters in the tragedies.

3.1 'It Is Better Not To Be Born Than To Be Born'

Ecclesiastes is well known for regarding 'the dead, who have already died, more fortunate than the living, who are still alive; but better than both is the one who has not yet been, and has not seen the evil deeds that are done under the sun' (Eccl. 4:2). Further, the book proclaims that 'a stillborn child is better off' than someone who lives a long life but 'does not enjoy life's good things' (6:3), and that 'the day of death [is better] than the day of birth' (7:1).

Aeschylus, on a number of occasions, has his tragic characters long for death: 'I do not refuse to become prey for the dogs, a dinner for the native birds, for he who dies is freed from evils that cry to be bewailed', sing the Chorus in *Suppliants* (800–803); 'It is better to die once for all than to suffer terribly all the days of my life', proclaims Io in *Prometheus Bound* (750–751). Several fragments from his lost plays strike a similar note, such as the advice that 'mortals are wrong to hate death; it is the greatest defence against life's many ills' (Aeschylus frag. 353).

The most pertinent line from Aeschylus in this connection—if indeed the line is from Aeschylus, as Stobaeus' ascription of it to that playwright has been called into question[4]—is fragment 466 (Stobaeus 4.53.17): 'Death is preferable to a wretched life, and it is better not to be born than to be born and suffer misery'.

But undoubtedly the classic presentation, within the world of the tragedies, of the thought that it would be better not to have been born is declaimed by the Chorus in Sophocles' *Oedipus at Colonus*:

> Whoever desires a greater share of life, not content with a moderate portion, is guarding, it is clear to me, a mistaken view. For the long days lay up, you can see, many things closer to pain, and you cannot see where pleasure lies, when anyone falls into more of life than he needs; but the deliverer brings an end for all alike, when the doom of Hades, with no wedding song, no lyre, no dances, is revealed, death at the last. Not to be born comes first by every reckoning; and once one has appeared, to go back to where one came from as soon as possible is the next best thing. For while youth is with one, carrying with it light-hearted thoughtlessness, what

---

4 See LCL vol. 505, p. 347.

painful blow is far away? What hardship is not near? Murders, civil strife, quarrels, battles, and resentment! And the next place, at the end, belongs to much-dispraised old age, powerlessness, unsociable, friendless, where all evils of evils are our neighbours. (*Oedipus at Colonus* 1211–1238)

Euripides tends to place the better-off-dead sentiment on the lips of his tragic heroines. In his *Trojan Women* Andromache declares:

Not to be born is the same, I say, as to die, and to die is better than to live in pain. For one who is dead feels no more pain than those who have never been born, since he has no sense of his troubles. But the one who enjoys good fortune and then falls into misery is distraught in mind because of his previous prosperity. (*Trojan Women* 636–640)

Also pertinent here is a Euripidean fragment in which an unidentified female character within an unidentified play enunciates the same opinion:

Not to be born is better than life for mortals. Shall I then bear children with the bitter pains of childbirth? If I do so and give birth to foolish children, I lament vainly as I watch them turn out bad; or if they are good, I lament when I see them die—or if they survive, my poor heart is worn down with fears for them. What then is so valuable in this? Is it not enough to have the distress of a single soul, and to bear the pains that it incurs? (Euripides frag. 908, 1–8)

3.2 *'Woman Is More Bitter Than Death'*

As for Qohelet's renowned 'misogynistic' utterance—'I found more bitter than death the woman who is a trap, whose heart is snares and nets, whose hands are fetters' (Eccl. 7:26)—we should perhaps not be surprised to find similar sentiments mouthed by assorted male characters penned by the male dramatists of ancient Athens.

Thus, for example, in his *Seven against Thebes*, Aeschylus has Eteocles castigate the frightened women of Thebes:

Whether in trouble or in welcome prosperity, may I not share my home with the female gender! When a woman is in the ascendant, her effrontery is impossible to live with; when she's frightened, she is an even greater menace to family and city. So now, with your running around in all directions like this, your clamour has spread panic and cowardice among the citizens; you are doing your very best to advance the cause of the enemy outside—the city is being sacked by its own people from within! That's the sort of thing you'll get if you live with women! (*Seven against Thebes* 187–195)

So too, in Aeschylus' *Agamemnon* (1636), Aegisthus snidely remarks that 'the entrapment was obviously a job for a woman', implying that women are particularly skilled at luring a man to his death, and in a fragment (Aeschylus frag. 470, though doubtfully ascribed to Aeschylus), a character opines that 'it is silence that gives women dignity', implying that a woman who speaks in public gives a distasteful display.

Perhaps we can partially exonerate Sophocles, for we have merely the following fragment of *Phaedra*: 'A man could acquire no plague worse than a bad wife nor any treasure better than a right-minded one, and each man tells the tale according to his own experience' (Sophocles frag. 682, 1–3).

But from Euripides, several vignettes can be brought forward. In *Orestes*, the Chorus bemoans that 'women are always an encumbrance to the affairs of men and make life harder to manage' (605–606). In *Iphigenia at Aulis*, Iphigenia declares that it is 'better to save the life of a single man than ten thousand women!' (1394). And three different fragments of this particular playwright's artefacts present characters putting forward Ecclesiastes-like attitudes in this respect. One protagonist advises his listeners that 'a sensible man should never put any trust in a woman' (Euripides frag. 671, 1–2). Another declares that 'a woman is the fiercest evil of all' (frag. 808, 1). And a third waxes more lyrical on the same theme: 'Terrible is the might of the sea's waves, terrible a river's, and hot fire's blasts; terrible is poverty, and terrible are countless other things—but nothing is so terrible an evil as a woman; there could be no such picture drawn, nor could speech describe it' (frag. 1059, 1–6).

4 Some Specific Vocabulary

In view of the passages assembled above, we might well be justified in saying that the book of Ecclesiastes shares a tragic vision of life with the Athenian dramatists. But perhaps we can go further than that, and say that in its Septuagintal guise the book also shares some specific vocabulary that was wielded by the classic tragedians.

4.1   *Futility* ($\mu\alpha\tau\alpha\iota\acute{o}\tau\eta\varsigma$)

It must be admitted that the key theme-word in the Greek version of Ecclesiastes, by which everything that may be observed or experienced is labelled as just so many examples of ματαιότης, 'futility' or 'pointlessness', is not to be found in Greek literature prior to this work. It would seem that the translator of the book may have coined a new nominal form to render the nuances of the Hebrew sage's enigmatic term הבל, a word which literally means 'breath' or 'vapour' but which is evidently deployed in the book of Ecclesiastes to denote 'transience' and 'insubstantiality', 'ineffectiveness' and 'futility'. Ματαιότης is an inspired choice to capture that aspect of the Jerusalem writer's thought, and though the particular form ματαιότης seems to make its first appearance in this specific book, it cannot fail to resonate with the cognate expressions much used by the tragedians, the adjective μάταιος, 'futile, empty' and the adverb μάτην, 'uselessly, pointlessly', both of which may carry the notion of something being done 'in vain'.

As for the adjective μάταιος, we find it deployed by Aeschylus, for example in his *Agamemnon* (387)—'Miserable Temptation forces her way in, the unendurable child of scheming Ruin, and every remedy is *in vain*'—and by Sophocles, for example in his *Antigone* (1339)—'Lead me out of the way, *useless* man that I am'—and by Euripides, for example in his *Iphigenia among the Taurians* (628)—'Poor man, whoever you are, your wish is *in vain*'. Especially to be noted is an expression in Euripides' *Phoenician Women* (1666), where he employs the combination of μάταια μοχθείς ('you toil *to no purpose*'), an example to which we shall return later. And we might also note the cry ὦ μάταια ('ah, *the futility!*'), to be heard in Sophocles' *Women of Trachis* (888).

As for the adverb μάτην, that is to be encountered with even greater frequency in the Athenian tragedies, but I will give just two pertinent examples from each of our tragedians. From Aeschylus' *Prometheus Bound* (1007): 'It looks as though, however much I say, I will say it *in vain*'; and from his *Eumenides* (144): 'Ah, how much I have suffered—and *for nothing!*' From Sophocles' *Electra* (772): 'It seems, then, that my coming was *in vain*'; and from his *Oedipus at Colonus* (259): 'What help comes from fame, or from a fine reputation that flows away *in vain?*' From Euripides' *Children of Heracles* (117): 'I too am luckless for having toiled so long *in vain*'; and from his *Trojan Women* (760): 'It was for nothing, it seems, that this breast of mine suckled you when you were in swaddling clothes, and all *in vain* was my labour and the pain of my toil.' Once again we see in Euripides the agonizing reflections of tragic figures on the purposelessness of their toil, and we might especially note that Sophocles' rhetorical question concerning the ebbing away of transient fame seems especially to evoke the notion of transience that so disturbs the sage of Jerusalem. But all of the examples I have given from the tragedians seem of a common vein with Ecclesiastes' bemoaning of his quintessential experience: 'I considered all that my hands had done and the toil I had spent in doing it, and again, all was *futility* (ματαιότης) and a chasing after wind, and there was nothing to be gained under the sun' (Eccl. 2:11).

Having noted that the noun ματαιότης as such does not appear in Greek literature prior to the book of Ecclesiastes, we should nonetheless be aware of the possibility that it may have been deployed by Euripides in his *Helen*, where we find the line (1056), 'How does that help us to escape with our lives? Your story seems a bit *pointless*'. Some critical editions suggest that the text here should read ματαιότης, 'your story seems one of *futility*', but perhaps we should accept the reading παταιότης, 'your story seems one of *obsoleteness*',[5] and thus allow the translator of Ecclesiastes the honour of introducing so fine a noun as ματαιότης into literary life, even while acknowledging its evident resonance over against the frequent usage of μάταιος and μάτην in the tragic visions of earlier Greek literature.

4.2   Toil (μόχθος)

When it comes to another key word in Ecclesiastes, however, found in both verbal and nominal forms, our Septuagintal wordsmith coins no new form, but employs already-standard Greek forms to communicate the message. I refer here to the rendering of the Hebrew root עמל, 'toil', to be met in Ecclesiastes' programmatic question, 'What do people gain from all the *toil* at which they *toil* under the sun?' (Eccl. 1:3), and in his summational statement, 'I hated all my *toil* in which I had *toiled* under the sun' (2:18), and in many other expressions. For these words, the translator chooses the noun μόχθος and its cognate verb μοχθεῖν, words that again cannot but call to mind the visions of the Athenian tragedians. Witness for example the *Libation-Bearers* of Aeschylus (1020): 'No mortal can complete his life unharmed and unpunished throughout, for some *troubles* (μόχθοι) are here now, and some will come later.' Or the *Women of Trachis* of Sophocles (1173): 'It said that at the time that is now alive and present my release from the labours that stood over me should be accomplished, and I thought that I would be happy; but it meant no more than that I would die, for the dead do not have *to labour*.' Or the *Medea* of Euripides (1261): 'The *toil* of bearing your children has come to naught, it was to no purpose that you bore your dear offspring.'

Time and again, then, the tragedians remind their audiences that mortals are born for toil and trouble, and they frequently speak of their protagonists labouring to no purposeful result. We might even remark that two striking features of Qohelet's particular turning of phrases are also to be found in the work of Euripides. Notice how the Athenian deploys a twofold usage of the μόχθος

---

5 See LCL vol. 11, p. 129.

stem in *Andromache* (133): τί μόχθον οὐδὲν οὖσα μοχθεῖς ('Why do you toil in vain, powerless as you are?'), somewhat redolent of Ecclesiastes' ἐν παντὶ μόχθῳ αὐτοῦ, ᾧ μοχθεῖ ('in all the toil at which one toils') and πάντα μόχθον μου ὃν ἐγὼ μοχθῶ ('all my toil at which I toiled'). And notice too, among the several variations that Euripides employs to articulate the notion of the futility of human effort, one that is especially resonant with Ecclesiastes in the expression mentioned above in the *Phoenician Women* (1666), namely μάταια μοχθεῖς ('toiling in vain'), an even closer juxtaposition of Qohelet's two key concepts than the Jerusalem sage's repetitions of the thought that all μόχθος is ματαιότης throughout the latter part of his second chapter.

4.3 *'Futility of futilities'* (*ματαιότης ματαιοτήτων*)

Having returned again to the insistent theme of ματαιότης—a theme which, through the agency of cognate adjectives and adverbs, is all too familiar to the consumer of classical Greek tragedy—a question that may arise is whether the thesis statement of Ecclesiastes, the striking expression ματαιότης ματαιοτήτων ('futility of futilities', a rendering of the Hebrew original הבל הבלים), would have made any sense or struck any chord with a Greek audience.

Our first thought might be that so seemingly Semitic a construction would strike a Greek reader as an unseemly barbarism, but in fact it would be readily understandable to a Hellenistic audience, not least on account of the oriental expression 'king of kings' (in its Greek guise of βασιλεὺς βασιλέων) being a readily-to-hand template for this kind of expression. Indeed we find such a style of titling the Supreme Power in Aeschylus' *Suppliants* (524–526), in which the almighty Zeus is addressed as ἄναξ ἀνάκτων, μακάρων μακάρτατε καὶ τελέων τελειότατον κράτος ('O king of kings, O most blest of the blest, O power most perfect of the perfect'). So too, in Aeschylus' *Persians* (681), the elders of Persia are addressed as πιστὰ πιστῶν ('trusted of the trusted' or 'most trustworthy ones'). Somewhat similarly, we find Sophocles on two occasions having certain protagonists addressed as κακῶν κάκιστε ('vilest of the vile' or 'most villainous of villains'), once in *Oedipus Tyrranus* (334) and then again in *Oedipus at Colonus* (1384). And in those two plays, we also meet such analogous expressions as κακὰ κακῶν ('evils of evils' or 'utter disasters', in *Oedipus at Colonus* 1238) and ἄρρητ᾽ ἀρρήτων ('horrible of horribles' or 'the most unspeakable thing', in *Oedipus Tyrannus* 465).

But among our Athenian triumvirate, Euripides seems most fond of the device of juxtaposing cognate words in order to emphasise the enormity of what is being expressed. Witness the following examples: δάκρυα δάκρυσι ('tears upon tears', twice in *Orestes* 335–336 and 1309, and twice again in *Helen* 195 and 366); πάθεα πάθεσι ('woes upon woes', also deployed twice in *Helen* 173 and 1163); θανάτους θανάτων ('deaths upon deaths', in *Orestes* 1007); and ἄχεά τ' ἄχεσι ('grief upon grief', in *Helen* 366). Or for piling it on even more, note ἄξονές τ' ἐπ' ἄξοσιν νεκροί τε νεκροῖς ('axles upon axles, corpses upon corpses', in *Phoenician Women* 1194–1195) and φόνος ἐπὶ φόνῳ ἄχεα ἄχεσιν ('slaughter upon slaughter, grief upon grief', in *Iphigenia among the Taurians* 198).

One might well say that, in the works of Euripides, 'woe lies on top of woe' (ἐπὶ δ' ἄλγεσιν ἄλγεα κεῖται, in *Trojan Women* 596), or that it is a case of 'speaking of misery on top of misery' (πρὸς κακοῖς ἐρεῖς κακά, in *Phoenician Women* 1704). Ecclesiastes' talk of 'futility upon futilities' sounds a similar note in his own presentation of the human predicament.

5 Conclusion

This study has brought forward significant examples of themes and of vocabulary that reverberate between the musings of Ecclesiastes and the dramatic scenes staged by the Athenian triumvirate of Aeschylus, Sophocles, and Euripides.

All in all, one might very well feel that Ecclesiastes—not least with its signature statement that 'futility' utterly overshadows the human condition, but equally throughout its bitter observations on the vicissitudes of life and the inevitability of death—seems very much at home in the company of the Greek tragedians.

The Disturbing Experience of Eliphaz in Job 4: Divine or Demonic Manifestation?

Mart-Jan Paul

1   Introduction

At the beginning of his first speech, Eliphaz responds to the bitter situation of Job with several observations and theological statements (4:1–11). In the second half of chapter 4, he strengthens his argument by appealing to a nightly apparition (4:12–21). In his speech to Job, Eliphaz believes he has a strong argument by citing a revelation he received.

In many commentaries, these words are construed as a divine message, similar to how Eliphaz considers them. Therefore, in these explanations, the vision of Eliphaz is associated with prophetic experiences and with the theophany traditions of the Sinai.[1] Recently, some publications express doubts about these associations.

Half a century ago, in 1961, the South-African scholar J.H. Kroeze, in his Dutch-language commentary on the book of Job, asked the question what God's purpose could be with such a revelation. He points to 42:7, which embodies a real revelation of God to Eliphaz: 'You have not spoken what is right, as my servant Job has', thereby correcting earlier statements by Eliphaz. Using the prologue of the book of Job for his argument, Kroeze says that Satan used storms, lightning, robbers—and friends. Therefore, he thinks it is possible that Satan (the Accuser)[2] influenced Eliphaz to hurt Job.[3] Repetition of the content of the vision several times in the book, gives more reason to doubt the genuineness of it as a divine message.[4]

---

1   E.g. J.E. Hartley, *The Book of Job* (NICOT), Grand Rapids 1988 and D.J.A. Clines, *Job 1–20* (WBC), Dallas 1989. For a literary analysis of the passage, see J.P. Fokkelman, *Major Poems of the Hebrew Bible at the Interface of Prosody and Structural Analysis*, vol. II: 85 Psalms and Job 4–14 (SSN, 41), Assen 2000.
2   J.H. Kroeze, *Het boek Job* (COT), Kampen 1961, 51.
3   Kroeze, *Job*, 82–83.
4   Kroeze, *Job*, 86. Joseph Hontheim gives a short remark in his commentary: 'Es handelt sich um eine teuflische Erscheinung'. The reader of the prologue can understand 'den höllischen Ursprung' of the vision. See *Das Buch Job: als strophisches Kunstwerk nachgewiesen*, Freiburg i. B. 1904, 94 (with a reference to a work of G. Gietmann from 1887). Kroeze mentions the work of Hontheim in his bibliography, but gives no reference to it in the cited pages.

In his commentary published in 1985, J. Gerald Janzen also points to the tension between the content of God's words about Job as spoken in the first chapters and this vision. 'What Eliphaz, of course, does not know is that in imputing to humankind the qualities of inevitable untrustworthiness and inevitable error, he (or his 'revelation') is speaking on one side of the issue already joined in the heavenly meeting between Yahweh and the Satan.'[5] He argues that from the perspective of the prologue, we may appreciate that the 'inspiration' of Eliphaz derives, not from God, but from the Satan. In an analogous illustration, Janzen points to the prophetic messages of Zedekiah and Micaiah, in 1 Kgs 22:5–28.[6]

A third publication pointing in this new direction is by James E. Harding in his 'A Spirit of Deception in Job 4:15?' He deals with the problem of the identity of the spirit, a matter that Eliphaz apparently took for granted.

> The reader of the whole book of Job, being aware of the role of YHWH in the narrative, might ask: *whose* spirit is this? Is this the spirit of YHWH that came upon the judges, Saul, and some of the prophets? Or, could it be an evil spirit from YHWH such as that which afflicted Saul? Given that Job 4:12–21 is concerned with a revelation, could this be a spirit of deception such as that which deceived Zedekiah ben Chenaanah in 1 Kgs 22:19–23?

Harding proposes another possibility construing the ghost as 'a spirit of uncleanness'. He refers to a parallel in Zech. 13:2 where a comparable spirit is associated with prophets who are condemned for speaking 'deception' (13:3) in the name of YHWH.[7] Harding, however, gives no clear answer to these questions and points to the ambiguity of the language and the indeterminacy for the reader.[8]

Georg Fohrer declares that any relation between the vision and the Satan is excluded. He refers to the work of Hontheim, but gives no counter-arguments, see G. Fohrer *Das Buch Hiob* (KAT), Gütersloh 1963, 142, n. 19.

5 J.G. Janzen, *Job* (Interpretation), Louisville 1985, 43.
6 Janzen, *Job*, 73–4.
7 J.E. Harding, 'A Spirit of Deception in Job 4:15? Interpretive Indeterminacy and Eliphaz's Vision', *Biblical Interpretation* 13 (2005), 137–66, esp. 150. Also R.S. Fyall states that Eliphaz's vision 'is not in fact God but the enemy masquerading as him'. See *Now my eyes have seen You: images of creation and evil in the book of Job* (NSBT, 17), Downers Grove—Leicester 2002, 37, cf. 146–47.
8 Harding, 'Spirit', describes 4:12–21 as 'the mediation of a problematic revelation' (161, cf. 165).

In this paper, I continue the exploration set out by Kroeze, Janzen and Harding and treat the question whether the disturbing experience of Eliphaz in Job 4 constitutes either a divine or a demonic manifestation. After a short remark about Satan, I will deal with several characteristics of the vision, the scope of the vision, and place the apparition of it in the perspective of demonic activity in general. I will focus on the character of the spirit or 'appearance' to Eliphaz and will point to the necessity of discernments of spirits.

2   Satan

In Job 1–2 the Satan (הַשָּׂטָן) is portrayed as one of the sons of God. He is among them the only figure identified by name and thus is somewhat distinctive from the others. In the Old Testament the word 'satan' is not always used *in malam partem* (e.g. Num. 22:22), and sometimes this creature seems to be portrayed only as an accuser (Zech. 3:1). Without reading back the later conceptualization of Satan as found in the documents from the intertestamental period into the story of Job 1–2, it seems save to interpret Satan in the Book of Job as not only an accuser or prosecutor in a legal context. He behaves as adversary of God as well as of Job, and tries to derive his goal through enacting calamities and the death of Job's children. However, only with the consent of God himself, the Satan can do this.[9] The role of Job as intercessor (1:5) is in marked contrast with Satan in the capacity of accuser and destroyer. Because in Old Testament times, the characterization of spirits was not as clear as in later times, I will in this article use the term 'satanic' and 'demonic' interchangeably as manifestations of spirit.[10]

---

9   In the encounter between the Satan, as one of the sons of God, and YHWH, the problem arises about the true relation between piety and prosperity. The agreement of God with the proposal is difficult to understand, and seems a paradox, but for the narrator Satan has the right to ask critical questions and YHWH is in the right to have the problem probed (cf. Abraham in Gen. 22). See Clines, *Job 1–20*, 19–25 and C.L. Seow, *Job 1–21: Interpretation and Commentary* (Illuminations), Grand Rapids, MI 2013, 255–57, 263.

10 Cf. G.J. Riley, 'Demon', in: K. van der Toorn, B. Becking, P.W. van der Horst (eds), *Dictionary of Deities and Demons in the Bible* (*DDD*), Leiden ²1999, 235–40. Originally, the Greek word δαίμων referred to a 'distributor (of fate)' or just a 'divine being', in the Ancient Near East it is applied to describe negative ghosts or spirits. For the Greek translation of the relevant Hebrew words in Job, see J.G. Gammie, 'The Angelology and Demonology in the Septuagint of the Book of Job', *HUCA* 56 (1985), 1–19.

3 Who Received the Vision?

It is impossible to deal here with the varied linguistic details of the vision, but some insights into several characteristics are required for a proper discussion. One of these is the question who received the vision. Most commentators accept the usual view that Eliphaz is the recipient. However, N.H. Tur-Sinai suggests another view.[11] He is followed by H.L. Ginsberg[12] and especially by Gary V. Smith.[13] The last author points to the fact that the vision is quoted again in Eliphaz's second speech in 15:14–16 and in a later speech attributed to Bildad in 25:4–6, and notes that interpreters always have had difficulty integrating this vision into the flow of the arguments between Job and his comforters.

Smith asks: '[I]f this is a divine revelation to Eliphaz which solves the riddle of Job's suffering, why is Eliphaz condemned by God at the end of the dialogue in 42:7?'[14] This author does not want to consider the possibility that this was a false vision inspired by 'the Satan' of the prologue, while no scholar takes such a position. I think the question of Smith is a good one, but a different answer is possible, as indicated in the publications by Kroeze and Janzen.

Smith shows several examples of unmarked quotations and tries to establish that Eliphaz quotes a vision received by Job. He sees a tension between the message of the vision with on one hand, its emphasis on the total depravity of the universe, and on the other, the rules of righteousness mentioned by Eliphaz. Eliphaz did not think that Job was suffering so severely because he was human; he believed Job was suffering because he had committed serious and grave sins, sins that he needed to confess to God (22:5–11, 15). The sudden destruction of a person, like a moth, and the death of individuals without wisdom (4:20–21) also contradict, according to Smith, the logical connection between sin and punishment, which was a part of Eliphaz's tradition.

The friends claimed that God treats righteous and unrighteous people differently but Job saw that destruction and pain came to them both (9:22–24). Smith concludes that in its essential teaching, the vision corresponds more with the thinking of Job than that of Eliphaz.

In my evaluation of this position, I argue for the traditional view that Eliphaz received the vision, and was not quoting Job.

---

11   N.H. Tur-Sinai, *The Book of Job: A New Commentary*, Jerusalem 1957.
12   H.L. Ginsberg, 'Job the Patient and Job the Impatient', in: *Congress Volume Rome 1968* (SVT, 17), Leiden 1968, 88–111, esp. 105–7. He sees Job 4:12–21 as a continuation of 3:3–26.
13   G.V. Smith, 'Job IV 12–21: Is it Eliphaz's Vision?', *VT* 40 (1990), 453–63.
14   Smith, 'Eliphaz's Vision?', 453.

1. Eliphaz continued his speech in chapter 5. It is not clear in these verses that he reacted to a quotation expressing a wrong view. Although it is possible that quotations were not marked, in this case it is very likely to see the content as a continuation and elaboration of the words and vision portrayed in chapter 4.
2. It is not necessary to see a tension between the words about the depravity of mankind and the view on a different treatment of just and unjust persons. Both arguments can be used against Job's view that he is a righteous person, and that the calamities are not caused by his sinful behaviour.
3. The message of the vision is repeated several times, especially in 15:14–16, in the second speech by Eliphaz. There again, the words are fitting in the argument and no correction of these is discernible. It is even possible that Eliphaz's question 'Have you listened in the council of God?' (15:8) alluded to the message he received in a special way. The content of the revelation in 4:17–18 becomes the bedrock of Eliphaz's position in 15:14–16, which re-emphasizes the impossibility of human purity or righteousness in view of the sinfulness of all beings beneath God himself.
4. The message of the vision reoccurs in 25:4–6, at the end of a short speech attributed to Bildad. The place at the end indicates that Bildad did not want to correct the content but used it as an argument.
5. Job did not accept the reasoning by Eliphaz. Although in 9:2 Job asked the question how it is possible for a man to be righteous before God, he altered the message of the vision, because in the same chapter Job mentioned several times his own position (vv. 15, 20, 21) and disagreed with the situation on earth.
6. Elihu, another friend, became angry because Job held himself to be righteous in his own eyes (32:1). In his argument against Job, Elihu referred to God's speaking in a dream, in a vision of the night (33:14–15). This can be considered as a support for Eliphaz's appeal to a vision.

Based on these arguments, it seems most likely that the vision had been received by Eliphaz and not by Job.

4 Wind or Spirit?

Another question we have to consider is the translation of the word רוּחַ with 'wind' or 'spirit'. It is possible to translate verse 15 'Then a wind swept past my face, a whirlwind made my body quiver.' The word רוּחַ is usually feminine;

when masculine, it generally refers to a wind or breath (1:19; 41:8; etc.).[15] However, sometimes the masculine form is used for a spirit. This is the case in Isa. 57:16; 63:10–11; Ps. 51:12–13; Job 20:3. Also in 1 Kgs 22:21 a masculine רוּחַ is mentioned.

Therefore, we need to look here beyond grammatical gender for the proper understanding of this noun. If רוּחַ refers to 'wind', it cannot really be the subject of the verb עמד in 4:16, which would entail that the subject of the verb is missing. As suggested by David Clines, maybe the word תְּמוּנָה can be the subject.[16] However, it seems easier to carry the meaning 'spirit' through 4:15–16. In this case, רוּחַ is the subject of עמד. For that construction, several parallels can be adduced. In Dan. 8:15, Daniel sees Gabriel, who 'stands before me'. In Zech. 3, several figures 'stand' in the heavenly scene. In 1 Kgs 22:19–23, the prophet Micaiah sees the host of heaven standing before YHWH. One of the spirits went forth and stood before YHWH (v. 21).[17] The word תְּמוּנָה can refer to the vague visibility of the spirit. While Eliphaz was seeing this, he heard a voice (v. 16b).

Based on these considerations, I prefer the translation of 'spirit' as found in verse 15, although we have to leave open the possibility that both senses of רוּחַ may be intended. Despite this ambiguity in the text, someone in the vision speaks and gives his meaning.

5   The Extent of the Vision

It is clear that the verses 12–21 form the account of the revelation. In the verses 12–16 the circumstances are given. At the end of verse 16 a voice is introduced. The content of the message is found at least in verse 17, but may be seen extending to verse 21. Most scholars and translations regard verse 17–21 as the 'divine' speech as heard by Eliphaz, but some regard only verse 17 as the word of revelation. And the verses 18–21 serve as wisdom's extensions of it, in their formulation by Eliphaz.[18] I prefer the view of the majority, being that the spirit uttered the verses 18–21, because the content of the verses 18–21 is not easily deduced out of verse 17.

---

15 Clines, *Job 1–20*, 107, 111.
16 Clines, *Job 1–20*, 111.
17 Harding, 'Spirit', 146–50.
18 Clines, *Job 1–20*, 133–34; Harding, 'Spirit', 140.

6 Demonic Activity in General

The main question in this paper is the character of the spirit or 'appearance' as that came to Eliphaz. As already stated, most scholars see the message in the verses 17–21 as a divine word. However, I want to explore another possibility. In the last decennia, more attention is being given to views on demonic activity and allusions to it in the Ancient Near East and in the Old Testament.[19]

In the book of Job, we sometimes find remarkable allusions to demonic activities. Scott B. Noegel wrote an article on Job 3:5, and suggested the translation 'day-demons' instead of the usual 'blackness of the day'.[20] In Job 3:8 the mythological monster Leviathan can be aroused by magic. In Job 5:7 several scholars see a reference to Resheph. Clines writes in his commentary:

> Since in Joban language the deity Death (Mot) has a 'firstborn' (18:13) and is entitled 'the king of the terrors' (18:14),[21] who are underworld demons, it is entirely likely that the 'sons of Resheph' had the same function. On this view, Eliphaz is saying that when humans beget trouble for themselves they let loose (metaphorically speaking) the underworld demons of pestilence to fly high to earth in order to attack mortals.[22]

More possible references to demonic forces can be seen in the mention of Rahab (9:13; 26:12) and the gliding serpent (26:13). Eliphaz's speech in 15:17–24

---

[19] Recent publications on magic, demons and spirits are for instance, the above mentioned *DDD* and the Brill series *Studies in Ancient Magic and Divination*. A new publication, available on the internet, is J. Eggler and Ch. Uehlinger (eds), *Iconography of Deities and Demons in the Ancient Near East*: http://www.religionswissenschaft.uzh.ch/idd/prepublication_4.php.

Cf. P.K. McCarter, 'Evil spirit of God', in: *DDD*, 319–20: 'Another *rūaḥ* that should be mentioned in this regard is the "wind" that brushes the face of Eliphaz in his sleep,... This spirit, which seems to operate quite independently of God, has a discernible form..., comparable to the appearance of the ghost or spirit of Samuel to Saul (1 Sam. 28).'

[20] S.B. Noegel, 'Job iii 5 in the Light of Mesopotamian Demons of Time', *VT* 57 (2007), 556–62. He mentions the explanation of Rashi and Ibn Ezra. They understood the expression as 'like demons that rule by day'. Cited in support is Deut. 32:24.

[21] Calamity and Disaster in 18:12 can be seen as demons who are waiting for the wicked man to stumble. Disease and 'the Firstborn of Death' are as two underlings of Death that go out in the world looking for victims. In the view of Clines, they are demons like Calamity and Disaster in v. 12. (*Job 1–20*, 416–18).

[22] Clines, *Job 1–20*, 142.

mentions no vague spirits or mere metaphors of death, but horrifying presences that torment the living.[23]

It is not possible to evaluate these suggestions here, but I do note a new tendency to detect references to demonic activities and follow up on this development.

7 Arguments for Demonic Activity in Job 4

If in Job 3 and 5 references are being made to spirits, is it possible to think about such a possibility in Job 4 as well? Did Eliphaz receive a vision of a demon or negative spirit, although he himself was convinced of its divine origin?

1. The vision was frightening. This phenomenon corresponds with the evil spirit that afflicted Saul and with the spirit he met in Endor (1 Sam. 28). It is true that divine manifestations and apparitions of angels of God evoke strong emotions, but in such cases usually the words 'Do not fear' are spoken (Gen. 15:1; 21:17; 26:24; Judg. 6:23; Dan. 10:12).
2. Shalom M. Paul adduces several examples to illustrate the second half of verse 15, and describes it as a hair-raising encounter.[24] His illustrations are taken from the Mesopotamian world and refer to ghosts and evil demons. These horrifying encounters with supernatural beings points to the same interpretation in Job 4.
3. As already stated, in 42:7 Eliphaz was rebuked, because he did not speak what was right. It seems likely therefore that the content of the vision and the implications were not right. It raises the issue what the origin of the wrong message was.
4. The main question treated in the vision is: Can mortals be righteous before God? Can human beings be pure before their Maker? (v. 17). The unspoken answer on these questions is: No. This dogma is placed in interrogative form for emphasis. While this revealed truth seems so obvious that its being stated is trite, it is central to Eliphaz's thinking. Thus he will repeat it in each of his speeches (15:14–16; 22:2). His approach allows him to reject Job's defence of his innocence from the start without directly

---

23 The 'terrors' are not simply the plural of the abstract noun 'terror', but the personified spirits of vengeance, denizens of the underworld, ruled over by 'the king of terrors' (18:14). See Ibid., 357.
24 S.M. Paul, 'Job 4:15—A Hair Raising Encounter', ZAW 95 (1983), 119–21.

disputing whether Job is a sinner.[25] However, in the context of the whole book, he is in opposition to the declarations of God in the chapters 1–2. Of course, this raises questions about the redaction of the book, whether or not the framework was later added to the dialogues. But in the final form, the reader senses the tension between the expressions. YHWH declared Job's being 'a blameless and upright man who fears God and turns away from evil' (1:8; 2:3). Eliphaz undermines the righteousness of Job and does not believe in his innocence.

5. In general, the Old Testament allows for people to be righteous before God, e.g. Abraham in Gen. 15:6. Even Eliphaz admits the distinction between the upright people and the sinners or fools (4:6–7; 5:2–3; 15:2; 22:2–4). Bildad in 25:5 refers to the vision and makes the very general statement: 'even the moon is not bright and the stars are not pure in his sight', having the conclusion 'how much less a mortal' (v. 6).

6. While the usual basis for the thought of human unworthiness in the Old Testament is humanity's sinful disposition, the vision seems to ground the doctrine of human insignificance on humanity's inferiority before God.[26]

7. The vision states that God puts no trust in his servants, and that He charges his angels with error (v. 18). Regarding the servants on earth, chapters 1–2 show that God puts a great trust in Job, to such an extent that Satan is allowed to test the loyalty of this servant. Therefore the content of verse 18 is in contradiction with the first chapters.

8. Does God charge his angels with error? The idea of 'fallen angels' is later developed in the intertestamental literature (e.g. 1 Enoch 6–9), but the story of the union of the 'sons of God' with the 'daughters of men' in Gen. 6:1–4 is a possible background for this assessment of angels' reliability.[27] More texts can be adduced for God's judgment of 'heavenly beings' ('sons of God'; Job 1:6),[28] e.g. Ps. 82 and Isa. 24:21. However, in these cases several reasons are adduced for the punishment. The claim in the vision goes further, for God puts no trust in his servants and charges his angels with error. This statement is so general that it is more than likely a complaint by one of the criticized messengers than a word spoken by a dedicated and obedient angel.

---

25 Hartley, *Job*, 113.
26 Kroeze, *Job*, 86 and Hartley, *Job*, 113.
27 Maybe Isa. 14:12–15; see N.C. Habel, *The Book of Job* (OTL), Philadelphia 1985, 129. Cf. J. Doedens, *The Sons of God in Genesis 6:1–4*, Ph.D. dissertation, Kampen 2013, 191.
28 For 'sons of God', see 1:6; 2:1; 38:7.

9. The next words in the vision use the argumentation form of *a maiore ad minorem*: humans are portrayed as dwellers in houses of clay. The last sentences point to the possibility of a sudden and unpredictable death. Humans can be crushed like a moth; many people die devoid of wisdom (vv. 19–21). The words can be read as general statement or as a possibility.[29] In the last case, they are an indirect appeal to prepare for death and to become wise. However, in the vision these words serve as a strong warning to understand the fragile situation of mankind and for Job the message is not to think he is above this situation. As such, for him there is no hope and no escape. This fits better in the context of accusations by a demon than in the context of heavenly messengers, who usually point out to recipients a way how to behave.[30]

10. In the vision, the notions of sin, guilt, and the confession of guilt are absent. The only message is distrust. Whereas there is no appeal to confession of guilt, yet Eliphaz advises Job to go to God (5:8). The first chapter portrays how Job sanctified his children and offered burnt offerings for them, so to restore the relationship with God (1:5). In 7:20–21, Job speaks about the possibility that transgression may be pardoned. To this the words of Elihu can be adduced. He speaks about God's action in a dream or vision, with the goal that He may turn the people from pride, to spare their souls from the Pit (33:14–18). In the vision these elements are not mentioned.

11. No prophet in the Old Testament refers to a spirit as source of his message.[31]

12. In the totality of the book of Job, the first two chapters give us a view of a heavenly council. Satan received consent to attack Job and his family. After the first attack the writer concluded 'In all this Job did not sin or charge God with wrongdoing' (1:22). After the second attack on Job's health, the conclusion is 'In all this Job did not sin with his lips' (2:10). In the remaining 40 chapters of the story, Satan is no longer mentioned. Could it be likely that he stopped with his activities? Can Satan only use extreme circumstances, or does he use more subtle means also? The last possibility is often mentioned in later literature.[32] With regard to the

---

29   Clines, *Job 1–20*, 135.
30   It is true that Eliphaz pointed out such a direction, but it is not in the vision.
31   Habel, *Job*, 127–128.
32   E.g., 1 Chron. 21:1.

book of Job I refer to the words of Kroeze, already mentioned, that Satan used storms, lightning, robbers—and friends.[33]

13. In the entire book of Job, God is silent during the sufferings of Job, until chapter 38, while He allows his servant Job to be tested. It is not likely that He attacks his own servant in the meantime.

14. In 7:13–14, Job complained that he was scared with dreams and terrified with visions. It is very likely that he too had hair-raising encounters, with very spooky apparitions. The consequence is that he prefers to die (v. 15). Of course, Job thinks that these visions are given by God, as is clear from the next verses (esp. vv. 20–21). Here again we cannot adduce similar experiences by the prophets. In the case of Jeremiah, he wants to die because of the reactions of man, not because of the visions he received (Jer. 20:14–18). It seems that Job had comparable negative experiences, caused by a demon.

I conclude that is possible to evaluate the vision of Eliphaz in a more negative way than he himself was aware of. A demonic manifestation in the vision is a serious possibility.

8 Strategy of the Book

In case Eliphaz is misguided, it is possible to ask why neither Satan nor a demonic activity are explicitly mentioned in chapter 4. Why is it so difficult to grasp the negative meaning of this vision, easily understood as a theophany?

The first reason lies in the relation between the vision and the prologue. For the dialogues in this chapter are usually explained without a strong connection to the prologue. Yet, looking at the strategy of the book as a whole, the reader is given a double focus. First, he is shown the heavenly discussions and the satanic background of the calamities in the first two chapters. Second, the following chapters concentrate on the situation on earth and the reader comes to see that Job and his friends are not aware of the heavenly background for the problems on earth. Provided with this double focus, the reader views whether

---

33 In the history of interpretation, Behemoth and Leviathan in Job 40–41 have often figured as personifications of evil (cf. 3:8). Maybe it is possible to connect them with the Satan in the first chapters. See Fyall, *Now my eyes*, for a strong defense of this view. Clines is more reserved, *Job 38–42*, Nashville 2011, 1186. For a discussion of the usual identifications with a hippopotamus and crocodile, and the relevance for the relation with Satan, see my article 'Behemoth and leviathan in the book of Job', *Journal of Creation* 24 (2010), 94–100.

or not Job and his friends can grasp the background. The reader not only reads the dialogues, but tries to combine both points of view. This is the strategy of the book. Without this understanding, it is possible for readers to mistake Satan's subtle attacks on Job.

The second reason for the absence of the mention of Satan or demonic activities is that Elifaz is convinced of the positive origin of the received revelation. Only his view is presented, and Job does not have the knowledge of the happenings in the first two chapters to contradict Elifaz. The reader has to interpret several allusions to demonic activities and to wait until 42:7 to hear God's verdict against the friends: 'You have not spoken of me what is right'.

9   Examples in the Old Testament

Does the above-mentioned interpretation present a unique case, or can more experiences in the Old Testament be found to substantiate this suggestion? A dream or vision can be used for God's communication with mankind. However, sometimes people are misguided.

A first example can be deduced from Deut. 13. If prophets or those who divine by dreams stimulate Israel to serve foreign gods, the people of Israel are not allowed to listen. In that case, YHWH is testing his people, to know whether they indeed love YHWH their God (13:1–5). What is important to note in the formulation of this law, is the prospect that the spokesman will have received a message in a dream. It is clear from the admonition that knowing the content is the most important way to discern the reliability of the message.

An interesting narrative is told in 1 Kgs 22 (// 2 Chron. 18). King Jehoshaphat of Judah and the king of Israel (Ahab, see vv. 20, 39–40) made plans to attack Ramoth-gilead. They received a positive advice to do so by 400 prophets and by Zedekiah son of Chenaanah (vv. 1–12). At a later moment Micaiah, the son of Imlah spoke of his vision whereby Israel would be scattered on the mountains, like sheep that have no shepherd. In his explanation of it, he spoke of YHWH sitting on his throne with all the hosts of heaven standing beside Him. In that council, a spirit promised to entice Ahab, saying: 'I will go out and be a lying spirit in the mouth of all his prophets'. Of course Zedekiah disagreed with this message, but for us the point is, that sometimes prophets can be deceived. One of the tests to see who is speaking the truth is the outcome of the prophecies (vv. 17–28).

Zedekiah asked: 'Which way did the spirit of YHWH pass from me to speak to you?' (v. 24). Apparently, Zedekiah believed he had received an authentic revelation! However, in the description of the book of Kings he is revealed as deceived in his meaning and advice.

This story from 1 Kgs 22 is especially relevant for the interpretation of the story in Job, because it contains a comparable pictorial of a heavenly council. The difference is of course that Micaiah spoke about a messenger of God, and in the book of Job it is an action by Satan.

The third reference is to Zech. 13. YHWH will cut off the names of the idols from the land and will remove the prophets and the unclean spirit (v. 2). This combination of 'prophets' and 'unclean spirit' is remarkable. The unclean spirit is a spirit inspiring the false prophets who engage in prophesying lies in the name of YHWH.[34] In Zechariah the consequence is that fathers and mothers accuse their sons of speaking lies. In the next verse their activity is related to visions (v. 4).

In the Old Testament we find several references to negative spirits. According to Judg. 9:23, God sent an 'evil spirit' between Abimelech and the Shechemites. Its task was to cause the Shechemites to become traitorous toward Abimelech and turn on him. An 'evil spirit' also came upon Saul once the spirit of YHWH had left him (1 Sam. 16:14). Though not involving prophecy in these cases, the notion of harmful, evil spirits is very much at home in the Old Testament.

10 Conclusion

On the base of the arguments I have put forward, it seems likely that a negative or demonic spirit (related to Satan) tried to follow up the negative works of the first chapter. This was done in a subtle way: that is, through words of friends, who were influenced by their own thoughts and by a dream, which is perceived by them as a divine message. The statements in Job 4:17–21 are formulated as revelation, but in the context of the book of Job a discernment of spirits is necessary. By drawing up a perspective on the role of demonic influence in Job 4, it is possible to have a new interpretation of an old text,[35] with consequences for the interpretation of the entire book. The framework and the dialogues are more connected than usually thought.

---

34 E.H. Merrill, *Haggai, Zechariah, Malachi: An Exegetical Commentary*, Chicago 1994, 329–30.

35 Cf. M.J. Paul et al. (eds), *Bijbelcommentaar Ezra—Job* (Studiebijbel OT, 6), Veenendaal 2009, 437–43, 884–86.

Acquiring Wisdom: A Semantic Analysis of Its Metaphorical Conceptualisations

Pierre Van Hecke

1   Introduction and Methodology

> Where then does wisdom come from? And where is the place of understanding? (Job 28:20, NRSV)

Not only the book of Job, but all of wisdom literature asks the question how wisdom can be acquired, how knowledge and insight should be pursued and how they can be found. The present article aims at analysing how this quest of wisdom is conceptualized in the Classical Hebrew wisdom literature. In other words, it will address the questions which Hebrew terms and expressions are used to describe the human pursuit of wisdom and what these terms and expressions reveal about the way in which the quest for wisdom and even wisdom itself are understood.[1]

Wisdom and the acquisition of it are highly abstract concepts. As with many abstract concepts, it is difficult, if possible at all, to describe them in direct, literal terms. For this reason, metaphors are very frequently used in conceptualising them. For example, in the introductory paragraph of this article, several expressions have been used for the pursuit of wisdom which, although highly conventional in English, they are metaphorical in origin. Wisdom cannot literally be *acquired, pursued* or *found,* or at least not in the way real estate can be acquired, a car can be pursued or lost keys can be found. Yet, these terms were used for want of literal terms which would exclusively and unequivocally describe the 'acquisition' of wisdom. In the course of the last decades, Cognitive Linguistics has made a strong case that these metaphorical expressions cannot be regarded as mere substitutions for more literal terms. Rather, their usage affects the way in which we conceptualise (the acquisition of) wisdom. Speaking of the pursuit of wisdom, for example, implicitly conceptualises

---

[1] This contribution will not deal with the conceptualisation of wisdom as a gift from God, rather than the result of human effort. This conceptualisation is a late development in the Biblical tradition according to seminal work by G. von Rad, *Weisheit in Israel*, Neukirchen 1970, 70.

it as a valuable and desirable object, which can only be 'obtained' at the cost of a lot of sustained effort, as with the pursuit of wild animals. The aim of this article is therefore not only to analyse the different expressions for the pursuit of wisdom, but also, and more importantly, to expound the conceptualisations they involve.

In spite of previous, thorough studies on wisdom vocabulary by, among others, Whybray[2] and Fox,[3] a systematic semantic analysis of the expressions for *acquiring* wisdom is still lacking. It is this lacuna the present article aims to fill. An article-length analysis like the present one cannot provide an exhaustive analysis of all the expressions in their contexts. It will rather present a survey of the extant material in its totality, aiming to lay bare its systematicity and interconnections. An attempt has been made, however, to be as exhaustive as possible in registering the data, in spite of the fact that no list of cases exists and that such a semantic list is harder to compile than one of lexical or morphological features in the text. In a first step, all the verses featuring wisdom terms as חכמה, בינה, דעת in the Classical Hebrew literature (Hebrew Bible, Ben Sira, Dead Sea Scrolls) were listed with the help of concordance tools, and all the expressions for the acquisition of wisdom to be found in these verses were registered. Additionally, the major wisdom songs and hymns as Proverbs 8, Job 28, Ben Sira 6, 14 and 51, were surveyed in their entirety, again extracting the terms and expressions for wisdom acquisition. In a second step, all the instances of the words and expressions for the acquisition of wisdom retrieved in the first phase (e.g. קנה) were registered, and all their usages in the context of wisdom which had remained unnoticed in the first phase were added. In spite of this procedure, the present article does not pretend to be more than an initial survey, which—much like archaeological surveys—remains superficial, and does not pay sufficient attention to all the individual findings. Yet surveys and overviews are important in that they bring to light relations and links between the expressions under investigation which would remain unnoticed in more detailed—and potentially more myopic—studies of individual expressions. Expressions on what it takes concretely to reach wisdom, or on what is the content of wisdom, will not be taken into consideration in the present contribution.

---

2 R.N. Whybray, *The Intellectual Tradition in the Old Testament* (BZAW, 135) Berlin, New York 1974.
3 M.V. Fox, 'Words for Wisdom', *Zeitschrift für Althebraistik* 6 (1993), 79–91.

2.1 Seeking and Finding Wisdom

A first common group of expressions describes the process of the acquisition of wisdom in terms of searching and finding, as in the words of personified Wisdom herself in example (1).

(1) Prov. 8:17 ומשחרי ימצאנני
Those who seek me diligently, find me.[4]

The verbs most commonly used for the process of seeking wisdom are בקש[5] and דרש,[6] with a number of terms occurring just once or twice: חפש (Prov. 2:4) and the already mentioned שחר (Prov. 8:17; 4Q525 2 ii+3 3).[7] The resulting 'finding' of wisdom is commonly expressed with the verb מצא, as in example (1) above.[8] Also the verb חקר in Sir. 6:27 (A) is to be understood as referring to the result of the searching, rather than as the searching itself. Two arguments can be given for this interpretation: firstly, as I have argued elsewhere,[9] the verb does not designate 'searching for' something, but rather 'penetrating it completely' and its result 'knowing it completely'. Secondly, Sir. 6:27 contains three pairs of verbs, in which the second is, in my opinion, always the continuation of the first. The second and third pair thus read 'search and find' and

---

[4] All biblical translations are taken from the NRSV unless mentioned otherwise.

[5] Prov. 2:4 (search her as silver); 14:6; Qoh. 7:25; Sir. 4:12 (A); 6:27 (A); 51:13 (11QPs^a and B); 51:26 (B).

[6] Qoh. 1:13; Sir. 6:27 (A); 51:14 (11QPs^a); 4Q525 2 ii+3 2.

[7] To this list, one might wish to add the verb תור, which, next to its meaning of 'spying', is used a number of times with reference to the process of mental investigation (Qoh 1:13; 2:3; 7:25). Since its object is not wisdom or knowledge itself, but refers to the method of investigating (1:13; 7:25) or to the investigation of a particular issue, I do not include it in the main text of this contribution.

[8] Prov. 2:5; 3:13; 8:9, 17, 35; 24:14; Sir. 51:16 (11QPs^a), 26, 27 (B). Compare with Sir. 6:18, not extant in any of the Hebrew manuscripts (except for the two final words in MS C), see R. Egger-Wenzel, 'Ein neues Sira-Fragment des MS C', *Biblische Notizen* 138 (2008), 107–14. The Greek reads: τέκνον ἐκ νεότητός σου ἐπίλεξαι παιδείαν καὶ ἕως πολιῶν εὑρήσεις σοφίαν translated by Skehan as 'My son, from your youth embrace discipline; thus you will gain wisdom in graying hair' (P. Skehan and A.A. Di Lella, *The Wisdom of Ben Sira* [AB, 39], New York 1987, 190). This translation, which stresses the importance of discipline in the search for wisdom and the long time and old age it takes to acquire it (see ibid., 192) is to be preferred over translations as that of the NRSV 'My child, from your youth choose discipline, and when you have gray hair you will *still* find wisdom' (italics mine).

[9] P. Van Hecke, 'Searching for and Exploring Wisdom: A Cognitive-Semantic Approach to the Verb ḥāqar in Job 28', in: E. van Wolde (ed.), *Job 28: Cognition in Context* (Biblical Interpretation Series, 64), Leiden 2003, 139–62.

'hold fast to her and do not let her go'. Also the two first verbs דרש וחקר should then be read as a pair of verbs expressing the search and its result 'inquire and know completely', and not as the first two of three verbs expressing the process of searching, followed by one verb of finding, as Skehan's translation seems to imply.[10]

Although the conceptualisation of seeking and finding wisdom may come across as very natural, since most languages will use terms of searching and finding with reference to intellectual quests, it is interesting to ask what this conceptualisation implies. A first implication is that wisdom and knowledge metaphorically speaking have a location, but that this location is not readily known or seen by people, so that it demands a conscious effort to 'search' and 'find' them. This conceptualisation of the quest for wisdom is in keeping with the common representation of wisdom and knowledge themselves as deeply hidden, described convincingly by Greenstein.[11] It comes as no surprise then that the search for wisdom is compared to the search for hidden treasures (Prov. 2:4) or to the most extreme and labour-intensive form of searching known in Antiquity, namely the digging for precious metals or stones, as in Job 28:1–12 or again in Prov. 2:4. Searching for wisdom thus has the aim of bringing out what is in origin hidden or that of which the location is unknown. A second implication of describing the quest for wisdom as searching is that one does not commonly search for something in order to simply be familiar with the object's location, but rather to stay in its vicinity, because of its qualities (e.g. search for water), or to take possession of it (e.g. search for gold). Both aspects are also present in the metaphorical searching for wisdom, as will be demonstrated in the following paragraphs.

2.2 Turning to Wisdom

In several cases, wisdom's location is not conceptualised as unknown or hidden, but as clear for all to see, as is most notably the case in Prov. 9:1 and Sir. 14:23–27 in which wisdom is said to build/to have a house. In that case, the acquisition of wisdom is no longer regarded as searching for wisdom, but as turning towards wisdom—of which the location is now known—with the purpose of staying in its proximity. Physical nearness is used in many languages to

---

[10] Skehan and Di Lella, *Ben Sira*, 190: 'Search her out, discover her; seek her and you will find her'. Moreover, I am not convinced that the imagery used in verses 26–28 is that of hunting (ibid., 194), even though this metaphor is used elsewhere in the book (14:22), as will be argued below.

[11] E. Greenstein, 'The Poem on Wisdom in Job 28 in Its Conceptual and Literary Contexts', in: van Wolde, *Job 28*, 253–80; esp. 258–63.

metaphorically conceptualise relationship, intimacy and influence, as testified by very common expressions like *My sister and I are very close; We have a close collaboration*.[12] Drawing on a similar conceptualisation, wisdom literature invites people to turn to wisdom's place (2), to remain at her doorsteps (3), to become neighbours with her (4) and even to dwell in her habitation (5).

(2) Prov. 9:4[13] מי־פתי יסר הנה
Whoever is simple, let him turn in here.[14]

(3) Prov. 8:34 אשרי אדם שמע לי לשקד על־דלתתי יום יום לשמר מזוזת פתחי
Happy is the one who listens to me, watching daily at my gates, waiting beside my doors.

(4) Sir. 14:24–25 החונה סביבות ביתה והביא יתריו בקירה
ונטה אהלו על ידה ושכן שכן טוב
[Happy the person] Who encamps near her house and fastens his tent pegs next to her walls; Who pitches his tent beside her and lives as her welcome neighbor.[15]

(5) Sir. 14:26–27 וישים קנו בעופיה ובענפיה יתלונן
וחוסה בצלה מחרב ובמעונותיה ישכן
Who builds his nest in her leafage and lodges in her branches;
Who takes refuge from the heat in her shade[16] and dwells in her home.

It is interesting to observe that in Prov. 8:34 and Sir. 14:24–25 (examples 3 and 4) the searchers for wisdom are portrayed as humans, waiting at doors and pitching tents as human beings do, while in the immediately following verse 26 and possibly also in 27a (example 5), they are depicted as birds, building nests

---

12   G. Lakoff and M. Johnson, *Metaphors We Live By*, Chicago 1980, 52: 'INTIMACY IS CLOSENESS'.
13   See also Sir. 15:1 (A), the verse immediately following examples (3) and (4) for a similar conceptualisation of moving towards wisdom. Verse 7 of the same chapter stresses that the impious, by contrast, do not (wish to) move towards wisdom.
14   My translation.
15   Ben Sira's translations are taken from Skehan and Di Lella, *Ben Sira* unless mentioned otherwise.
16   For צל as economic protection, compared to wisdom's protection, see Qoh. 7:12.

and spending the night in the branches of a tree.[17] Verse 27b returns to the image of wisdom herself having a home,[18] but in contrast to verses 24–25 people are no longer invited to live as her neighbours, but rather to dwell in her home itself. Whether described as pitching tents or as building nests, both metaphors share the common aspect of coming to live in Wisdom's immediate vicinity.

Since proximity or closeness is a reciprocal relation—if A is close to B, than B is close to A—it comes as no surprise to find instances in which it is wisdom itself that remains close to the wise (חכמתי עמדה לי Qoh. 2:9), and even comes to rest in the heart of the wise (בלב נבון תנוח חכמה Qoh. 14:33).

In contrast, Qohelet's failed attempts to become wise are described as a distance between wisdom and himself (והיא רחוקה Qoh. 7:23), while Sir. 15:8 stresses that wisdom is far from the impious, since they will not be able to attain her (לא ידריכוה), as the preceding verse 7 indicates.

2.3 Pursuing Wisdom

In all of the aforementioned cases, wisdom was regarded as having a static location in space—whether hidden or known—which people are to search for and to draw near to. In several other instances, however, wisdom is conceptualised as a moving entity, and the quest for wisdom takes the form of a pursuit. The following examples can be adduced:

(6) Sir 14:22 (A) לצאת אחריה בחקר וכל מבואיה ירצד
[21 Happy the person who ponders her ways in his heart and pays attention to her paths]
Pursuing her like a scout and lying in wait at her entrances.[19]

(7) 4Q525 2 ii–3 5 אשרי אדם השיג חכמה
Happy the man who overtakes wisdom[20]

(8) Sir. 4:19b אם יסור מאחרי אשליכנו
If he strays from behind me, I will cast him off.

In example (6), the person searching for wisdom is described as a tracker or a hunter—reading בחקר as כחקר in accordance with the Greek ὡς ἰχνευτής, thereby highlighting the attention, focus and patience involved in the search

---

17   Skehan and Di Lella, *Ben Sira*, 264.
18   Compare with Bar 3:15.
19   My translation of 22b.
20   My translation.

for wisdom. Given the personification of wisdom as a young bride later in the poem (Sir. 15:2), a double entendre may be intended, understanding the 'going out after' in an amorous sense, as running after a beloved.[21] I will return to the conceptualisation of wisdom as a lover in paragraph 2.7. Whether or not this connotation plays a role in the present verse, it is clear that wisdom is seen as a moving entity (an animal or a person), as is also made clear by the preceding verse 21 in which reference is made to wisdom's ways and paths to which the wise is urged to pay attention. A similar conceptualisation can be found in example (7), in my opinion. Even though the hiphil of נשג can designate both the reaching of a place and the overtaking of a moving object, the verb's common collocation with רדף in the Hebrew Bible shows that the latter meaning is clearly dominant.[22] This interpretation is to be favoured in example (7), as becomes clear when the two following sentences are taken into consideration ויתהלך בתורת עליון ויכן לדרכיה לבו, in which *walking* in the ways of the Law, and thus pursuing it, is mentioned.[23] Example (8) is text-critically complicated as MS A proposes two versions of the Ben Sira verse side by side. In the second version, represented here, wisdom demands its 'followers' not to stray from behind her, in other words, not to give up pursuing her. Besides the examples proposed above, the conceptualisation of acquiring wisdom as walking after her is possibly also found in Sir. 51:18 and 20 (11QPsa). The difficult verb שחק in verse 18 can best be read in accordance with Exod. 30:36 and Job 14:19 as meaning 'to pulverise, to make into thin dust'; the full expression אשחקה then refers to wearing wisdom's paths, by treading them continuously.[24] The verb טרתי of verse 20 is likewise problematic, although most scholars follow Sanders, the editor of the Psalm scroll in the DJD, in reading it as a contraction of טרדתי, deriving from the rare verb טרד with the meaning of 'pursuing'.[25] Also here,

---

21 For an extensive discussion of the conceptualisation of running after, see my article 'Are People Walking After or Before God? On the Metaphorical Use of אחרי הלך and לפני הלך', *Orientalia Lovaniensia Periodica* 30 (1999), 37–71.

22 Gen. 44:4; Exod. 14:9; 15:9; Deut. 19:6; 28:45; Josh. 2:5; 1 Sam. 30:8; 2 Kgs. 25:5 Ps. 7:6; 18:38; Jer. 39:5; 52:8; Lam. 1:3; Hos. 2:9. Interestingly, the last case uses the terms in a (metaphorical) amorous sense.

23 The verb נשג (hiphil) with the object חכמה is also at the top of the recto of folio III of MS C, which looks like the second part of Sir. 6:18, given the fact that the folio continues with 6:19. Since the expression occurs without any further context, it is difficult to make any claims concerning its conceptualisation.

24 A similar meaning is found in Sir. 6:36 with reference to wearing someone's doorstep. Given the difficulty of this interpretation, some commentators have preferred to read a different verb here, namely שחק or חשק, see Skehan and Di Lella, *Ben Sira*, 575.

25 J.A. Sanders, *The Psalms Scroll of Qumran Cave II (11QPsa)* (DJD, 4), Oxford 1965.

then, the acquisition of Wisdom, so extensively described in the final acrostic of the book of Ben Sira, is conceptualised as pursuing it.

2.4 Watching Wisdom

The acquisition of wisdom is not only conceptualised as a physical movement towards wisdom, but also as the (attempt at) visually perceiving it.[26] This conceptualisation is in keeping with the former, as the process of searching for and pursuing typically also involves visual perception; both metaphors are often found together, therefore. Moreover, cross-linguistically knowledge and acquaintance with something are very commonly described as seeing, one only has to think of expressions as *I see what you mean; She provided me with a new insight*.[27] Typically, then, also Hebrew wisdom literature, and the book of Ben Sira in particular, conceptualises the acquisition of wisdom as watching it carefully. Some examples:

(9) Sir. 14:20 (A) אשרי אנוש בחכמה יהגה ובתבונה ישעה
Happy the person who meditates on Wisdom, and fixes his gaze on understanding.

(10) Sir. 15:7 (A) לא ידריכוה מתי שוא ואנשי זדון לא יראוה
Worthless people will not attain to her, the haughty will not behold her.

Both examples are taken from the central poem on the acquisition of wisdom in Sir. 14:20–15:10. Whereas the first verb of this poem is to be taken literally—הגה referring to the murmuring soliloquizing of a sage—the visual language in the second half of the verse is obviously metaphorical, as understanding is not something that can literally be seen. Visual metaphors occur at several occasions in the same wisdom poem: in 14:22 'watch sneakily/lie in wait for wisdom (רצד)'; in 14:23 'peep through wisdom's window (שקף hiphil)', and in

---

[26] Expression dealing with listening to or learning from wisdom are purposely not included in the present contribution on the metaphorical conceptualisations of the quest for wisdom. In my opinion, these expressions are metonymic rather than metaphorical: they do not conceptualise the acquisition of wisdom in terms of something else. Rather, listening to and learning from wisdom *stands for* listening to and learning from the people teaching this wisdom. For expressions of listening or paying attention to wisdom, see Prov. 2:2; 5:1; 8:33.34; Sir. 4:15; 14:21.23; 51:16 (11QPs^a); expressions of learning from wisdom, see Prov. 30:3; Sir. 51:15 (B).

[27] M. Fortescue, 'Thoughts about Thought', *Cognitive Linguistics* 12 (2001), 15–45.

15:7, cited in full above, in which the visual metaphor is juxtaposed to a spatial one. The common verb נבט (hiphil) is probably used in a metaphorical way in Sir. 51:20 (B) to indicate gazing on wisdom. Even though the context is too broken to make any definite claims, this interpretation is supported by the preceding verse in which the first person claims not to have turned his face from wisdom (הפך in MS B, שׁוּב hiphil in 11QPs^a). Another occurrence of the metaphorical use of the verb נבט hiphil is found in 4Q300 1 ii 3, where fools are said not to have *watched* the root of wisdom, and their vision is sealed. A final reference to the watching or observing of wisdom may occur in Prov. 4:13 (נצר),[28] although the context of the verse speaks about seizing wisdom and not letting her go, which seems to suggest that the verb should be understood as 'keeping' or 'guarding' wisdom here.

2.5 *Acquiring Wisdom*

Of a very different nature is a group of expressions explicitly conceptualising the acquisition of wisdom, well precisely as *acquisition*, namely as acquiring it as a valuable commodity. This group of metaphorical expressions is particularly common; the verb most frequently used in Classical Hebrew literature to conceptualise the acquisition of wisdom is קנה,[29] as in the following example:

(11)   Prov. 4:7   ראשׁית חכמה קנה חכמה ובכל־קנינך קנה בינה:
       The beginning of wisdom is this: Get wisdom, and whatever else you get, get insight.

When used non-metaphorically, the verb most often designates economic acquisition through buying or exchange of goods. Most commentators argue that in the case of the collocation קנה חכמה, the verb has the more general meaning of acquiring or getting, without economic overtones.[30] While it goes without saying that in acquiring wisdom no money is involved,[31] I would argue that it does more right to the semantic potential of the texts not to completely downplay the economic background of the term. Firstly, the verb קנה is not the only term taken from the conceptual domain of economic interaction used in the conceptualisation of one's dealing with wisdom, and seeing the broad range of economic terms gives a better insight in the way in which this pursuit of wisdom was conceived of in the Hebrew Bible. Moreover, having an eye for

---

28 See also Prov. 3:1, 21; 5:2.
29 Prov. 1:15; 4:5, 7; 15:32; 16:16; 17:16; 18:15; 19:8; 23:23; Sir. 51:20, 21, 25 (B).
30 E. Lipiński, קנה, ThWAT 7, 63–71.
31 As Sir. 51:25 (B) explicitly states: 'gain wisdom for yourselves, without money'.

the underlying conceptualisations can also make the reader and the researcher more aware of other, overlooked instances of the same type of metaphors. The two following examples show how economic language is used to speak about the pursuit of wisdom.

(12) Prov. 23:23   אמת קנה ואל־תמכר חכמה ומוסר ובינה:
Buy truth, and do not sell it; buy wisdom, instruction, and understanding.

(13) Qoh 7:11–12   טובה חכמה עם־נחלה ויתר לראי השמש:
כי בצל החכמה בצל הכסף ויתרון דעת החכמה תחיה בעליה
Wisdom is as good as an inheritance, an advantage to those who see the sun.
For the protection of wisdom is like the protection of money, and the advantage of knowledge is that wisdom gives life to the one who possesses it.

In the first example (12), the verb קנה is placed in parallel with מכר, which has an almost exclusively economic meaning of 'selling' in its other occurrences, and thus strengthens the economic metaphorisation of the acquisition of wisdom (and other virtues) in the present verse. In his commentary on the book Job, Clines qualified the terminology used here as 'the unembarrassed adoption of the language of the marketplace'.[32] Example (13) portrays wisdom as an inheritance and as bringing advantage and protection. In his extensive study on the vocabulary of Qohelet, Schoors has argued that verse 11 does not defend the idea that wisdom can be inherited, but rather that it is as good as possessions.[33] The terms expressing 'advantage' in these verses, the cognates יתר and יתרון, are commercial in origin, as again Schoors has demonstrated, and as a result 'this commercial meaning colours also the metaphorical connotations it mostly adopts in Qoh'.[34] Verse 12a even explicitly equals wisdom's protection with that of money/silver.[35] A very similar expression can be found in Prov. 3:14, in which it is argued that the סחר of wisdom is better than that of silver, the Hebrew term literally designating either the trading of goods or the

---

32   D. Clines, *Job 21–37* (WBC, 18A), Nashville, TN 2006, 918.
33   A. Schoors, *The Preacher Has Sought to Find Pleasing Words. A Study of the Language of Qohelet. Part II. Vocabulary* (OLA, 143), Leuven 2004, 403.
34   Ibid., 426.
35   Sir. 51:28 (B) goes even a step further in claiming that whoever acquires wisdom, will acquire silver and gold.

ACQUIRING WISDOM

profit gained from such commercial traffic.[36] Also here, then, the acquisition of wisdom is conceptualised in what are essentially economic terms. The most extended description of the quest of wisdom in economic terms can be found in the second stanza of Job 28 (verses 12–19), after a first stanza in which this quest is compared to the digging for precious metals and minerals, as mentioned before. This chapter ultimately denies the possibility of ever acquiring wisdom, but this did not prevent the author to use a variegated metaphorical language describing it in terms of 'bartering and buying'.[37] Without discussing the passage at length, the terms put in bold below should be mentioned:

(14) Job 28:15–19

לא־יתן סגור תחתיה ולא ישקל כסף מחירה׃
לא־תסלה בכתם אופיר בשהם יקר וספיר׃
לא־יערכנה זהב וזכוכית ותמורתה כלי־פז׃
ראמות וגביש לא יזכר ומשך חכמה מפנינים׃
לא־יערכנה פטדת־כוש בכתם טהור לא תסלה׃ פ

15 It cannot be gotten for gold, and silver cannot be weighed out as its price.
16 It cannot be valued in the gold of Ophir, in precious onyx or sapphire.
17 Gold and glass cannot equal it, nor can it be exchanged for jewels of fine gold.
18 No mention shall be made of coral or of crystal; the price of wisdom is above pearls.
19 The chrysolite of Ethiopia cannot compare with it, nor can it be valued in pure gold.

Some of the highlighted terms are straightforwardly economic in origin: the noun מחיר is mostly used in the literal sense of 'price' or 'hire',[38] while the noun תמורה is commonly used for the exchange of goods. Also the verb שקל 'to weigh' is most frequently used in the specific meaning of weighing an amount of silver in order to pay with it, to the extent that the verb metonymically also came

---

36 The evaluation of wisdom as more precious than silver, gold and pearls is quite common the book of Proverbs: 4:7; 8:10, 11, 19; 16:16. The 'gain' of wisdom is not only described in trading/economic terms, as in the present verse (see e.g. Sir. 51:28 [B]), but also repeatedly in agricultural terms, viz. as the yield of wisdom conceptualised as a plant, see paragraph 2.8 on Cultivating Wisdom below.

37 Clines, *Job 21–37*, 918.

38 The use of the term מחיר in the context of the acquisition of wisdom is also found in Prov. 17:16.

to mean 'to pay' in a number of contexts.[39] The meaning of the rare verb סלה, which outside of this pericope only occurs in Lam. 4:2 in the form סלא, is hard to determine exactly: HAL proposes 'to pay', a suggestion rejected by Clines in favour of the meaning 'to weigh' and hence 'to value'.[40] Semantically speaking, these options are obviously closely related, as the price paid is in accordance with the value attributed to the object. The contexts of all three instances of the verb leave no doubt, however, that the verb is economic in origin. The verb ערך, finally, has the rather broad core meaning of 'to arrange', going for example from 'dressing' tables over 'drawing' battle arrays to 'drafting' arguments in court. From the meaning of 'ordering' objects, a less frequent meaning of 'to value, to evaluate', often in economic terms, was derived,[41] which is applicable here. A particular case of economic vocabulary is the noun מֶשֶׁךְ, of which the meaning is debated. The noun only occurs here and in Ps. 126:6, where it probably has the meaning of the sower's seed-carrying bag.[42] Commentators and translators therefore propose the same meaning in Job 28: 'a pouch of wisdom fetches more than rubies'.[43] Others connect the noun's meaning more closely to the verb's meaning of 'pulling up' and read the verse as comparing the acquisition of wisdom with the 'fishing' of corals.[44] As I have argued elsewhere,[45] in particular on the basis of the specific economic meaning of the verb משך and its cognate noun משיכה in Mishnaic Hebrew, the noun מֶשֶׁךְ should be translated as the 'acquisition/buying' of wisdom.[46]

What are the metaphorical implications of this very common use of economic vocabulary to describe the acquisition of wisdom? As in the case of the conceptualisation of the quest for wisdom as 'searching', also the economic

---

39   See e.g. Zech. 11:12: וישקלו את־שכרי שלשים כסף 'So they weighed out as my wages thirty shekels of silver', the point being not only that the silver was weighed, but also that the wages were paid to the prophet.

40   Clines, *Job 21–37*, 902.

41   The noun עֵרֶךְ underwent a similar semantic development from 'order' to 'value', the latter meaning having become quantitatively dominant.

42   So HAL, 610, proposing the semantic development 'pull off (skin)' > 'leather' > 'leather bag'.

43   Clines, *Job 21–37*, 893.

44   S.R. Driver and G.B. Gray, *A Critical and Exegetical Commentary on the Book of Job together with a New Translation* (ICC), Edinburgh 1921, 196; TOB: 'Et mieux vaudrait pêcher la sagesse que les perles'.

45   P. Van Hecke, *From Linguistics to Hermeneutics: A Functional and Cognitive Approach to Job 12–14* (SSN, 55), Leiden 2011, 315.

46   In the same vein, also the verb משך could be read, as in Mishnaic literature, as meaning 'to buy' in some instances, see e.g. Exod. 12:21; Jer. 31:13.

metaphors conceptualise wisdom as difficult to acquire, as coming at a high cost and effort. This is what differentiates acquiring or buying from simply taking into one's possession: it involves a serious investment, a (financial) effort on the part of the acquirer. Even though the two groups of metaphors (spatial and economic) are very different from each other, they share a number of higher-level characteristics and are therefore what Lakoff and Johnson would call 'coherent' metaphors.[47]

2.6 Grasping Wisdom

Just as the search for wisdom could result in staying in its vicinity, as described above, its finding as well as its acquisition results in a different form of vicinity, namely its possession. This possession is often conceptualised as grasping it and holding on to it, as the two following examples illustrate.

(15) Sir. 6:27b (A)   והחזקתה ואל תרפה
                           Grasp her and do not let her go.

(16) Prov. 3:18   עץ־חיים היא למחזיקים בה ותמכיה מאשר:
                           She is a tree of life to those who lay hold of her; those who hold her fast are called happy.

Although one could argue that the grasping is not a conceptualisation of the *acquisition* of wisdom, per se—and hence not in place in this contribution—the immediate context of example (15), viz. Sir. 6:26–27b, leave no doubt that the pursuit of wisdom is described here. Next to the verbs חזק hiphil[48] and תמך 'to grasp'[49] and the negative of the verb רפה '(not) to let lose',[50] featuring in the examples above, also the verbs נצר 'to guard, to keep' (Prov. 4:13) and the difficult hiphil of פוק (Prov. 3:13) express a similar conceptualisation.

2.7 Loving Wisdom

In most of the metaphors treated above, wisdom is conceptualised as an object.[51] Given the frequent personification of wisdom (as Lady Wisdom) in

---

47   Lakoff and Johnson, *Metaphors We Live By*, 97–105.
48   Also in Prov. 4:13.
49   Also in Sir. 4:13.
50   Also in Prov. 4:13.
51   Admittedly, pronominal and verbal forms referring to wisdom are grammatically feminine in Hebrew (as the word 'wisdom' is feminine, and Hebrew lacks the neuter), making it not always easy to decide whether a personification of wisdom is intended or not.

Classical Hebrew literature, it does not come as a surprise that also the acquisition of wisdom is repeatedly conceptualised as becoming acquainted and even loving her/it. A few examples illustrate this point.

(17) Prov. 7:4   אמר לחכמה אחתי את ומדע לבינה תקרא:
Say to wisdom, 'You are my sister', and call insight your intimate friend,

(18) Sir 4:12 (A)   אהביה אהבו חיים ומבקשיה יפיקו רצון מייי
Those who love her, love life, and those who seek her out win the Lord's favor.

In the first example, the book of Proverbs invites the addressee to become acquainted with wisdom as with a close relative or friend, and thus to 'familiarise' oneself with her. In other instances, the book of Proverbs urges the reader to come to 'love' wisdom (8:17, 21: 29:3). It is in the book of Ben Sira, however, that the desire to acquire wisdom is conceptualised in explicitly amorous and even erotic terms, see e.g. the following example:

(19) Sir. 51:19 (11QPs^a)   חריתי נפשי בה ופני לוא השיבותי
I burned with desire for her, and I did not turn away my face.

This erotic language has been observed by several authors in Sir. 51, and some authors, including the editor of the acrostic in the DJD series, J.A. Sanders, recognized many more allusions to erotic language, which would be emended or interpreted differently in later stages.[52] Di Lella, in his commentary, is much more reluctant to accept such allusions.[53] Recently, Balla analysed all of the explicit wisdom poems in Ben Sira and found sexual or erotic metaphors in each of them.[54] One example is the famous verse 6:19.

(20) Sir 6:19a (A)   כחורש וכקוצר קרב אליה וקוה לרב תבואתה
As though plowing and reaping,[55] draw close to her; then await her bountiful crops.

---

52   Sanders, *Psalms Scroll.*
53   Skehan and Di Lella, *Wisdom of Ben Sira*, 579.
54   I. Balla, *Ben Sira on Family, Gender, and Sexuality* (Deuterocanonical and Cognate Literature Series, 8), Berlin, New York 2011, 169–218.
55   Skehan follows the Greek in his translation and renders 'sowing'.

Balla argues that the 'ploughing' and 'sowing' (as the LXX has it) are themselves metaphorical euphemisms for sexual intercourse with personified Wisdom.[56]

2.8 Cultivating Wisdom

In my opinion, however, the expressions used in example (20) can better be understood as agricultural metaphor for the quest for wisdom, rare though it may be. For one thing, this reading fits better with the second part of the verse:

(21) Sir 6:19b (A)   כי בעבדתה מעט תעבוד ולמחר תאכל פריה
                     For in cultivating her you will labor but little, and soon you will eat of her fruits.

It is unconvincing to continue reading an erotic metaphor in 19b: firstly, the term עבד is the common term for tilling the ground (in continuity with the plowing and sowing/reaping of the previous line), but is never read as a euphemism for sexual intercourse; secondly, it is difficult to explain what it would mean that wisdom's lover would only have to labour little before being able to enjoy her fruits; thirdly, the terms תבואה and פרי usually refer to the yield of agricultural harvest, and are also used elsewhere to speak about wisdom's gains.[57] Moreover, wisdom is conceptualised as a plant yielding fruit also elsewhere in the book of Ben Sira, most notably in Sir. 24 (not extant in Hebrew) in which wisdom sings her own praises. In the verses 13–17, wisdom compares herself to a number of trees and plants, inviting those who yearn for her to eat her fruits.[58]

2.9 Carrying (the Yoke of) Wisdom

A final group of metaphors is only found in Ben Sira and in the Dead Sea Scrolls and conceptualises the pursuit of wisdom as carrying wisdom('s yoke) and accepting its fetters.

(22) Sir 6:25 (A)   הט שכמך ושאה ואל תקץ בתחבולתיה
                     Stoop your shoulders and carry her and be not irked at her bonds.

---

56   Balla, *Family, Gender and Sexuality*, 184–85; see J. Rogers, 'As Ploughing and Reaping Draw Near to Her', *OTE* 13 (2000), 364–79.

57   תבואה in Prov. 3:14 and 8:19, פרי in Prov. 3:14, although the terms could be also be taken to have a more economic meaning in these cases, viz. as 'revenue'.

58   The concept of eating and drinking from wisdom's produce is also found in Prov. 9:5 and in Sir. 51:24. Since it is not the acquisition of wisdom that is conceptualised in these cases, I do not deal with them in more depth here.

(23) 4Q421 Ia ii–b 10   עול חכמה
    the yoke of wisdom

Example (22) is part of the long admonition to strive for wisdom in Sir. 6, and is the last of a series of expressions referring to wisdom's weight and bonds. In verse 20–22, the poet describes how the stupid and fool cannot stand the weight of wisdom as a burdensome stone (verse 21 אבן משא), and rather throw off its burden. Verse 22 affirms with a rare word-play that instruction (מוּסָר) is true to her name, namely that it is a bond (מוֹסֵר).[59] In verse 24, only extant in Greek, the advice is then given to voluntarily put one's feet into her net, and one's neck into her collar, followed by the admonition of verse 25 quoted above. In verses 29–30, it is subsequently made clear how this net, collar, yoke and bonds will ultimately become the wiseman's apparel and adornment. The same advice is given at the end of the book, viz. in 51:26(B): וצואריכם בעלה הביאו ומשאו תשא נפשכם 'Submit your neck to her yoke, and may your soul carry its burden'.[60] Although the context of the expression עול חכמה in example (23) is broken, there is little doubt that the same conceptualisation is intended.

3   Conclusion

The survey presented in this contribution has demonstrated that the acquisition of wisdom is conceptualised with a large variety of metaphorical expressions. Many of these individual expressions share what metaphor studies would call a common source domain (e.g. spatial movement, economic transaction, agriculture) and can thus be regarded as belonging to a single consistent *conceptual* metaphor. This survey has attempted to provide a systematic overview of these different groups of metaphors and to show how they conceptualise the acquisition of wisdom in a consistent way. In the course of the presentation of the material, it has become clear, however, that these different groups mutually overlap. To name a few examples: the 'pursuit' of wisdom (2.3) partly overlaps with the 'love' for wisdom (2.7), when wisdom is conceptualised as a woman, and the wise as amorously running after her. The 'agricultural' (2.8) and 'economic' (2.5) conceptual metaphors share the concept that the 'acquisition' or the 'cultivation' of wisdom will 'bring profit' or 'bear fruit'.

---

59   I consider this wordplay more probable and more fitting in the context (the word מוּסָר actually occurring in verse 30), than the one proposed by Skehan and Di Lella, viz. reading מוּסָר as the homonym hophal participle, meaning 'withdrawn, turned away'.

60   Second part of the verse translation mine.

But also on a more abstract level, the metaphorical conceptualisations presented here display a strong degree of coherence, even if they do not portray the pursuit of wisdom in a single consistent image (pursuing animals and cultivating trees can hardly be united as one single image). What most metaphors have in common, however, is that they conceptualise wisdom as difficult to obtain, and the quest for it hence as demanding a strong effort, but one that is ultimately rewarding. Wisdom is alternatingly conceptualised as a hidden object that needs to be found, as an evasive animal or person that needs to be pursued, as an expensive object that comes at a high cost, as a plant that needs to be cultivated. The reward of these efforts is that one can enjoy its company, possess and grasp it, and profit from its fruits. The final group of metaphors (Carrying Wisdom's Yoke) obviously shares the concept of hardship with the other groups (wisdom is initially hard to bear), but seems to lack the concept of reward. What reward comes from bearing fetters? It is not without reason, then, that Sir. 6:29–30 steps outside of the metaphor and promises that wisdom's fetters will eventually become its bearers' adornment.

Finally, the survey presented above has again pointed to the necessity of avoiding both minimalist and maximalist positions when it comes to studying metaphors. The former will attempt to find more general or abstract meanings for metaphorically used terms, so as to undo them from their metaphorical potential. For example, when one does not recognise the economic background of the most common verb קנה 'to buy' in the context of wisdom, one may miss the overwhelming consistency across different metaphorical expressions conceptualising the acquisition of wisdom in terms of an economic activity. A maximalist position, on the other hand—typical for research dealing with one particular conceptual metaphor—may see the realisation of this metaphor in more expressions than was probably intended, and thus overstretch the metaphor's and the text's meaning potential. While there is no doubt that amorous and erotic language is used to describe the quest for wisdom, some scholars found instances of this conceptualisation also where they probably were absent, as I argued for example with regard to Sir. 6:19. In the end, however, this comes to show that the study of metaphor will always to some extent remain a matter of (informed) interpretation.

Aristobulus and the Universal Sabbath

J. Cornelis de Vos

1   Introduction

The Jewish exegete and philosopher Aristobulus lived in the second century BCE, probably in Alexandria. He was, as far as we know, the first Jew who used the allegorical method in commenting on the Bible. Aristobulus connected— just as his famous successor Philo of Alexandria about a century later—Jewish biblical tradition with the Hellenistic culture, and especially with philosophy. 'It was his intention to show that the Jewish Torah could, by the aid of the allegorical explanation, be made explicable and acceptable for philosophically skilled Greeks.'[1]

We know that Aristobulus wrote a large work.[2] Unfortunately, of this large work only five fragments are left. All five of them are passed on by Eusebius of Caesarea (ca. 263–ca. 339).[3] Parts of the fragments are also passed down by Clemens of Alexandria (ca. 150–ca. 215), who is, however, far less precise than Eusebius.[4] So I will adhere to the text of Eusebius in this contribution.

---

1   It was the intention of Aristobulus 'zu zeigen, daß sich mit Hilfe der allegorischen Auslegungsmethode die Thora der Juden in einer auch für philosophisch gebildete Griechen annehmbaren Weise erklären lasse' (N. Walter, 'Fragmente jüdisch-hellenistischer Exegeten: Aristobulos, Demetrios, Aristeas', in W.G. Kümmel [ed.], *Jüdische Schriften aus hellenistisch-römischer Zeit*. Bd. 3: *Unterweisung in Lehrhafter Form*. Lief. 2, Gütersloh 1975 [2. Aufl. 1980], 257–99 at 263).
2   Clemens of Alexandria, *Strom.* 5.99.7; cf. also Walter, 'Jüdisch-hellenistische Exegeten', 263.
3   The first fragment occurs within a larger quotation of Anatolius of Laodicaea († 282).
4   Therefore I only list the fragments in Eusebius; see for a full list of sources and testimonies N. Walter, *Der Thoraausleger Aristobulos: Untersuchungen zu seinen Fragmenten und zu pseudepigraphischen Resten der jüdisch-hellenistischen Literatur* (TU, 86), Berlin 1964, 7–9: frag. 1: Eusebius, *Hist. eccl.* 7.32.17–18; frag. 2: *Praep. ev.* 8.10.1–17; frag. 3: *Praep. ev.* 13.12.1–2; frag. 4: *Praep. ev.* 13.12.3–8; frag. 5: *Praep. ev.* 13.12.9–16 (partly also in *Praep. ev.* 7.14.1).—See for editions of the fragments of Aristobulus: A.-M. Denis, 'Fragmenta pseudepigraphorum quae supersunt graeca: Una cum historicorum et auctorum Judaeorum hellenistarum fragmentis', in: M. Black and A.-M. Denis (eds), *Apocalypsis Henochi Graece: Fragmenta pseudepigraphorum quae supersunt graeca* (PVTG, 3), Leiden 1970, 45–246 at 217–28; C.R. Holladay (ed.), *Fragments from Hellenistic Jewish Authors*. vol. 3: *Aristobulus* (Pseudepigrapha Series, 13), Chico, CA 1995.—See further K. Mras (ed.), *Eusebius Werke*. Bd. 8: *Die Praeparatio Evangelica* (GCS, 43), Berlin 1982; E. Schwartz and T. Mommsen (eds), *Eusebius Werke*. Bd. 9: *Historia Ecclesiastica* (GCS, 9), Berlin 1999; O. Stählin and L. Früchtel (eds), *Clemens*

In the following I will focus on fragment 5, which deals with the seventh day of creation. My aim is to show that Aristobulus tried to overrule his Egyptian or Alexandrine contemporaries by stating that the Jewish Sabbath is a cosmic and noetic principle and that the Jewish God, and only the Jewish God, created the cosmos and has pervaded this cosmos ever since.

2 The Seventh and the First Day of Creation

2.1 *In Short: How the Seventh and First Day Are Connected*

In fragment 5, Aristobulus connects the seventh day of creation with the first day. He argues as follows: God has given the seventh day as a day of rest to all humans. Rest enables contemplation. Contemplation has to do with knowledge, knowledge with light, and light comes from wisdom. As the light was created on the first day, the seventh and the first days are 'actually' the same. The cosmos was created in seven days, thus, the principle of seven not only stands for the noetic order but also for the cosmic order.

This was the short version. Aristobulus needed a few words more—although not that many—and presupposed some contemporary philosophical insights. Here comes the longer outline:

2.2 *God as Creator of the Whole Cosmos*

Aristobulus writes that God has established the whole cosmos (5:9). This is, right at the beginning of the fragment, a universal claim that the Jewish God is the creator of the universe. We know that with 'God' (ὁ θεός) he really meant 'his' God because in fragment 4, he replaced the word 'Zeus' in a quotation of Aratus with 'God'; directly after the quotation, he even admits that he replaced

---

Alexandrinus. Bd. 2: *Stromata Buch I–VI* (GCS, 52), Leipzig 1985; Stählin and Früchtel (eds), *Clemens Alexandrinus*. Bd. 3: *Stromata Buch VII und VIII; Excerpta ex Theodoto; Eclogae propheticae; Quis dives salvetur; Fragmente* (GCS, 17), Leipzig 1970.—See for translations of Aristobulus' fragments: A.Y. Collins, 'Aristobulus', in J.H. Charlesworth (ed.), *The Old Testament Pseudepigrapha.* Vol. 2: *Expansions of the Old Testament and Legends, Wisdom and Philosophical Literature, Prayers, Psalms, and Odes, Fragments of Lost Judeo-Hellenistic Works*, London 1985, 832–42; Holladay, *Aristobulus*; Walter, 'Jüdisch-hellenistische Exegeten'.— Introductions to the fragments of Aristobulus in the aforementioned translations, in A.-M. Denis, *Introduction aux pseudépigraphes grecs d'Ancien Testament* (SVTP, 1), Leiden 1970, 1216–37; and in K.M. Woschitz, *Parabiblica: Studien zur jüdischen Literatur in der hellenistisch-römischen Epoche; Tradierung—Vermittlung—Wandlung*, Wien 2005, 94–107.

'Zeus' and explains that he did that because it is God, not Zeus, who pervades the whole cosmos (4:6–7).[5]

Aristobulus uses the verb κατασκευάζω (5:9) for 'to create' which means 'to furnish, to equip fully', and that fits the meaning of κόσμος as 'ordered' or even 'decorated world'.[6] It is noteworthy that Aristobulus uses the derivate κατασκευή in the last paragraph of fragment 4 to denote the constitution of 'our', that is, the Jewish, law. This implicitly suggests a connection between the cosmos and the law although we do not know how much text there was, originally, between the fourth and the fifth fragment.

In a sophisticated way, Aristobulus makes clear that God had not only created the cosmos but that he also associated it with the pre-existent wisdom in some way:

> And one of our ancestors, Solomon, said more clearly and better that wisdom existed before heaven and earth. (frag. 5:11)

This is an allusion to Prov. 8:22–31.[7] Aristobulus does not mention God nor does he make the connection between God and wisdom explicit as in Proverbs where the personified wisdom is the object of God's acting. The Old Greek of Proverbs interpreted קנה in Prov. 8:22 that can mean both 'to acquire/to buy' and 'to create/to produce' as 'to create' (κτίζω) (sc. Wisdom).[8] This is probably also what Aristobulus means since in paragraph 9 he had said that God has established the whole cosmos, both heaven and earth; and he repeats this in similar words in paragraph 12. If God is the creator of the whole universe, he must also have created wisdom, even if it has a pre-existent origin. Since all

---

5   Cf. Acts 17:22–34 and the quotation of Aratus in v. 28.
6   H.G. Liddell et al., *A Greek-English Lexicon: Compiled by Henry George Liddell and Robert Scott. Revised and Augmented Throughout by Sir Henry Stuart Jones with the Assistance of Roderick McKenzie and with the Cooperation of Many Scholars*, Oxford 1996 (= LSJ), s.v. κατασκευάζω and κόσμος. LSJ renders as a second group of meanings of κόσμος 'ornament, decoration'.
7   Holladay (*Aristobulus*, 227–28 n. 128) is less sure about the allusion. He also considers Wisd. 6:22 and 9:9 as possible alluded texts (ibid., 227 n. 128).
8   See W.A. VanGemeren (ed.), *New International Dictionary of Old Testament Theology & Exegesis*, Grand Rapids, MI 1997 [repr. 1998], s.v. קנה.—Whether or not the translation of Proverbs into Greek was extant at Aristobulus' lifetime is not certain. The translation was probably made at the end of the second century BCE and, thus, post-dated Aristobulus; see F. Siegert, *Zwischen Hebräischer Bibel und Altem Testament: Eine Einführung in die Septuaginta* (Münsteraner Judaistische Studien, 9), Münster 2001, 42; cf. N. Fernández Marcos, *The Septuagint in Context: Introduction to the Greek Version of the Bible*, Atlanta, GA 2009, 314–15.

light has its origin in wisdom (5:10), God on the first day created the light out of his wisdom. This brings us to the next part.

2.3 Sabbath, Light, and Leisure

2.3.1 Life Is Troublesome

God has given rest to mankind because life is troublesome (κακόπαθος) for all (5:9). Later on, Aristobulus equates this rest with Sabbath (5:13). Such an explanatory statement of the Sabbath in 5:9 cannot be found in the biblical Sabbath commandments of either Decalogue version (Exod. 20:8–11; Deut. 5:12–15).[9] The word κακόπαθος, here translated with 'troublesome',[10] should rather be connected to the theory of ἀπάθεια, the avoidance of bad passions, namely distress, fear, lust, and delight that was one of the central concerns of the Stoa.[11] Aristobulus, thus, implicitly claims that the Sabbath is a day without κακοπάθειαι, without bad passions. The antonym of κακοπάθειαι is εὐπάθειαι; this is a technical term in the Stoic philosophy and points to sereneness that can only be achieved without being disturbed by passions (ἀτάραχος, cf. 5:10) and by living and acting according to the rational nature of the cosmos, the λόγος.[12] This implies—if it is allowed to interpret him in a Stoic way[13]—that for

---

9   At most, we could say that it is an amalgamation of the two explanatory statements: Creation/cosmos (Exod. 20:11) is connected with hardship of labour in Egypt (Deut. 5:15).

10   LSJ, s.v. κακοπάθεια κτλ.

11   M.-P. Engelmeier, 'Apathie', in J. Ritter (ed.), *Historisches Wörterbuch der Philosophie*, Basel 1971, 1:429–33, esp. 1:430–31. Also for the Cynics and Sceptics, ἀπαθεία was an important virtue. However, Aristobulus has more traits in common with the Stoics than with the Cynics and the Sceptics as will become clear in the following.

12   Cf. M. Forschner, 'Stoa; Stoizismus 1', in J. Ritter and K. Gründer (eds), *Historisches Wörterbuch der Philosophie*, Basel 1998, 10:176–84 at 182; for εὐπάθειαι G. Lieberg, 'Lust, Freude 1.', in J. Ritter and K. Gründer (eds), *Historisches Wörterbuch der Philosophie*, Basel 1980, 5:552–55; and for ἀταραξία in the late Stoa H. Reiner, 'Ataraxie', in Ritter, *Historisches Wörterbuch der Philosophie*, 1:593; Holladay, *Aristobulus*, 277 n. 126.

13   Aristobulus is called 'the Peripataean' by Clemens of Alexandria (*Strom.* 1.72.4) and Eusebius (*Praep. ev.* 9.6.6; 13.12.1). However, 'Grundlos nennen ihn die alten und die meisten modernen Gelehrten einen jüdischen Peripatetiker: man müsste schon einen sehr weiten Begriff dieser Bezeichnung zulassen, wenn sie nicht unmöglich sein soll; auch der Lehre des Peripatos stellte A. [Aristobulus] die Worte Salomons als besser und klarer (!) gegenüber und fühlte und nannte sich selbst einen Israeliten: darauf geht ἣ καθ' ἡμᾶς αἵρησις (Eus. 666 d), deren theologischer Grundanschauung alle Philosophen zustimmen, und deren Ausfluss das ganze jüdische (καθ' ἡμᾶς) Gesetz ist' (A. Gercke, *Aristobulus* 15 [Paulys Realencyclopädie der classischen Altertumswissenschaft, München 1895], 919–20). See also note 11.

Aristobulus the Sabbath is the day *par excellence* to exist in accordance with the *logos*, with the cosmic order.

2.3.2 God Gave Rest to Mankind

The word ἀνάπαυσις in 'God gave rest (ἀνάπαυσις) to mankind' (5:9; see also 5:13; cf. 5:11) means 'rest' but has the connotation 'upwards' by the prefix ἀνά. It is, in contradistinction to κατάπαυσις, a rest with an upward perspective, a rest which connects the resting subject with the transcendental sphere.[14] We may presume that Aristobulus used this word deliberately because the Septuagint of Gen 2:2–3 uses the verb καταπαύω for God's resting at Sabbath—with the prefix κατά, 'downwards', instead of ἀνά. Connected with this meaning of ἀνάπαυσις, κακόπαθος also gets a philosophical meaning.

2.3.3 God Created the Light

At the end of 5:9 Aristobulus equates the seventh day with the first day. However, the relative clause ἥ δὴ καὶ πρώτη is difficult to understand. It is difficult in two aspects: firstly, relating to syntax; and, secondly, relating to the discursive structure.

Is πρώτη an attributive adjective to φωτὸς γένεσις or a predicative adjective to ἥ? In the first case, it should be translated '[…] which (day) indeed is also the first […] beginning/creation of light'.[15] In the second case, it should be: '[…] which (day) indeed is also the first […]—(it is) the beginning/creation of light.'[16] I opt for the second translation because, firstly, ἑβδόμην ἡμέραν is apparently intentionally positioned at the end of the first clause in order to highlight the association of 'seventh' with 'first'. Secondly, the first genesis/creation/beginning is, in fact, pleonastic. Therefore I translate: 'which (day)

---

14 Later in history, ἀνάπαυσις became a technical term in Gnosis; see J. Helderman, *Die Anapausis im Evangelium Veritatis und in anderen Schriften der Nag Hammadi-Bibliothek: Eine vergleichende Untersuchung des valentinianisch-gnostischen Heilsgutes der Ruhe im Evangelium* (Nag Hammadi Studies, 18), Leiden 1984; S. Hagene, 'Der Weg in die eschatologische Sabbatruhe (Mt 11,28–30; Hebr 3,7–4,13 und 'Evangelium Veritatis')', in: K. Löning and M. Fassnacht (eds), *Rettendes Wissen: Studien zum Fortgang weisheitlichen Denkens im Frühjudentum und im frühen Christentum* (AOAT, 300), Münster 2002, 317–44.

15 Thus E.H. Gifford (ed.), *Eusebii Pamphili Evangelicae praeparationis libri 15*, Oxford 1903.

16 Thus Walter, 'Jüdisch-hellenistische Exegeten'; Collins, 'Aristobulus'; and Holladay, *Aristobulus*, 236–37 n. 160.

indeed might φυσικῶς[17] be called[18] the first (day), the creation of light, by which (light) all things can be seen together at the same time'.

Now I proceed to the problem of the discursive structure. The question at hand is: Why does Aristobulus connect the seventh day with the creation or beginning of light? And what does 'light' mean here precisely? To begin with the second question: does 'light' as an antonym of 'heavy' stand for a life without trouble, without bad passions?[19] Or does 'light' stand as an antonym of 'dark' for the ability to see? What speaks for the first interpretation is the foregoing explanatory statement that God gave the Sabbath, because life is troublesome (κακόπαθος); the subsequent phrase, in which 'seeing' is stressed speaks for the second interpretation. As 'light' is usually connected with seeing and metaphorically with understanding, either κακόπαθος must be understood differently, or the relative clause should be connected to a former thought in the paragraph. The word ἀνάπαυσις, the transcendence-oriented rest, presents itself as this former thought. Thus, the last sentence of 5:9 can also be *seen* in this *light*. Light enables seeing. That is easy enough to understand. But there is also a more philosophical interpretation. Τὰ πάντα, 'all things/the whole [cosmos]', relates to the works of creation that can be observed together at the same time (συνθεωρέω) because ἀνάπαυσις of the seventh day and φῶς of the first day are in some sense the same. All the works of creation, to which also the rest belongs—in antique ontology, everything that can be said has a counterpart in reality—point to divisions: the order of days, that is of time; and the order of things. Aristobulus explicitly goes into the divisions in 5:12:

> For it [the legislation] signifies that in six days he [God] made heaven and earth and all things which are in them in order that he might manifest the times and foreordain what precedes what with respect to order.

The verb συνθεωρέω in 5:9, literally 'to observe at the same time' also means 'to contemplate'.[20] Later on, Aristobulus states that humans have knowledge

---

17 See below (4.1.) on φυσικῶς.

18 See on ἄν + optative in a subordinate clause E. Bornemann, *Griechische Grammatik* ed. E. Risch, Braunschweig 1978 [2. Aufl. 2008], § 230.3–4.

19 See LSJ, s.v. φάος II: '*light*, as a metaph. for deliverance, happiness, victory, glory, etc'.

20 LSJ, s.v. συνθεωρέω. This reminds us of the Aristotelian *philosophia contemplativa* and his use of the verb θεωρεῖν; see L. Kerstens, 'Kontemplation', in J. Ritter (ed.), *Historisches Wörterbuch der Philosophie*, Basel 1976, 4:1024–26 at 1024. It points to observing the world as if you are God; see W. Kullmann, *Aristoteles und die moderne Wissenschaft* (Philosophie der Antike, 5), Stuttgart 1998, 248.

of human *and divine* things by this wisdom (5:12)—a thought that is well-documented in Stoic writings.[21] Not unlike God, humans can see all cosmic divisions together at the same time as one cosmic order. The day of leisure is the day of philosophy which is the day on which the (spiritual) light enables the noetic view of the whole cosmos. The instrument, the light, comes from wisdom. Since wisdom is pre-existent, it pervades the cosmos in time and matter. This has happened from the first day on, from the day God created the light.[22]

3 Ἕβδομος λόγος: An Ontological or an Epistemological Principle?

Before we proceed, we must dwell on the expression ἕβδομος λόγος that we find in 5:12 and 15. There is a lot of discussion about the meaning of this collocation.[23] The question is whether it points to a human faculty of perception, to the cosmic order, or to both.

There are a couple of parallels to ἕβδομος λόγος in early Jewish literature (Jesus Sirach, Philo, Testament of Reuben), with which Nikolaus Walter and Carl R. Holladay have already dealt extensively.[24] Thus, I can draw on their analyses. There are sources that support ἕβδομος λόγος or a similar conception with respect to the number of seven as referring to human faculties of perception and others as referring to the cosmic order. Thus there is no well-defined conception of ἕβδομος λόγος in the early Jewish literature.

The combination ἕβδομος λόγος itself occurs in Sir. 17:5, in the so-called Greek-II text.[25] This verse reads:

> They [humans] received [from the Lord] the use of the five works [ἐνεργήματα] of the Lord,
> as the sixth he gave them understanding [νοῦς] and divided it to them,

---

21 Holladay, *Aristobulus*, 232–33 n. 144.
22 It is possible that Aristobulus alludes with his equation of the first and seventh day of the week to the the seventh day of the month that was a feast of Apollo and that was equated with the first day of the month. Further, Apollo was associated to the sun, that is, with light, which reminds us of the association of Aristobulus' first-seventh day with the light; see Holladay, *Aristobulus*, 224–26 n. 123.
23 See the discussions in Walter, *Thoraausleger*, 68–81; and Holladay, *Aristobulus*, 236–37 n. 160.
24 See the previous note.
25 Text: J. Ziegler (ed.), *Sapientia Iesu Filii Sirach* (Septuaginta: Vetus Testamentum Graecum. Auctoritate Academiae Scientiarum Gottingensis editum, 12/2), Göttingen 1980.

and as the seventh the word [τὸν ἕβδομον λόγον] as the translator of his works. (Transl. Skehan/Di Lella)[26]

However, this text does not combine the seven 'works' of humans with the seventh day of creation. This is different in Philo's *Hypothetica*. There he explains what the Jews do and do not do on Sabbath (7.12–20). In *Hypoth.* 7.20 the combination ἕβδομος λόγος occurs, although here with respect to the seventh year, that is, the Sabbath year. Nevertheless, this comment is interesting for us because 'both physicians, and investigators of natural history, and philosophers, [...] discuss this law about the seventh year, as to the effect which it has on the nature of the universe, and especially on the nature of man' (transl. Yonge).[27] We see a combination of the elements seven, cosmos, and human being.

However, we do not have a connection of a concept of ἕβδομος λόγος with at least the seventh day of creation in the aforementioned parallels. So we have to look for thematically closer parallels. The closest ones can be found in the works of Philo: *Creation* 117, *Abraham* 28–30, and *Alleg. Interpr.* 1.16–19. In his treatment of the creation of the world, Philo, when commenting on the seventh day of creation, deals extensively with the number seven (*Creation* 89–127). After a long introduction on the number itself that is based on Pythagorean speculations on numbers, he shows where in nature seven can be found.[28] He then writes that apart from the leading faculty (τὸ ἡγεμονικόν) humans have seven faculties, 'namely five senses, the faculty of speech (φωνητήριον ὄργανον), last that of generation (τὸ γόνιμον)' (*Creation* 117; transl. Colson/Whitaker).[29] Philo uses the soul theory of the Stoics who knew eight abilities of the soul, the five senses, the faculty of voice, the faculty of procreation, as well as the leading faculty ἡγεμονικόν, where the senses come together and which is the

---

[26] P.W. Skehan and A.A. Di Lella, *The Wisdom of Ben Sira: A New Translation with Notes* (AB, 39), New York 1987, 276. G. Sauer, *Jesus Sirach/Ben Sira* (ATD Apokryphen, 1), Göttingen 2000, 141, who seems to imply that λόγος is in Sir 17:5 the 'Möglichkeit der Reflexion'.

[27] C.D. Yonge, *The Works of Philo: Complete and Unabridged* new updated ed., 9th print, Peabody, MA 2008.

[28] See on number speculation among Pythagoraeans an on the speculation on the number seven among Jews in the tradition of the Pythagoraeans, among others, Walter, *Thoraausleger*, 160–62; Holladay, *Aristobulus*, 225–26 n. 123; L. Doering, *Schabbat: Sabbathalacha und- praxis im antiken Judentum und Urchristentum* (TSAJ, 78), Tübingen 1999, 310–11; Woschitz, *Parabiblica*, 99–100; 102–5.

[29] F.H. Colson and G.H. Whitaker (eds), *Philo*. Vol. 1 (LCL, 226), Cambridge, MA 1929 [2004].

possibility of reflection.³⁰ He deliberately mentions the leading faculty apart from the other senses so that he can connect the seventh day of creation in an allegorical way with seven parts of the human soul.³¹

Philo does something similar in *On the Life of Abraham*.³² He explains that Noah means 'rest'. He then writes that God gave 'the seventh day, which the Hebrews call Sabbath, the name of rest' (*Abraham* 28; transl. Colson).³³ He connects the number of seven with the five human senses, the faculty of speech (προφορικὸς λόγος), and with 'the dominant mind' (ἡγεμόνον νοῦς) (*Abraham* 29–30). Whereas Philo was dependent on the eightfold Stoic division of the Stoa in *On the Creation of the World*, here, in his *Allegorical Interpretation*, he presents a sevenfold division whereby the seventh is the νοῦς.³⁴ This reminds us of ἕβδομος λόγος since λόγος and νοῦς can be synonyms in Stoic thought.

An even closer parallel can be found in Philo's allegorical interpretation of the biblical text about the seventh day of creation. Again, the soul is only divided into seven parts, of which the seventh is 'the holy Reason of which Seven is the keynote [ὁ κατὰ ἑβδομάδα ἅγιος λόγος]' (*Alleg. Interpr.* 1.16; transl. Colson/Whitaker).³⁵ Now we have the λόγος as a seventh part, just like in fragment 5 of Aristobulus.³⁶ The interesting thing is that Philo follows this by connecting seven with light: 'God both blesses and makes holy the dispositions set in motion in harmony with the seventh and truly Divine light' (*Alleg.*

30   H. von Arnim (ed.), *Stoicorum veterum fragmenta* (Sammlung wissenschaftlicher Commentare), Leipzig 1903–1905 [München 2004], 1:39, Nr. 143, 2:225–7, Nrs. 823–33; cf., for example, Porphyrius (SVF 2:226, nr. 830): αὐτίκα οἱ μὲν ἀπὸ τῆς Στοᾶς ὀκταμερῆ τὴν ψυχὴν θέντες καὶ πέντε μὲν μέρη τὰ αἰσθητικὰ λαβόντες, ἕκτον δὲ τὸ φωνητικὸν καὶ ἕβδομον τὸ σπερματικόν, τὸ λοιπὸν τὸ ἡγεμονικὸν [...]; see further J. Annas, *Hellenistic Philosophy of Mind* (Hellenistic Culture and Society, 8), Berkeley 1992, 61–70, and Walter, *Thoraausleger*, 69.
31   Cf. *Worse* 168, 172, 173; *Agriculture* 30; QG 1.75.
32   See Walter, *Thoraausleger*, 69–70.
33   F.H. Colson (ed.), Philo. Vol. 6 (LCL, 289), Cambridge, MA 1935. I am not sure if this phrase can be singled out as a gloss as Walter (*Thoraausleger*, 73–74) and others with him state.
34   Cf. *Heir* 225 where Philo writes that the soul has three parts that are each divided into two, 'making six parts in all'. The seventh part is 'the holy and divine Word, the All-severer' (ibid.). This All-severer (τομεὺς [...] ἁπάντων) alludes to the λόγος (that is, the divine Word) as the one who severs the three animals of the covenant in Gen 15:9–11 (*Heir* 215; cf. 219); text and translation: F.H. Colson and G.H. Whitaker (eds), *Philo*. Vol. 4 (LCL, 261), Cambridge, MA 1932 [2005]. It is not really clear which six parts Philo means. It could be νοῦς, θύμος, and ἐπιθυμία or ψυχή, λόγος, and αἴσθησις (each part divided into two).
35   Colson and Whitaker, *Philo*. Vol. 1.
36   A few paragraphs before, however, Philo described the soul as consisting of seven parts, the five senses, the organ of speech, and the genital organ (*Alleg. Interpr.* 1.11). Please note that Philo does not have a consistent theory of the soul.

Interpr. 1.17). This divine light maintains the existence of the world and continually renews its creation (1.18)—in Philo's own words:

> [T]he reason why the man that guides himself in accordance with the seventh and perfect light is both of good understanding and holy, is that the formation of things moral ceases with this day's advent. For indeed, the matter stands thus; when that most brilliant and truly divine light of virtue has dawned, the creation of that whose nature is of the contrary kind comes to a stop. But we pointed outh that God when ceasing or rather causing to cease, does not cease making, but begins the creating of other things, since He is not a mere artificer, but also Father of the things, that are coming into being. (*Alleg. Interpr.* 1.18, transl. Colson/Whitaker)

We definitively have a connection of a noetic and a cosmic meaning of seven mediated by 'the holy Reason' that can be equated with 'the divine light'. This is quite an exact thematic parallel to Aristobulus' fifth fragment.[37] Nikolaus Walter even goes so far as to write that the Philonic text expresses the same thought as in fragment 5, that the divine order coins the number seven that works both in cosmos and in the human ψυχή.[38]

Nevertheless, and somewhat surprising, Walter comprehends ἕβδομος λόγος in Aristobulus' fifth fragment as a cosmic principle, not as parts of the soul. His three main arguments are:[39] (1) This understanding fits the content better than the other two concepts, and one is not dependent on external Stoic evidence; (2) Walter cannot imagine that Aristobulus would have said: God has established the seventh day to indicate that the human soul has seven parts or to point to the *logos* as the leading principle of that soul; (3) all the quotations from pagan authors at the end of fragment 5 deal with seven as a cosmic principle.

I agree with the arguments of Walter except with the second. Of course, Aristobulus did not want to express that God established the seventh only to indicate that the human soul has seven parts; and, yes, the quotations at the

---

37   See Walter, *Thoraausleger*, 78: 'Der ganze Zusammenhang (schon von 1 2 ab) ist ohne Zweifel mit Aristobulos' F 5 (PE XIII 12,9–16) thematisch verwandt'. Cf. also *Spec. Laws* 2.59: 'For seven reveals as completed what six has produced, and therefore it may be quite rightly entitled the birthday of the world, whereon the Father's perfect work, compounded of perfect parts, was revealed as what it was'; transl. F.H. Colson, *Philo*. Vol. 7 (LCL, 320), Cambridge, MA 1937 [2006].

38   Walter, *Thoraausleger*, 78.

39   Walter, *Thoraausleger*, 71.

end of fragment 5 are all about seven as a cosmic principle (although 5:15 also connects the ἕβδομος λόγος with truth and knowledge of truth). However, it is very likely that Aristobulus points to the *logos* with the seven-structure as the cosmic order *and* as the leading principle of the soul. Cosmic and eidetic, or ontological and epistemological principles are not to be separated here.[40] The *logos* of the soul is in alignment with the *logos* of the whole cosmos. The cosmos is divided and ordered according to the seven-structure, and this seven-structure is the eidetic principle to see this cosmic structure together (συνθεωρεῖν), to contemplate the cosmos. In 5:15, the text already mentioned, it sounds like this:

> He [Homer] thereby signifies that away from the forgetfulness and evil of the soul, by means of the principle of seven [ἕβδομος λόγος] in accordance with the truth, the things mentioned before are left behind and we receive knowledge of the truth, as has been said above.

The phrase 'As has been said before' refers to 5:12 which means that knowledge of the truth can be equated with knowledge of human and divine things.[41] The cosmological principle clearly functions also as an epistemological principle.[42]

So, in fact, we do not really need the works of Philo to comprehend the seven-principle in Aristobulus' fifth fragment as both noetic and cosmological. However, Philo, though not only he, teaches us that the number seven was typically connected to the seven faculties or to seven of the eight faculties of the human soul. Philo, just like Aristobulus, dwells, in addition, on the meaning that God created the world in six days and gave rest, the Sabbath, on the seventh day. We do not know exactly whether Philo knew the works of Aristobulus. In case he did not know them, he probably knew the speculations

---

40   Cf. Doering, *Schabbat*, 312: 'In jedem Fall handelt es sich in F 5,9 um einen Brückenschlag von Ontischem und Noetischem, von göttlichem Schöpfungswerk und menschlicher Erkenntnis: Der siebte Tag erschließt den Kosmos. Auch wenn das Licht bereits am ersten Tag geschaffen ist, wird es >Uns< doch erst im siebten Tag zugeeignet'.

41   Differently Holladay, *Aristobulus*, 237 n. 160: προειρημένα—Holladay favours this form from the apparatus instead of προείρηται—in 5:15 refers to the immediately foregoing context.

42   It seems as if Walter suffered from 'Systemzwang'. In a footnote he opts, just like Binde (R. Binde, *Aristobulische Studien* [Programme des Königlichen Evangelischen Gymnasiums zu Groß-Glogau], Glogau 1869–1870, 2:15–16) and I myself for both alternatives: 'Meint man, an der Übersetzung von λόγος mit "Vernunft" festhalten zu müssen, so ist Bindes Übersetzung von ἕβδομος λόγος mit "auf das Siebenverhältnis [aller kosmischen Vorgänge] sich gründende Vernunft" [...] erwägenswert' (Walter, *Thoraausleger*, 75 n. 3).

of Aristobulus about the meaning of the Sabbath and therewith of the seventh day. So I think we may connect Aristobulus and Philo as they probably lived in the same city, the same Jewish-Hellenistic milieu, and wrote about similar themes in a similar way.[43]

Much of Aristobulus' thought reminds us of Stoic thought.[44] Therefore, the understanding of ἕβδομος λόγος in the Stoic sense is likely. The innovation of Aristobulus is that he combines both the Stoic soul theory and the Stoic conception of λόγος with the seventh day of creation and the Sabbath as a simultaneously cosmic and noetic principle.

4   Φυσικῶς and ἔννομος

Besides ἕβδομος λόγος, there are two other key concepts that must be scrutinized: φυσικῶς and ἔννομος.

4.1   *Φυσικῶς*

Φυσικῶς belongs to one of the methods of allegoresis, a method to deal with an allegory.[45] Allegory, as is well-known, is a trope whereby one thing is used to speak of another. That what is said or written does not (only) have the meaning of the content on the plain text level, but another, deeper meaning (ὑπόνοια).[46] What other meanings? The Stoic allegorical method worked mainly with two kinds of allegoresis: the psychological and the physiological. The first form implies that what is said or written refers, in fact, to the soul, the *psyche*. The second form implies that what is said or written refers, in fact, to nature.

---

43   P. Borgen, 'Philo of Alexandria', in M.E. Stone (ed.), *Jewish Writings of the Second Temple Period: Apocrypha, Pseudepigrapha, Qumran, Sectarian Writings, Philo, Josephus* (CRINT 2/2), Assen 1984, 233–82, here 274–79. Borgen even mentions Aristobulus a predecessor of Philo (ibid., 274).

44   But not everything. Aristobulus also uses Pythagoraean and Peripatetic thought.

45   Different: Doering, *Schabbat*, 310 n. 140: 'Hier geht es nicht eigentlich um Allegorie, sondern um Arithmologie'.

46   See, among others, M. Hay, 'Defining Allegory in Philo's Exegetical World', SBLSP 33 = 130 (1994), 55–68, at 55–56; B.L. Mack, 'Weisheit und Allegorie bei Philo von Alexandrien', *Studia Philonica* 5 (1978), 57–105; M.R. Niehoff, *Jewish Exegesis and Homeric Scholarship in Alexandria*, Cambridge 2011; Niehoff, 'Jüdische Bibelexegese im Spiegel alexandrinischer Homerforschung', BN 148 (2011), 19–33; F. Siegert, 'Early Jewish Interpretation in a Hellenistic Style', in M. Sæbø (ed.), *Hebrew Bible, Old Testament: The History of Its Interpretation*. Vol. 1: *From the Beginnings to the Middle Ages (until 1300); Antiquity*, Göttingen 1996, 130–98.

In 5:9, the seventh day is called φυσικῶς⁴⁷ the first day; thus, it is, in fact, the first day according to nature, in a natural way, or more specifically: according to the laws of nature.⁴⁸ The question at hand is: What does 'nature' exactly mean here? Of course, Aristobulus knew that days are natural time divisions. But how, then, did he comprise 'nature'? The simplest definition of 'nature' is 'the things that are, reality'. For the Stoa, on which, as we have seen, Aristobulus heavily draws, nature is both the whole cosmos as well as the human *physis*.⁴⁹ The human *physis* as part-nature corresponds to the cosmos as all-nature. As is well-known, virtue or 'the good' in Stoic ethics is achieved by living according to nature. All-nature is shaped by the divine *logos*, which is the same as the divine cosmic law or order which pervades all things.⁵⁰

It is clear that for Aristobulus the 'seven-logos', which I translated as 'seven-principle', is the *logos* par excellence, the source of order and of virtue; and since all-nature corresponds to the human nature, the 'seven-logos' is also the epistemological source of the previously mentioned goods which humans can comprehend with their intellect (νοῦς).

4.2 Ἔννομος

The law for the Stoics is the law of nature; wisdom or virtue is living according to nature or the law of nature. One does not, in fact, need a written version of this law. Aristobulus being a Jew has a written version of the law, which he calls 'our legislation' (5:11) and to which he also refers with the expression 'our books' (5:13). In 5:12 he equates the law of nature and the written Jewish legislation, the Torah:

> And it [the legislation] has shown plainly that it [the seventh day] is ἔννομος for us as a sign of the seven-principle which is established around us, by which we have knowledge of human and divine matters.

---

47   Cf. Aristobulus at Eusebius, *Praep. ev.* 8.10.2 (= Fragment 2:2).
48   See Walter, 'Jüdisch-hellenistische Exegeten', 270 n. 2b: '"seinem Wesen, seinem wirklichen, eigentlichen Sinne nach"; für Aristobulus heißt das in den fraglichen Fällen: allegorisch (vg. PseuAris 143f. 171; Philon, Post C 60 u.ö.)'; Siegert, 'Early', 139: 'being said with a deeper meaning belonging to natural science'; Collins, 'Aristobulus', 841 n. b: 'or "in a way corresponding to nature"'.
49   F.P. Hager, 'Natur I', in J. Ritter and K. Gründer (eds), *Historisches Wörterbuch der Philosophie*. Bd. 6, Basel 1976, 421–41, 433–34.
50   L. Brisson, 'Natur, Naturphilosophie', in H. Cancik (ed.), *Der neue Pauly: Enzyklopädie der Antike*. Bd. 8, Stuttgart 2000, 728–36.

Aristobulus does not use νόμος, 'law', or νομοθεσία, 'legislation', here. Instead he uses ἔννομος. Ἔννομος which means 'ordained by law, legally, legally binding' is not the law itself; it is only the *expression* of the law of nature which is identical with the seven-principle.[51] By the way, if he had said: 'our law ordains' and so on, he would not have convinced his non-Jewish contemporaries.

5 Contextualising the Universal Sabbath Claim

In fact, Aristobulus overrules his non-Jewish contemporaries with his Sabbath speculations—I would say in a rather sophisticated way. He did that by proclaiming and defending. He proclaimed the following things:

(1) He proclaimed the Jewish God
    a) as the creator of the whole cosmos;
    b) as the creator of the light out of his pre-existent wisdom
    c) and as the creator of the Sabbath as a potentiality to devote oneself to wisdom; in other words, as the day of contemplation;
    d) as the creator of the logical structure of nature, that is, the seven-structure, by which he pervades the whole cosmos.
(2) He proclaimed the seven-structure both
    a) as an ontological
    b) and as an epistemological principle.
(3) He proclaimed the Jewish law as an expression of the logical structure of the world and of knowledge.

I now come to the defending part. This was also an apology of the Jewish law, traditions and customs. By proclaiming the Sabbath as a day of rest, he defended

(1) the custom of the Jewish Sabbath in its non-Jewish, probably Alexandrian, surrounding;
(2) the Jewish law as the most basic book of philosophy;
(3) a Jewish ancestor, Solomon, as the one who verbalised this philosophy earlier, clearer, and better than the Greek philosophers.
(4) He shows that ancient Greek poets already borrowed from the Torah in stressing the importance of 'seven'.

---

51 Against Holladay, *Aristobulus*, 230 n. 141: 'inherent law of nature' (ibid. 185); see the refutation in Doering, *Schabbat*, 314.

Text and Translation of Aristobulus, Frag. 5

In: Eusebius, *Praep. ev.* 13.12.9–16[52]

9 [Eusebius:]
Τούτοις ἑξῆς μεθ' ἕτερα ἐπιλέγει·

[Aristobulus:]
Ἐχομένως δ' ἐστὶν ὡς ὁ θεός, <ὃς> τὸν ὅλον κόσμον κατεσκεύακε, καὶ δέδωκεν ἀνάπαυσιν ἡμῖν, διὰ τὸ κακόπαθον εἶναι πᾶσι τὴν βιοτήν, ἑβδόμην ἡμέραν, ἢ δὴ καὶ πρώτη φυσικῶς ἂν λέγοιτο φωτὸς γένεσις, ἐν ᾧ τὰ πάντα συνθεωρεῖται.

10 μεταφέροιτο δ' ἂν τὸ αὐτὸ καὶ ἐπὶ τῆς σοφίας· τὸ γὰρ πᾶν φῶς ἐστιν ἐξ αὐτῆς.

καί τινες εἰρήκασι τῶν ἐκ τῆς αἱρέσεως ὄντες<τῆς> ἐκ τοῦ Περιπάτου λαμπτῆρος αὐτὴν ἔχειν τάξιν· ἀκολουθοῦντες γὰρ αὐτῇ συνεχῶς ἀτάραχοι καταστήσονται δι' ὅλου τοῦ βίου.
11 σαφέστερον δὲ καὶ κάλλιον τῶν ἡμετέρων προγόνων τις εἶπε Σολομῶν αὐτὴν πρὸ οὐρανοῦ καὶ γῆς ὑπάρχειν· τὸ δὴ σύμφωνόν ἐστι τῷ προειρημένῳ.

τὸ δὲ διασαφούμενον διὰ τῆς νομοθεσίας ἀποπεπαυκέναι τὸν θεὸν ἐν αὐτῇ, τοῦτο οὐχ, ὥς τινες ὑπολαμβάνουσι, μηκέτι ποιεῖν τι τὸν θεὸν καθέστηκεν, ἀλλ' ἐπὶ τῷ κατὰ πεπαυκέναι τὴν τάξιν αὐτῶν οὕτως εἰς πάντα τὸν χρόνον τεταχέναι.

9 [Eusebius:]
Following these things, after other (remarks), he adds:

[Aristobulus:]
And connected (with this) is (the fact) that God, who has established the whole cosmos, has also given us as a rest— because life is troublesome for all—, the seventh day, which (day) indeed might φυσικῶς be called the first (day) also, the creation of light, by which (light) all things can be seen together at the same time.

10 And the same thing might be said metaphorically about wisdom also. For all light has its origin in it.

And some of those belonging to the Peripatetic school have said that it (i.e., wisdom) holds the place of a lantern; for as long as they follow it unremittingly, they will be calm through their whole life.
11 And one of our ancestors, Solomon, said more clearly and in a better way that wisdom existed before heaven and earth; which indeed agrees with what has been said above.

And it is plainly said by our legislation that God rested on it (i.e., the seventh day). This does not mean, as some interpret, that God no longer does anything. It means that, after he had finished ordering all things, he so orders them for all time.

---

[52] Text: K. Mras (ed.), *Eusebius Werke*. Bd. 8: *Die Praeparatio Evangelica* (GCS, 43,1–2), Berlin 1954/1956. The translation leans on A.Y. Collins, 'Aristobulus', OTP 2: 832–42.

12 σημαίνει γὰρ ὡς ἐν ἓξ ἡμέραις ἐποίησε τόν τε οὐρανὸν καὶ τὴν γῆν καὶ πάντα τὰ ἐν αὐτοῖς, ἵνα τοὺς χρόνους δηλώσῃ καὶ τὴν τάξιν προείπῃ τί τίνος προτερεῖ.

τάξας γὰρ, οὕτως αὐτὰ συνέχει καὶ μεταποιεῖ.

διασεσάφηκε δ' ἡμῖν αὐτὴν ἔννομον ἕνεκεν σημείου τοῦ περὶ ἡμᾶς ἑβδόμου λόγου καθεστῶτος, ἐν ᾧ γνῶσιν ἔχομεν ἀνθρωπίνων καὶ θείων πραγμάτων.

13 δι' ἑβδομάδων δὲ καὶ πᾶς ὁ κόσμος κυκλεῖται τῶν ζωογονουμένων καὶ τῶν φυομένων ἁπάντων· τῷ δὲ σάββατον αὐτὴν προσαγορεύεσθαι διερμηνεύεται ἀνάπαυσις οὖσα.
διασαφεῖ δὲ καὶ Ὅμηρος καὶ Ἡσίοδος, μετειληφότες ἐκ τῶν ἡμετέρων βιβλίων ἱερὰν εἶναι.
Ἡσίοδος μὲν οὕτως·
    πρῶτον ἔνη τετράς τε καὶ ἑβδόμη ἱερὸν ἦμαρ·
καὶ πάλιν λέγει·
    ἑβδομάτη δ' αὖτις λαμπρὸν φάος ἠελίοιο.

14 Ὅμηρος δὲ οὕτω λέγει·
    ἑβδομάτη δή ἔπειτα κατήλυθεν, ἱερὸν ἦμαρ·
καὶ πάλιν·
    ἕβδομον ἦμαρ ἔην καὶ τῷ τετέλεστο ἅπαντα
καί·
    ἑβδομάτῃ δ' ἠοῖ λίπομεν ῥόον ἐξ Ἀχέροντος.

12 For it (i.e., the legislation) signifies that *in six days* he (i.e., God) *made heaven and earth and all things which are in them* in order that he might manifest the times and foreordain what precedes what with respect to order.
For, having set all things in order, he maintains and alters them so (i.e., in accordance with that order).
And it (i.e., the legislation) has shown plainly that it (i.e., the seventh day) is ἔννομον for us, as a sign of the seven-principle which is established around us, by which we have knowledge of human and divine matters.

13 And indeed all the cosmos of all living beings and growing things revolves in series of sevens. That it is called 'Sabbath' means in translation 'rest'.

And both Homer and Hesiod, having taken information from our books, say clearly that the seventh day is holy.
Hesiod (speaks) so:
    To begin with, (the) first, (the) fourth, and (the) seventh, (each) a holy day;
and again he says:
    And on the seventh day (is) again the bright light of the sun.

14 And Homer speaks so:
    And then indeed the seventh day returned, a holy day;
and again:
    It was the seventh day and on it all things had been completed.
and:
    And on the seventh morning we left the stream of Acheron.

15 τοῦτο δὴ σημαίνων, ὡς ἀπὸ τῆς κατὰ ψυχὴν λήθης καὶ κακίας ἐν τῷ κατὰ ἀλήθειαν ἑβδόμῳ λόγῳ καταλιμπάνεται τὰ προειρημένα καὶ γνῶσιν ἀληθείας λαμβάνομεν, καθὼς προείρηται.

16 Λίνος δέ φησιν οὕτως·
ἑβδομάτῃ δ' ἠοῖ τετελεσμένα πάντα τέτυκται.
καὶ πάλιν·
ἑβδόμη εἰν ἀγαθοῖς καὶ ἑβδόμη ἐστὶ γενέθλη
καί·
ἑβδόμη ἐν πρώτοισι καὶ ἑβδόμη ἐστὶ τελείη
<καί·>
ἑπτὰ δὲ πάντα τέτυκται ἐν οὐρανῷ ἀστερόεντι, ἐν κύκλοισι φανέντ' ἐπιτελλομένοις ἐνιαυτοῖς.

[Eusebius:]
Τὰ μὲν οὖν Ἀριστοβούλου τοιαῦτα.

15 He (i.e., Homer) thereby signifies that away from the forgetfulness and evil of the soul, by means of the seven-principle in accordance with the truth, the things mentioned before are left behind and we receive knowledge of the truth, as has been said above.

16 And Linus speaks so:
And on the seventh morning all things were made complete;
and again:
(The) seventh (day) is of good quality and (the) seventh (day) is birth;
and:
(The) seventh (day) is among the prime (numbers) and (the) seventh (day) is perfect;
<and:>
And all seven (heavenly bodies) have been created in the starry heaven, Shining in their orbits in the revolving years.

[Eusebius:]
Such then are the remarks of Aristobulus.

Divine Judgment and Reward in Ecclesiastes

Stuart Weeks

In Ecclesiastes 8:12–13, Qohelet expresses with unusual clarity, by his standards, the opinion that things will work out well for those who fear God, but not for the wicked: whoever has no fear before God will fail to prolong his own life. This claim is sandwiched, however, between an acknowledgment that sinners may sometimes get away with it for a very long time (8:10–12), and an observation that what happens to the righteous and wicked seems sometimes to be the wrong way round, so that people do not always get what they deserve, or deserve what they get. In 3:16–17, similarly, the claim that God will judge follows straight after an observation that guilt seems to occupy the place of innocence, and directly before a reminder that humans see only annihilation, like animals, for all of themselves (3:18–21).[1] In general, although Qohelet seems to insist on the reality of a divine judgment, he seems also to present it as something that runs counter to common human experience. It is, furthermore, a belief that seems to sit uncomfortably with his insistence that humans, in possession of limited lives over which they have little control, should focus their attention on finding pleasure in what they do. When 11:9 famously brings both beliefs together by calling on the young to follow their hearts, but also to remember that they will be brought to a reckoning for their actions, there

---

1   3:19–20 recount straightforwardly enough the single מקרה of humans and animals, emphasizing that both die identically, and both decompose (cf. 9:2–3, where there is a single מקרה for all humans). The following verse 21, however, raises the possibility that there is an indiscernible difference between them: nobody can know whether, although they apparently share a single רוח (3:19), the רוח of humans will actually rise at death and that of the animals sink. The reference is presumably to the idea that human breath returns to God, stated in 12:7, but the point is that any actual or potential distinction between humans and animals at death remains invisible, while the similarities between their ends are manifest. Correspondingly, it seems unlikely that the much more obscure 3:18 should be read as a statement that humans actually *are* identical to animals. I read לברם האלהים as coordinate with ולראות…המה, so God is going to distinguish, while they (humans) are going to see something else for themselves (להם): that they are cattle (שהם בהמה). The difficulties arise largely from the word-order of the last clause: שהם בהמה המה להם, which is surely geared more to rhythm and assonance than to clarity. The deferment of the subject has provoked many readers, ancient and modern, to take לראות as a hiphil form, and so to retain God as subject, but this not only renders המה redundant and problematic, it also suggests that the writer was careless enough to introduce a confusing ambiguity through unusual and unnecessary syncopation of the ה.

may be no strict contradiction, but the juxtaposition is curious, and each part of the verse seems to undermine the force of the other. It is little wonder that Qohelet's assertions about judgment have played a significant role in discussions about the coherence of Ecclesiastes, and in theories about the redactional history of the book.[2]

I do not intend to argue in this paper that divine judgment is, on the contrary, a central element in Qohelet's thinking, or that it does, in fact, sit comfortably with all that he has to say. It seems possible, indeed, that some of the points to which Qohelet seems much more attached might be expressed more clearly and persuasively if he did not introduce judgment as a complication. That is not a good reason to assume that we are dealing with the work of some pious redactor in the references to judgment, but it does raise important questions about the reason why Qohelet should have chosen to adopt a theme so alien to much else in his speech, and it is my purpose in this short paper to suggest that it serves not as an idea that he wishes to promote, but as an assumption that he expects his readers to hold. Divine judgement, in other words, is a theological *datum*, which Qohelet feels obliged to square with his ideas. He does, in fact, find ways in which to use it as evidence for the case which he is trying to make, but because it is not itself the focus of his interest, he fails either to deal with it systematically or to pursue properly certain of its implications:

If we want to know what Qohelet understands by divine judgment, we have to look beyond his few explicit declarations on the matter, and to investigate

---

[2] It has been a major criterion for those scholars who see redactional layers in the book. So, for instance, when Galling lists examples of the changes made by his hypothetical redactor QR^2, the list is itself almost a list of the book's references to judgment; see K. Galling, 'Der Prediger', in: E. Würthwein, K. Galling, and O. Plöger, *Die fünf Megilloth* (HAT, 1/18), Tübingen ²1969, 73–125, esp. 76. More recently, M. Rose, *Rien de nouveau: nouvelles approches du livre de Qohéleth. Avec une bibliographie (1988–1998) élaborée par Béatrice Perregaux Allisson* (OBO, 168), Göttingen, Fribourg 1999, remarks (p. 472), that 'dans l'*ensemble* du livre, il y a tout un réseau de petits textes dans lesquels le second relecteur fait allusion à un «jugement»..., et ces remarques interprétatives bâties sur ce thème ne constituent pas des gloses isolées, mais, à leur tour, font partie intégrante de tout le travail que j'ai attribué à mon «Théologien-Rédacteur»'. Similarly, the theme also serves for some other scholars to identify 'orthodox' sayings quoted by Qohelet; so, e.g., R. Gordis, *Koheleth—The Man and His World: A Study of Ecclesiastes*, New York ³1968, 105. Interest in this theme is often linked to its appearance in the epilogue, at 12:14. The relationship between monologue and epilogue is outside the scope of this paper (see S. Weeks, *Ecclesiastes and Scepticism* [LHBOTS, 541], New York, London 2012, 171–72), but the possibility that a later epilogist believed in divine judgment does not, of course, preclude the possibility that Qohelet held the same view, so is not in itself evidence for the secondary character of the theme.

the constraints imposed by his other opinions or assumptions. Accordingly, I want to begin here by addressing briefly some more general questions about the relationships between God, humans and the world in Qohelet's monologue, before turning to issues more directly implicated in the nature and process of judgment. In this context, probably the most helpful place to begin is with the issue that Qohelet himself uses to conclude his monologue in chapter 12: the inevitability of human death. His evocative images of tearing, crushing and breaking in 12:6 betray his own resentment of this end, and Qohelet is not one to 'go gentle into that good night'. What drives this resentment, however, is not a love of life, but a desire to gain something from it—and so to offset the work involved. Humans each blink into existence for a short while 'under the sun', then face virtual extinction. In Sheol, the place of the dead to which all humans go, they will know nothing and receive nothing, losing even their loves, hates and resentments (9:5–6, 10), and when they pass from life into Sheol, they will carry nothing with them (cf. 5:14 [ET 5:15]),[3] but leave behind even their body and breath (12:7). No sort of resurrection is imagined, and all human achievement must, correspondingly, lie in the short interval between the non-existence that precedes birth and the effective annihilation associated with death. Since living involves effort and potential hardship, furthermore, it can also constitute a loss for the individual,[4] which is why a miscarried child, who comes into existence but passes straight to death, may be better off than a human who has lived for many years (6:3–6), and why the dead, or, better still those not yet born, may be more fortunate than those who currently endure the world (4:2–3; cf. 7:1).[5] Qohelet does not regard life itself, therefore,

---

3   In 5:12–16 (ET 5:13–17), the story is initially of a man whose wealth, set aside against a rainy day (if that is the sense of שמור לבעליו לרעתו, cf. 1 Sam. 9:24), is lost, leaving him with a son but no possessions. The man was not 'working for the wind', however, and so when 5:15 draws a moral from the story, building up to a commendation of pleasure in 5:17–19, it becomes apparent that this is not an account of some individual with unusually bad luck, but a parable about the circumstances of all humans. The problem is not that we risk losing everything if we are unlucky, but that we are all ultimately going to find ourselves in the same predicament. We are 'working for the wind' because it is not possible to take anything substantial with us, and it is true of every individual that שילך בידו מאומה לא ישא בעמלו (5:14).

4   This may be the implication of ענין רע in 1:13; 4:8: cf. 5:13 (ET 5:14), where it seems to refer to a business deal that has resulted in a loss. It is surely the sense of חסרון לא יוכל להמנות in 1:15, where achievement under the sun is 'an incalculable loss' (חסרון לא יוכל להמנות), to be contrasted with the 'profit' (יתרון) that Qohelet is looking for (1:3; cf. 2:11).

5   The possible contradiction to his position, in 9:3–6, is very obscure, and, as often in this book, the interconnection of the parts is made difficult by a plethora of כי s. I render the central section, rather tentatively: 'And also the heart of humans is bursting to do wrong, and confusion

as desirable in its own right, but it represents for him a brief opportunity for humans to achieve something beneficial for themselves, which ceases when they die. They can take advantage of this opportunity or they can squander it, but in any case, death robs them of any further chance to enhance their existence or to correct their mistakes.

From the idea that we leave our possessions behind us when we die, Qohelet goes on to deduce that they are never really, in any meaningful sense, our own, and to align this with an idea of the world as a continuous series of interactions and processes, within which individuals play merely a brief, discontinuous role. This idea is elaborated in the first chapter, where the nature of the world is illustrated by examples of phenomena in which the accomplishment of a task is distinguished from completion of a greater task: the sun travels across the sky each day, for instance, but never finishes its travelling, while rivers flow continually to the sea but never fill it. In this world, actions contribute to larger actions, and are not an end in themselves, so that past, present and future form a seamless whole.[6] When we die, as Qohelet comes to understand when he considers his own work in the next chapter, what we have done remains behind because it is part of that changeless world, not part of us. So it is that, although Qohelet himself thought his efforts to create a business and a personal fortune were on his own behalf,[7] the simple fact of his death will grant control of them to some successor, who contributed nothing to that creation (2:18–19, cf. 2:21).

---

is in their heart. While they are alive, and each has their back toward the dead (cf. Ezek. 8:16)—for which will stay joined to all the living? (cf. σ′)—there is a sense of security (בטחון), that it is better for a live dog than the dead lion, that the living know they will die, but the dead know nothing at all.' Qohelet uses the section to move between two different points: the problems caused by the absence of any obvious differences between the fates of people who have behaved in different ways, and the need to take pleasure in life because there is nothing to be found or gained in death. He does so *via* the sense of the living that what they have is better than what awaits them, and he does not disagree with their understanding of death, which provokes his own most eloquent exhortation to find pleasure in living one's life. It is not so clear, however, that he shares their idea that life is always better, and the reference to a dog may be a dig at such thinking. The passage, incidentally, is not about hope, and it is very unlikely that בטחון can have that sense: G ἐλπίς might allow it, but, as the NT usage tends to show, the Greek has a strong connotation of confidence or expectation also; those scholars who cite y. Berakhot 12–14, on the other hand, generally fail to observe that this tractate is not demonstrating such a sense in later Hebrew (as a casual reading of Jastrow might suggest) but is itself interpreting Qohelet and imposing an equivalence with תקוה, in an attempt to show that sinners (even those who attacked the Temple) still have a chance to repent whilst they are alive.

6   See Weeks, *Ecclesiastes and Scepticism*, 44–57.
7   Note the constant repetition of לי in 2:4–8.

Even if what we make persists, it is only ever in our possession temporarily, and can never be removed from the world. As Qohelet understands it, in fact, we are not, in reality, working for ourselves, but are in effect employed as workers on some greater project, beyond our comprehension: we use, shape and recycle what is in the world, but can never add to it, or, crucially, take anything away for ourselves.[8] At the end of our lives, therefore, we can keep nothing material as compensation for our efforts, and this is what provokes Qohelet's famous commendation of pleasure: we cannot find gain in things, but only by taking pleasure in what we do while we are alive. No profit is ultimately possible, but we can have a share in the world while we live, at least at the level of emotion or sensation, which itself balances our pain and efforts.[9]

None of these ideas requires a concept of divine judgment, and in some ways they are all difficult to reconcile with such a concept. To be sure, the exclusion of any general post-mortem judgment or retribution does not itself set Ecclesiastes apart from other literature of its time—although it does provoke an apparent condemnation of Qohelet's ideas in some subsequent Jewish works.[10] If the reward and punishment of humans has to occur within the world, however, then Qohelet's conceptualization of the world becomes problematic. Divine reward is commonly associated with material prosperity, but the meaningless material prosperity of Qohelet's world can hardly be a mark of divine favour in itself. This issue seems to be recognized in the monologue, where Qohelet draws a distinction between real and apparent prosperity: those

---

8   See especially 1:9–10; 3:14–15.

9   See especially 2:10; 3:22; 5:17,18; 9:9. Qohelet uses the term חלק, which A. Schoors describes (drawing on M. Fox's discussion) as 'an existential category referring to man's portion in this life under the sun, which mainly consists in the enjoyment potential of one's wealth'. See *The Preacher Sought to Find Pleasing Words: A Study of the Language of Qoheleth, Part II Vocabulary* (OLA, 143), Leuven, Paris, Dudley 2004, 198–200, and cf. M.V. Fox, *A Time to Tear Down and a Time to Build Up: A Rereading Of Ecclesiastes*, Grand Rapids and Cambridge 1999, 109–11. Fox states the relationship with 'profit' rather well (p. 112): 'If somebody opens a store that provides him with sufficient take-home pay to keep going day to day *and no more*, never producing a surplus and putting the business in the black, Qohelet would call the take-home pay the man's "portion." He would even allow that the food and drink he buys with it is "good." Yet by Qohelet's severe accounting, the business realizes no profit.' It is important to emphasize also, however, that although Qohelet uses financial language, חלק is potentially accessible to all, not just the wealthy, and lies in the pleasure to be achieved from what we do, not simply in enjoyment of what we earn from it (see, e.g., 9:9–10).

10 Most notably Wisdom of Solomon and 1 Enoch; cf. Weeks, *Ecclesiastes and Scepticism*, 174–75.

who seem to have much may in fact be very badly off, because they can take no pleasure in what they own (6:1–6). Since the ability to take pleasure is itself granted by God, it could potentially be used as a means of creating or avoiding such situations, and so rewarding and punishing individuals without changing their outward status. When he raises the subject in 2:26, 5:18 (ET 5:19) and 6:2, however, Qohelet does not explicitly or unambiguously link the granting or withholding of pleasure to ideas of retribution. Although we might see it as an obvious way to locate such divine action within Qohelet's thought, he does not take the opportunity himself; the language which he uses in 2:26, indeed, seems carefully chosen to suggest that what is granted to an individual will depend on God's attitude towards them, without stating that his attitude itself necessarily depends on their behaviour.[11]

More generally, in fact, it is striking that very little in the book as a whole is attributed directly to divine retribution: a lot of bad things happen to people in the course of Qohelet's many anecdotes and illustrations, but often through what seems like chance, or the natural course of events. In a world where things occur as a consequence of plans and processes beyond human awareness, of course, nothing happens without some element of divine involvement, and a sort of determinism runs through Qohelet's thought.[12] In some sense, therefore, every event may be attributed to God. Most events, however, are not attributed to direct divine action or response, and the problems which Qohelet identifies in the world, such as the oppressions discussed in 4:1, are not taken to imply a failure of divine power or justice in dealing with human behaviour. In general, moreover, retribution is not linked to specific actions, and the warning about breaking vows, in 5:3–5 (ET 5:4–6), is exceptional when

---

11 The person to whom good things are granted is טוב לפני, 'good before the face of' God, as opposed to the חוטא. This vocabulary recurs in 7:26, where one sort of person will escape the dangerous woman, and the other be ensnared by her, but it is not the classic vocabulary of righteousness and wickedness, and in 9:2, the טוב and the חוטא form a pair of their own, distinct from both צדיק + רשע and טוב + טהור. Indeed, טוב לפני means something like 'good in God's opinion', which might be 'whoever pleases him' or 'whomever he pleases' (cf. בטוב לו in Deut. 23:17), while חוטא, although commonly translated 'sinner', can have a range of meanings, as commentators have usually observed: Gordis, for instance, thinks it means more 'fool' than 'sinner', while Seow thinks of a 'bungler' or 'loser', and Fox speaks of an 'offender'; see Gordis, *Koheleth*, 227–28; C.L. Seow, *Ecclesiastes: A New Translation with Introduction and Commentary* (AB, 18C), New York, London, Toronto, Sydney, Auckland 1997, 141–42; Fox, *A Time to Tear Down*, 189–91.

12 This has been explored most thoroughly by D. Rudman, *Determinism in the Book of Ecclesiastes* (JSOTSup, 316), Sheffield 2001, although I think that he overstates the consistency of the book in this respect; see Weeks, *Ecclesiastes and Scepticism*, 152–59.

it speak of divine anger and the potential effect on personal prosperity.[13] That offence, however, which involves God directly, was itself probably considered exceptional by many ancient readers,[14] and later in 9:2, Qohelet himself singles out oath-taking as a special sort of behaviour. Although he does not say so directly, Qohelet seems to envisage retribution as something more typically disassociated from particular actions.

This is what seems to lie behind 8:10–13, where Qohelet observes that humans behave badly not just because they forget the behaviour of the wicked, but also because there is no swift and visible penalty for doing something wrong. This is regarded as a problem of course, and perhaps it was one that was quite widely recognized in the ancient world: Plutarch devoted a whole work to it.[15] Delay offers the possibility, however, that the consequences of any action may be outweighed by those of subsequent actions, and this may be just as well: Qohelet has already noted in 7:20 that nobody is so righteous that they never sin, and the punishment imposed on a sinner, according to 8:13, is premature death. If wrongdoing attracted instant retribution, then presumably everyone would be wiped out very swiftly. It seems that we are supposed instead to visualize judgment more as a process of tallying and balancing different actions. This has the unfortunate consequence that people can potentially get away with sinning for quite a long time, but it offers the compensation that occasional sins are unlikely to bring destruction. Indeed, Qohelet probably exploits this fact in 7:15–18, when he observes that the righteous man may 'perish through his righteousness', and urges against becoming very righteous. If sin does not bring instant destruction, then, equally, righteousness does not confer instant protection, and it is better to avoid dangerous acts of righteousness than to be killed, even though excessive wickedness or folly will itself lead to premature death. For Qohelet, retribution is, in effect, not attached to particular actions but to the overall record of each individual.

---

13   For the expression מעשה ידיך, see Deut. 16:15; 24:19 where it is something that may be blessed by God.

14   Oath-breaking was regarded as a way to anger the gods even in the classical cultures which did not more generally emphasize or accept that human morality was subject to divine judgment. See, e.g., J.H.W.G. Liebeschuetz, *Continuity and Change in Roman Religion*, Oxford 1979, 40–42; J.D. Mikalson, *Athenian Popular Religion*, Chapel Hill 1983, 31–38.

15   *On the Delays of the Divine Vengeance* (Περὶ τῶν ὑπὸ τοῦ θείου βραδέως τιμωρουμένων, often known by its Latin title *De Sera Numinis Uindicta*). There is a useful discussion of this work and its relevance to more general questions about retribution in J. Gwyn Griffiths, *The Divine Verdict: A Study of Divine Judgement in the Ancient Religions* (SHR, 52), Leiden 1991, 77–84.

Obviously, that sits uncomfortably with some of the modern ideas that have been put forward about the mechanisms of reward and punishment in wisdom literature and elsewhere, but it is hardly a very novel belief in itself. Despite the claim of the psalmist never to have seen the righteous forsaken (Ps. 37:5), Jewish literature is not short of instances where good people go through bad times, only finally receiving material favour from God; equally, the wicked sometimes wait a long time for their come-uppance. Such situations often present a further dimension to the problem, however: divine response may seem to be deferred not merely because it would be impractical for consequences always to follow immediately upon causes, but because individuals may have to continue to suffer undeservedly when their suffering is part of some greater process. This is made explicit, of course, in the story of Joseph, whose initial travails are hardly a proportionate response to his admittedly irritating priggishness at the start of the story, but prove essential to the survival of his family, and are presented as the consequence of a divine plan (Gen. 45:5–8; 50:20).

In fact, the divine control of long-term processes or events is quite widely attested in narrative, and wisdom literature itself sometimes makes explicit the idea that God effectively controls what humans do.[16] That seems incompatible with any notion of instant retribution, or of consequences inherent in each action, because if the course of human lives were subject to frequent or inevitable change on the basis of human behaviour, that would imply that any human action could disrupt God's purposes. It should not surprise us, therefore, that Qohelet, who is very interested in divine control of the world and of humans, should accept and even exploit the fact that divine judgment cannot simply consist of a response to each human action. When he touches in 7:14 on the fact that individuals may experience both good times and bad, indeed, Qohelet understands such inconsistency not in terms of response, but in terms of divine purpose: circumstances change unpredictably in order to forestall the possibility of prediction.

Such determinism also raises, however, issues of responsibility that may be difficult to reconcile with any belief in judgment. Without going in to the theological and philosophical issues ourselves, we may acknowledge, at least, that it is not straightforward to praise or blame someone for an action when performance of that action (or, indeed, the motivation behind it) was the inevitable component of some divine plan. Qohelet himself makes some strong statements along these lines, not only claiming in 9:7 that human work is in some way already approved by God, but also in 3:11 that God has made everything 'fine in its time'. This claim probably summarizes the message of the preceding

---

16   So, e.g., Prov. 16:9; 20:24.

3:1–8, Qohelet's famous list of times: when everything that we do is done in fulfilment of a divine purpose, then nothing that we do can be considered other than the proper, appropriate action at that time—whatever we might think of each action in the abstract. Qohelet does not, however, make any explicit attempt to square this with his pronouncements about judgment, even though there would seem to be a significant tension involved, and we might go so far as to say that he shows no awareness at all of the many problems involved in issues of free will and determinism.[17] To be fair, though, the same is equally true of many other ancient writers who speak freely both of divine action and of human accountability. We should certainly not presuppose that an author in this period would have found it difficult to hold both ideas, but we must also understand that they are not connected, and that Qohelet's general ideas about the world and about divine action would not naturally have led him to an emphasis on divine judgment.

Clearly, then, there are significant constraints upon the way that divine judgment can operate in the world as Qohelet conceives it. With no promise of heaven or hellfire to come, it must occur within the world. At the same time, though, if personal circumstances and material possessions are essentially meaningless, it cannot be manifested straightforwardly through such things—which is, of course, why the wholly undeserving may just inherit them. Since human actions contribute toward greater divine plans, furthermore, the requirements of retribution have to be balanced against the need to work through those plans, and this combines with simple practicality to ensure that judgment is not simply a swift response to each action. Qohelet holds open the possibility that it may affect the capacity of each individual to take pleasure in what they are doing, but does not press that point, and, indeed, he remains rather vague throughout upon the subject of just what consequences might flow from divine judgment. In 7:17, wickedness and folly result in dying 'when it is not your time' (בלא עתך), and in 7:26 the sinner will be caught by a woman reminiscent of the dangerous 'foreign woman' in Proverbs 1–9—this is described as 'more bitter than death', but it is not clear what will happen to the sinner as a result. According to 8:8, wickedness will not save its owner, while 8:13 suggests that, literally, 'there will not be good' for the wicked man, and that someone who fails to fear God will also fail to prolong his life, even if it appears that sinners are doing just that (8:12). Conversely, 7:18 and 8:12 both seem to suggest that fear of God will result in survival and in 'good'. This is all rather thin, and if it seems that the main consequence of being wicked is likely to be a premature death, then we may recall that Qohelet does not regard

---

17   See Weeks, *Ecclesiastes and Scepticism*, 68–72, 157–58.

death in itself as necessarily bad. Indeed, if we take his assumptions to their logical conclusion, then to be struck down before their time could potentially cut the losses of those who are failing to take pleasure in their lives, and so be a good thing for them. Qohelet seems happy to proclaim the reality of divine judgment, but he asserts no knowledge of the mechanisms, and has little to say about the consequences beyond what is self-evident: if judgment exists, then it must presumably result in good things for good people and bad things for bad, even if it is hard to specify just what is good or bad for someone living under Qohelet's sun.

There is just as little clarity about what criteria will be applied in the judgment of individuals, and Qohelet seems to affirm hardly more than that it is valuable to fear God and to avoid being wicked or foolish. These are, perhaps, encouragements to adopt a proper attitude more than they are admonitions to behave in a very particular way,[18] and there seems to be a similar idea behind the advice in 8:2–8, which moves from the need for caution and obedience in the presence of a king through to more general statements about the inevitability but unpredictability of judgment. The implication, perhaps, is that we must take seriously the aspect of fear in fearing God, living our lives in the knowledge that they are subject to judgment and punishment by a supremely powerful being, and that we have no real knowledge or control of our own. That may shape the choices that we make, and in such very specific matters as disobeying commands or breaking vows we might be well advised to avoid angering God, but it is not apparently intended to detract from the joy that we find in life more generally. Qohelet may be making a similar point in 11:9–12:1, where the joy to be found in youth must be set alongside knowledge of judgment and remembrance of one's creator. The preceding verse, 11:8, similarly sets a recollection of coming death alongside the joy to be taken in the course of a long life, and there we should probably not understand a contradiction between the two: it is death, after all, that should motivate us to take full advantage of life. In 12:1, God is to be remembered before the years come in which it is impossible to find pleasure, and so again seems to be linked with enjoyment of life. In this context, it seems hard to suppose that 11:9 alone is supposed to present knowledge of judgment as a sobering reminder to the young. Rather, Qohelet seems to view that awareness as an incentive to carefree enjoyment of life, probably not because we are going to be judged on how much we have enjoyed ourselves

---

18   See S. Weeks, *An Introduction to the Study of Wisdom Literature* (T&T Clark Approaches to Biblical Studies), London, New York 2010, 119–22; Weeks, *Ecclesiastes and Scepticism*, 87–88.

(as Seow suggests),[19] but because it reminds us that good times will not last forever, and, as he has already pointed out in 9:12, 'no person knows their time'. Judgment hangs over us, in Qohelet's view, but we do not know at what point our actions will be tallied, and can respond only with a healthy respect for the power of God, and with an urge to enjoy what we can, while we can.

In any case, divine judgment seems not only ill-fitting in the monologue, but also ill-defined: this is not a conclusion towards which Qohelet is working, and he seems to have little concern with any specific aspect beyond its existence. He does, however, regard that existence as significant in itself, and it is here, perhaps, that we can begin to identify the nature and limits of his interest in the theme. As we saw at the beginning of this paper, the two sections where Qohelet actually discusses divine judgment, in 3:16–21 and 8:10–14, emphasize its invisibility to humans. Both passages, furthermore, immediately precede commendations of joy, in 3:22 and 8:15–17, which urge humans to find pleasure in what they do because their ignorance precludes any other pursuit that might benefit them. When Qohelet appeals to divine judgment in these passages, then, it is as a demonstration of the limits placed on human understanding: he is not suggesting that the apparent absence of retribution raises questions about the justice of God, but that the indubitability of that justice illustrates the faultiness of human perception. This is part of the much broader theme in his monologue, summed up in his characterization of phenomena as *hebel*, which stresses the inability of humans to perceive the real significance of their actions in the world, and so to act appropriately for their own good. Some slight evidence is offered for the reality of judgment in Qohelet's claims about the ultimate survival of the pious, but essentially he is arguing that a belief in divine justice, confronted with the appearance of injustice in the world, must lead the believer to understand that appearances are deceptive, and that they are at risk of basing their behaviour on an illusion.

Qohelet is sometimes painted as an empiricist or natural theologian, and he does frequently appeal to his own experience for illustrations of his points. The more general case that he is making, however, is for the unreliability of human perception, and he is not afraid to rest that case on dogmatic statements or on ideas so commonplace in his own context that they are no more controversial than is, say, the theory of gravity in the present day. Just as he relies on his audience to share his suppositions that God exists and controls the world, for instance, so Qohelet also expects them to believe that God judges in some way, and to accept his conclusion that the hiddenness of that judgment shows how it is difficult for humans to understand their place in the world, or to act

---

19   Seow, *Ecclesiastes*, 371.

accordingly. This may succeed as a rhetorical strategy, of course, but it also leaves Qohelet in the position of maintaining an idea that seems to sit uneasily alongside many of his others, and with the problem that humans must apparently face judgment without being able to develop or to implement a proper understanding of what they are supposed to do in the world that might enable them to avoid punishment. If we see contradiction here, however, or some basic incoherence, then that is the very point: it is not supposed to provoke in us some urge to make sense of judgment, let alone to draw from their sheathes our redaction-critical knives; we are expected rather to accept that, if we believe God to be just, but perceive the world to be unjust, then the fault lies with our perception, not with our belief. If I see an apple fall upwards, that does not make gravity a myth: I am most likely standing on my head.

Index of Authors

Ackroyd, P.R.   53
Adams, S.   15
Albright, W.F.   58
Annas, J.   146
Anderson, W.H.U.   43
Arnim, H. von   146
Assis, E.   54

Balla, I.   134–35
Barbiero, G.   54
Barton, G.A.   95
Barton, S.C.   30
Baumgarten, J.M.   26
Beentjes, P.C.   1–19
Bergant, D.   54
Bernstein, M.J.   32
Bickerman, E.   82, 91
Binde, R.   148
Black, F.C.   54
Blenkinsopp, J.   65–66
Boccaccini, G.   12
Bolin, T.M.   88
Borgen, P.   149
Bornemann, E.   143
Braun, R.   95
Brenner, A.   59
Brisson, L.   150
Brooke, G.J.   20–33
Bruch, J.C.   50
Burton, J.   61–63

Carr, D.   57–58, 60, 65
Christianson, E.S.   51
Clements, R.A.   24
Clines, D.J.A.   34–42, 43, 108, 110, 113–14, 118, 130, 132
Clooney, F.X.   62
Coblentz Bautch, K.   30
Collard, C.   95
Collins, J.J.   20, 24, 29
Colson, F.H.   145–47
Crenshaw J.L.   43
Cropp, M.   95
Cross, F.M.   20
Curtis, J.B.   37

Davidson, R.   43
Day, J.   53
Dell, K.   43–52, 64–68
Denis, A.-M.   138
De Troyer, K.   31
De Vos, J.C.   138–54
Dijk-Hemmes, F. van   64
Di Lella, A.A.   123, 134, 145
Dillon, E.J.   43
Dobbs-Allsopp, F.W.   58–60
Doedens, J.   116
Doering, L.   145, 148–49, 151
Driver, S.R.   59, 132

Edgerton, F.   62
Egger-Wenzel, R.   123
Eggler, J.   114
Ehrensvärd, M.   57, 60
Eichrodt, W.   43
Eissfeldt, O.   53
Elgvin, T.   24
Engelmeier, M.-P.   141
Exum, J.C.   53–68

Fabry, H.-J.   21
Falk, D.   24
Férnandos Marcos, N.   140
Flint, P.W.   29
Fohrer, G.   109
Fokkelman, J.P.   69–81, 108
Forschner, M.   141
Fortescue, M.   128
Fox, M.V.   56–57, 60–61, 64, 67, 122, 159–60
Frame, D.   86
Fyall, R.S.   109, 118

Galling, K.   156
Gammie, J.G.   28
García Martínez, F.   20, 24, 26, 32
Garrett, D.   54
Gault, B.P.   67
Gercke, A.   141
Gerleman, G.   60
Gifford, E.H.   142
Ginsburg, H.L.   111

Goff, M.   23, 24
Goitein, S.D.   64
Good, E.M.   40
Gordis, R.   34, 37, 44, 53, 95, 156, 160
Gray, G.B.   132
Greenstein, E.   124
Griffiths, J.G.   161

Habel, N.C.   38–39, 116
Hagedorn, A.C.   52, 61
Hager, E.P.   150
Harding, J.E.   109
Harkins, A.K.   29
Harrington, D.J.   22, 23
Harrop, G.G.   39
Hartley, J.E.   108
Haspecker, J.   1
Hatton, P.   47–48
Haupt, P.   53
Hay, M.   149
Helderman, J.   142
Hempel, C.   21, 24, 29
Hess, R.S.   54
Hoglund, K.G.   47, 49
Holladay, C.R.   139–45, 148, 151
Holm-Nielsen, S.   31
Hontheim, J.   108
Hughes, J.A.   31
Hunter, A.G.   82–94
Hunter, R.   62
Hurwitz, A.   57

Janzen, J.G.   109
Jarick, J.   50
Jassen, A.   21, 31
Jastrow, M.   53
Johnson, M.   125, 133
Jokiranta, J.   21

Kampen, J.   23, 32
Keel, O.   63
Kerstens, L.   143
Koh, Y.-V.   51
Kovacs, D.   95
Kroeze, J.H.   108
Krüger, T.   46, 50, 52
Kullmann, W.   143
Kynes, W.   44, 50

Lakoff, G.   125, 133
Landsberger, F.   53
Landy, F.   54–55
Lange, A.   23, 24, 31, 32
LeCureux, J.T.   54
Lee, E.P.   47
Lee, J.A.L.   59
Lichtenberger, H.   15
Lieberg, G.   141
Liebeschuetz, J.H.G.W.   161
Lieu, J.M.   29
Lipiński, E.   129
Lloyd-Jones, H.   95
Longman, T.   54–55
Loprieno, A.   60–61

Macaskill, G.   24
Macchi, J.-D.   21
Machiela, D.   30
Mack, B.L.   149
Maier, G.   2
Marböck, J.   1
Martin, J.   9
Mason, E.   30
McCarter, P.K.   114
Meredith, C.   54, 56, 59
Merrill, E.H.   120
Middendorp, T.   3
Millard, A.R.   64
Mommsen, T.   138
Mras, K.   138, 152
Muilenberg, J.   23
Müller, H.-P.   61
Murphy, R.E.   65–66

Newsom, C.A.   26, 27, 28
Niditch, S.   64
Niehoff, M.R.   149
Nihan, C.   21
Nissinen, M.   21, 31, 61
Noegel, S.B.   58–60, 63, 114

Olyan, S.   2

Patrick, D.   37
Paul, M.-J.   **108–20**
Paul, S.M.   115
Perdue, L.G.   20, 23, 28, 43, 66

INDEX OF AUTHORS

Perry, T.A.   86, 87
Pope, M.H.   57, 60, 63
Popovic, M.   22
Priest, J.F.   43

Rabin, C.   62
Rad, G. von   43, 65
Ranston, H.   95
Reiner, H.   141
Reiterer, F.V.   3, 17
Rendsburg, G.A.   58–60, 63
Rey, J.-S.   24
Rezetko, R.   57, 60
Richter, H.   44
Riley, G.J.   110
Rogers, J.   15
Römer, T.   21
Rose, M.   156
Rückl, J.   21
Rudman, D.   160
Rudolph, W.   63

Sadgrove, M.   65
Sanders, J.A.   127, 134
Saur, G.   145
Sawyer, J.   2
Schiffman, L.H.   21
Schipper, B.U.   21
Schmidt Goering, G.   16
Schnabel, E.   11
Schofield, A.   30
Schoors, A.   130, 159
Schuller, E.M.   24, 26
Schulte, L.L.   31
Schwartz, E.   138
Schwienhorst-Schönberger, L.   95
Seow, C.L.   52, 110, 160, 165
Siegert, F.   140, 149–50
Skehan, P.W.   123, 145
Smend, R.   3
Smith, G.V.   111
Sommerstein, A.   95
Stadelamnn, H.   2
Stegemann, H.   22, 26

Sterling, G.E.   24
Stuckenbruck, L.T.   30

Teeter, A.   21
Thomas, S.I.   25, 30
Ticciati, S.   44
Tigchelaar, E.J.C.   24, 26, 27
Tooman, W.   21
Tov, E.   29, 31
Triplet-Hitoto, V.   21, 24, 25
Tur-Sinai, N.H.   111

Uehlinger, C.   114
Ulrich, E.   30

VanderKam, J.C.   29, 32
Van Hecke, P.   121–37
Van Leeuwen, R.C.   48
Voitila, A.   21

Walsh, C.E.   54
Walter, N.   138–39, 142, 144–48, 150
Weeks, S.   50, 95, 155–66
Weigold, M.   31
Weinfeld, M.   44
Westermann, C.   44
Wette, W.M.L. de   51
Whitaker, G.H.   145–46
Whitley, C.F.   95
Whybray, N.   38, 41, 45, 48, 65, 122
Wilde, A. de   39
Wise, M.O.   29
Wold, B.G.   30
Woschitz, K.M.   139, 145
Woude, A.S. van der   25, 32
Wright, B.G.   27

Yadin, Y.   1
Yarbro-Collins, A.   139, 142, 152
Yoder, C.   48–49
Yonge, C.D.   145
Young, I.   57–60, 63–64

Zakovitch, Y.   54, 60, 67
Ziegler, J.   144

Index of Textual References

Hebrew Bible

Genesis
1:28–30	83
2:2–3	142
2:7	93, 94
3:14	84, 94
3:15	94
3:19	84, 93
3:20	84, 93, 94
6:7	85
6:20	85
7:2	84
7:8	84
7:23	85
8:19	84
8:20	84, 88
9:1–3	83
10:8–12	92
10:12	93
12:10	89
15:9–11	146
24:30	40
30:14–18	60
42:14	36
44:4	127
45:5–8	162
48:13–14	90
50:20	162

Exodus
3:7	40
4:12	90
4:15	90
8–13	86
14:9	127
15:9	127
19:13	85
20:8–11	141
20:10	85
20:11	141
22:18	85
24:12	90
30:4	84
30:36	127
34:6–7	86

Leviticus
7:21	84
7:25–26	86
11:26–27	84
20:25	84
27:9–11	86
27:11	84
27:26–28	86
27:26–27	86

Numbers
3:13	86
8:17	86
18:15	86
23:22	5
24:8	5
25:11–13	6

Deuteronomy
4:17	86
5:12–15	141
5:14	85
5:15	141
5:32	90
13	119
13:1–5	119
14:6	84
16:15	161
17:11	90
17:20	90
19:6	127
23:17	160
24:19	161
28:14	90
28:26	85
28:45	127
33:4	14

INDEX OF TEXTUAL REFERENCES

Joshua
1:7	90
2:5	127
10:2	89, 93
23:6	90

Judges
9:23	120
13::8	90

1 Samuel
8	48
9:24	157
16:14	120
17:44	84
17:46	84
30:8	127

2 Samuel
14:19	90

1 Kings
4:20	63
4:20–25	63
4:33	63, 85
5:13	85
8:36	90
9:5	10
10:7	40
10:22–29	63
22	119
22:17–28	119
22:19–23	109

2 Kings
19:6	40
22:2	90
25:5	127

Isaiah
2:3	90
5:1–7	60
18:6	85
30:20–21	90
46:1	84
52:13	29
53:7	83

Jeremiah
6:2	60
7:33	85
15:3	85
15:4	85
19:7	85
20:14–18	118
27:5–6	86
28:9	90
28:14	86
28:26	90
31:13	132
34:20	85
39:5	127
52:8	127

Ezekiel
8:10	84
8:36	158
44:31	84

Hosea
2:9	127
14:6–8	60

Joel
1:18–21	86
2:12–14	86
2:21–24	85

Jonah
	82–94
1:7	92
1:17	88
2:9	93
2:10	88
3:7–8	85, 88
4:11	87, 88, 90, 93, 94

Micah
4:2	90
5:7	85

Habakkuk

1:16	84

Zechariah

11:12	132
13	120
13:2	120
13:4	120

Psalms

7:6	127
8:8	85
8:22–31	140
8:22	140
18:38	127
21:4	9
25:8	90
25:12	90
27:11	90
32:8	90
36:6 (7)	85
37:5	162
37:11	28
37:14	28
48:8 (9)	40
50:10–11	87
50:10	85
72	52
73:22	87
86:11	90
89:30	9
103:14	93
104:14	85
104:29	93
119:33	90
119:102	90
126:6	132
127	52
135:8	86
148:10	85

Job

1:8	116
1:15	37
2:3	116
3:5	114
4–5	45
4	108–20
4:12–21	108
5:7	114
5:9	36
6:5–6	44
6:24	90
7:13–14	118
7:15	118
8:11–12	44
9:10	36
10:9	93
10:16	36
11:6	37
12:7–10	86
12:7	37
12:12–13	44
13:1	40
14:19	127
15:14–16	111–13
17:5	44
19:25	41
19:26	41
19:27	41
22:2	115
23:9	90
23:13–14	35
25:4–6	112
28	44, 47
28:1–12	124
28:15–19	131
28:18	132
29:11	40
30	51
31	51
31:37	38
32	45
33:9–11	45
34:5–9	45
34:15	93
34:22	90
35:11	85
36:9	37
36:22	90
37:5	36
37:14	36
38:2	36
38:18	37

INDEX OF TEXTUAL REFERENCES

40:3–5	34	8:6–8	48
40:4	35	8:9	123
40:15–24	94	8:10, 11	131
40:19	94	8:16–17	47
42:1–6	**34–42**	8:17	123
42:2	35, 37	8:19	131, 135
42:3	35	8:22	94
42:4–6	35	8:33	128
42:4	38	8:34	125, 128
42:5	39	8:35	123
42:6	36	9	91
42:7	111, 115, 118	9:1–12	50
		9:1	124
Proverbs	31	9:4	125
1–9	45–46, 49–50, 163	9:5	135
		9:18	50
1:1	51	10:1	49, 51
1:10–19	45, 49	10:12	48
1:15	129	10:15	48
1:18a	50	10:22	48
2:1–22	45	11:4	48
2:2	128	11:28	48
2:4	123–24	12:10	87
2:5	123	14:6	123
2:9	49	14:20	48
2:19	49	15:32	129
3:1	129	16:9	162
3:13	123, 133	16:14	48
3:14	130, 135	16:16	129
3:16	90	16:32	48
3:18	133	17:16	129, 131
3:21	129	18:22	49
4:5	129	20:2	48
4:7	129, 131	20:12	40
4:13	129, 133	20:24	162
4:27	90	22:4	48
5:1	128	22:7	48
5:2	129	23:23	129–30
5:15–20	49, 66	24:30–34	45
6:6–8	47	25:1	51
7	50	26:4–5	47, 49
7:4	134	27:15	49
7:6–27	45	30:3	128
7:14–20	49	30:24–31	47
7:25–28	50	30:29–30	48
7:26	50	30:30	85
7:28	50	31:10–31	60, 67

INDEX OF TEXTUAL REFERENCES

Song of Songs		3:1–8	163
1:5	63	3:2–8	45
2:8–9	55	3:11	162
2:14	40	3:14–15	159
3:1–5	56	3:16–21	165
1:5	51	3:16–17	46, 155
3:2–3	67	3:18–21	83, 91, 155
3:6–11	55–56	3:18	155
3:7	51, 63	3:19–20	155
3:9	51, 58, 63	3:19	155
3:11	51, 63	3:20	93, 94
4–5	56	3:21	87, 155
4:3	59	3:22	159, 165
4:9	62, 65	4:1	160
4:12–5:1	56	4:2–3	157
5:1	65	4:2	101
5:6–7	67	4:5–6	44
6:4	57	4:8	157
6:5	62	4:9–12	44
8:6–7	52, 67	4:12	96
8:6	66	5:1–2	44
8:11–12	51, 63	5:3–5	160
		5:9–12	44
Ecclesiastes	23	5:12–16	157
1:1	51, 96	5:13	157
1:2	96	5:14	157
1:3	105, 157	5:15	97, 157
1:4–9	45	5:17–19	157
1:9–10	159	5:17–18	159
1:12–2:24	45, 51	5:17	97
1:12–2:26	100	5:18	160
1:12	51	6:1–6	160
1:13	123, 157	6:2	160
1:14	97	6:3–6	157
1:15	157	6:3	101
2:3	123	6:12	97
2:4–8	158	7:1–14	45
2:9	126	7:1–13	44
2:10	159	7:1–12	45
2:11	97, 105, 157	7:1–6	45
2:17	97	7:1	46, 101, 157
2:18–19	44, 158	7:7	44
2:18	105	7:11–12	130
2:21–26	91	7:12	125
2:21	158	7:13–14	45
2:24	44	7:14	162
2:26	160	7:15–18	161

INDEX OF TEXTUAL REFERENCES

7:15	98	11:8	164
7:16–17	100	11:9–12:1	164
7:17	163	11:9	100, 155, 164
7:18	163	11:23–29	46
7:20	161	12	157
7:23	126	12:1–7	97
7:25	123	12:1	100, 164
7:26	52, 102, 160, 163	12:6	157
		12:7	93, 99, 155, 157
8:2–8	164	12:8	96
8:7–17	98–99	12:9	45
8:8	99, 163	12:14	156
8:10–14	165	14:33	126
8:10–13	161		
8:10–12	155	*Lamentations*	
8:12–13	155	1:1	93
8:12	163	1:3	127
8:13	161, 163	4:2	132
8:15–17	165		
8:15	96	*Daniel*	
9:1	98	11:33–34	28
9:2	160–61	12:3	28
9:2–3	155		
9:3–6	157	*Nehemiah*	
9:5–6, 10	157	7:4	89, 93
9:5	96	10:37	86
9:6	96		
9:7	162	*2 Chronicles*	
9:9	52	6:27	90
9:9–10	159	34:2	90
9:11–12	96		
9:12–16	93		
9:12	98, 165	**Pseudepigrapha and**	
9:13–16	45	**Deuterocanonical Literature**	
9:13–14	92		
9:16	44	*Baruch*	
9:18	44	1:9–10	16
10:2	90, 91	3:15	126
10:4	92	4:1	13
10:16	48	7:29–31	2
10:17	48	24:18–22	14
10:18	44	24:23	13
10:20	48	24:25–27	14
11:1	44	33:7–15	16
11:3–4	44	34:21–35:12	2
11:5	46	35:22–36:22	17
11:7	46	45:6–26	2

Baruch (cont.)	
45:6–22	3
45:7	4–5
45:8	5
45:12	9
1 Enoch	
1–36	20
Judith	
4:1	86
4:10	85, 88
Sirach	22, 32
4:12 (A)	123, 134
4:13	133
4:19	126
5:15	128
6	136
6:18	123, 127
6:19 (A)	134–35
6:20–22	136
6:24	136
6:25 (A)	135–36
6:27 (A)	123, 133
6:29–30	137
6:36	127
8:17	134
8:21	134
14:20 (A)	128
14:22 (A)	126, 128
14:23–27	124
14:23	128
14:24–25	125–26
14:26–27	125–26
15:1 (A)	125
15:2	127
15:7 (A)	128–29
15:8	126
15:18	127
15:20	127
16:30	93
17:5	144–45
24	135
24:13–17	135
29:3	134
38:24	23
39:1–3	23
45:15	9
45:24c-25b	8
45:25c	8
45:25	6
50:1–24	2
50:24	9–10
50:27	2
51:13 (B)	123
51:16 (B)	123, 128
51:19	134
51:20 (B)	129
51:21 (B)	129
51:24	135
51:25 (B)	129
51:26 (B)	123, 136
51:27 (B)	123
51:28 (B)	130–31
Wisdom	
6:22	140
9:9	140

Ancient Greek Authors

Aeschylus

Agamemnon
387	104
1636	103

Eumenides
144	104

Libation-Bearers
1020	105

Persians
93–100	96
681	106
840–842	96

Prometheus Bound
49	97
750–751	101
1007	104

INDEX OF TEXTUAL REFERENCES

Seven against Thebes
187–195   102–103

Suppliants
524–526   106
800–803   101

Fragment 353   101
Fragment 399   97
Fragment 466   101
Fragment 470   103

Euripides

Alcestis
780–789   98

Andromache
133   106

Bacchae
280–283   100
397–399   100

Children of Heracles
117   104
611–617   99

Helen
173   106
195   106
366   106, 107
1056   105
1163   107

Heracles
503–507   99
637–650   99

Iphigenia among the Taurians
198   107
628   104

Iphigenia at Aulis
920–925   100
1394   103

Medea
1261   105

Orestes
335–336   106
605–606   103
1007   107
1309   106

Phoenician Women
1194–1195   107
1666   104, 106
1704   107

Suppliant Women
531–536   99

Trojan Women
596   107
636–640   102
760   104

Fragment 671   103
Fragment 808   103
Fragment 908   102
Fragment 1059   103

Fragmentum Grenfellianum   61

Sophocles

Antigone
1339   104

Electra
772   104

Oedipus at Colonus
259   104
607–620   97
1211–1238   101–102
1238   106
1384   106

Oedipus Tyrannus
334   106
465   106
1186–1196   97

INDEX OF TEXTUAL REFERENCES

Philoctetes
177–179   97
446–452   98
502–506   98

Women of Trachis
888   104
1173   105

Fragment 682   103

Stoicorum veterum fragmenta
1:39; Nr. 143   146
2:225–27; Nrs. 823–33   146
2:225; Nr. 830   146

Theocritus

Idylls   61–62

Qumran

Aramaic Levi Document
11:6–7   10

CD (Cairo Damascus Document)
III, 12–20   32
III, 18   27
XII, 20–21   28

1QpHab (Pesher Habakkuk)   27

1Q26 (Instruction)   25

1QS (Rule of Community)
III, 13   28
IX-XI   26
IX, 12   28
XI   26
XI, 3–4   26

1QSb (Rule of Blessings)   28

1QH[a] (Hodayot[a])   29
X-XVII   30
X, 34–35   28
XI, 26   28

XII, 12   31
XII, 19   31
XII, 5–29   31
XII, 28–29   31
XIII, 27   26
XIII, 28   26, 27
XX, 14–15   28
XX, 15–16   27
XXV, 34   28

4Q106 (Cant[a])   22

4Q107 (Cant[b])   58, 60

4Q171 (Pesher Psalms[a])   21, 27

4Q184 (Wiles)   23

4Q185 (Sapiential Work)   23

4Q258 (Rule of Community[d])   28

4Q264 (Rule of Community[j])   26

4Q270 (Damascus Document[e])
2 ii 13   26

4Q300 (Mysteries[b])   23
1 ii 3   129

4Q303–305 (Meditation on Creation)   24

4Q411 (Sapiential Hymn)   24

4Q413 (Comp. on Divine Providence)   24

4Q415–418 (Instruction)   23, 24, 25, 27

4Q416 (Instruction[b])
2 ii 8   26

4Q417 (Instruction[c])
1 i 2   26
1 i 13   26
1 i 25   26

INDEX OF TEXTUAL REFERENCES

4Q418 (Instruction[d])		Romans	
81+81a 17	28	16:20	94
177 7a	26		
		Hebrews	
4Q419 (Instruction-like Comp.)		3:7–4:13	142
	24		

Later Jewish Sources

4Q420 (Ways of Righteousness[a])		Aristobulus	138–54
	23	Frg. 2.2	150
		Frg. 4:6–7	139–40
4Q421 (Ways of Righteousness[b])		Frg. 5	152–54
	23	Frg. 5:9	140–43, 148, 150
1 12	28		
1a ii-b10	136	Frg. 5:10	140–41
		Frg. 5:11	140, 142, 150
4Q423 (Instruction[g])	25	Frg. 5:12	143–44, 148, 150
4Q424 (Instruction-like Comp.)		Frg. 5:13	141–42, 144, 150
	23		
		Frg. 5:15	148
4Q426 (Sapiential-Hymnic Work)			
	24	En Gedi Inscription	26
4Q525 (Beatitudes)	24	Philo of Alexandria	
2 ii+3 2	123		
2 ii+3 3	123	*Abraham*	
2 ii-3 5	126	28–30	145
		28	146
4Q528 (Hymnic or Sapiential Work B)		29–30	146
	24		
		Agriculture	
11Q5 (Ps[a])	23, 31, 123, 127–28, 134	30	146
		Alleg. Interpr.	
11Q19 (Temple[a])		1.11	146
LXIV, 6–8	26	1.16–19	145
		1.16	146
		1.17	146–47
New Testament		1.18	147
Matthew		*Creation*	
11:28–30	142	89–127	145
		117	145
Acts			
17:22–34	140		

Heir
215	146
219	146
225	146

Hypothetica
7:12–20	145
7:20	145

Spec. Laws.
2.59	147

Talmud

bBaba Bathra
15a	51

yBerakhot
12–14	158

Early Christian Writings

Clemens of Alexandria

Stromata
1.72.4	141
5.99.7	138

Eusebius

Hist. Eccl.
	138
7.32.17–18	138

Praep. Ev.
7.14.1	138
8.10–1-17	138
9.6.6	140
13.12.1–2	138
13.12.1	141
13.12.3–8	138
13.12.9–16	138

Evangelium Veritatis   142

Hindu Texts

Gita Govinda	62
Tiruvaymoli	62